The
European
Union

The
European
Union

From
Jean Monnet
to the Euro

EDITED BY DEAN J. KOTLOWSKI
INTRODUCTION BY JOAN HOFF AND
RICHARD K. VEDDER

OHIO UNIVERSITY PRESS
ATHENS

OHIO UNIVERSITY PRESS, ATHENS, OHIO 45701
© 2000 by Ohio University Press
Printed in the United States of America

Ohio University Press books are printed on acid-free paper ∞™

09 08 07 06 05 04 03 02 01 00   5 4 3 2 1

The publication of this book was made possible in part by
support from the Ohio University Contemporary History Institute.

Library of Congress Cataloging-in-Publication Data

The European Union: from Jean Monnet to the Euro /
edited by Dean J. Kotlowski.
    p.   cm.
    ISBN 0-8214-1331-7 (alk. paper)
    1. European Union. 2. European federation.
    3. Monnet, Jean 1888– . I. Kotlowski, Dean J.

JN30 .E9418 2000
341.242'2—dc21   00-025094

In memory of

*John Calhoun Baker (1895–1999) and
Elizabeth Evans Baker (1902–1990),
pioneers in higher education,
crusaders for peace*

 Contents

Acknowledgments   xi

Introduction   I
JOAN HOFF AND RICHARD K. VEDDER

Part I: An Overview of the European Union

The European Union   15
From Jean Monnet to the Euro
STEPHEN A. SCHUKER

Musings on the European   33
Economic and Monetary Union
HUGO M. KAUFMANN

Part II: Jean Monnet: Personality, Vision, and Legacy

The Man from Cognac   57
Jean Monnet and the
Anglo-American Mindset
HENRY H. H. REMAK

Jean Monnet and the Origins   79
of European Monetary Union
JOHN GILLINGHAM

Monnet and de Gaulle   87
The French Paradigm in the
Competitiveness between the
United States and the European Union
IRENE FINEL-HONIGMAN

Part III: The European Union: Social Dimension

The Euro and   99
European Social Policies
GEORGE ROSS

Equality in the European Union   117
and the United States
ELIZABETH F. DEFEIS

The Fundamental Social Rights   133
of Workers in the European Union
BERNARD D. REAMS JR.

Part IV: The European Union: International Impact

An American Perspective   149
on the Euro
LARRY NEAL

The Euro and the Dollar—   177
Partners or Rivals?
RODNEY THOM

Part V: The European Union, National Security, and NATO:
An Informal Roundtable

National Security and Defense   195
Implications of the European Union
A Continental European Perspective
GLENDA G. ROSENTHAL

National Security and Defense   199
Implications of the European Union
Looking Ahead
ELLEN L. FROST

The United States, NATO, and   203
the Lessons of History
FRANK NINKOVICH

National Security and Defense   213
Implications of the European Union
Summary, Commentary, and Discussion
JERALD A. COMBS

Contributors   217
Index   223

 _____ Acknowledgments

Many people gave their time, energy, and resources in preparing this volume. Nancy Basmajian, manuscript editor at Ohio University Press, did a superb job overseeing the many details of its publication, and Bob Furnish was a first-rate copyeditor. Shep Black at Ohio University's Alden Library assisted with the photographs, while Kara Dunfee at OU's Contemporary History Institute responded to my queries and pleas for help with efficiency and good humor. My good friend Carolyn Sherayko did an outstanding job compiling the index. In so many ways, Holly Panich served as the institutional memory for this project. Her warmth, generosity, and common sense eased its publication. I have learned much about editing books from another friend, Gillian Berchowitz, senior editor at Ohio University Press. Her experience, professionalism, and thoughtfulness made this a better book. Her sense of humor made the task of editing more enjoyable. I thank Joan Hoff, director of the Contemporary History Institute and professor of history at Ohio University, for encouraging me to undertake this project and offering sound advice and timely assistance. Finally, the John and Elizabeth Baker Peace Studies Program and Contemporary History Institute provided financial support for both the 1999 Baker Peace Conference and the publication of this collection. Ohio University is indeed fortunate to have such splendid patrons, institutions, and friends.

DEAN J. KOTLOWSKI

John Calhoun Baker and Elizabeth Evans Baker.
Photograph courtesy of Archives and Special Collections, Ohio University Libraries.

 _____Introduction

JOAN HOFF AND RICHARD K. VEDDER

Since the Contemporary History Institute at Ohio University sponsored the Baker Peace Conference on European integration in the winter of 1999, the euro has been born amid great fanfare, and the economic unification of Europe that has occurred at an accelerating pace since the Treaty of Rome in 1957 has continued. Yet in some respects, the euphoria and hype associated with the beginning of the euro has subsided. The euro sank significantly in value during its first year, suggesting that the world, if not Europe itself, was not terribly bullish on the new currency. This strengthened the voices opposed to currency unification and other perceived infringements on sovereignty in Great Britain and in several smaller nations outside the euro bloc. At the beginning of 2000 the euro stood at 0.9932 to the dollar.

Adding insult to injury, the greatest economic success stories in Europe at the close of the century were outside or on the fringes of the euro bloc and in some cases even the European Union (EU). The Celtic tiger, Ireland, continued to outdistance most of the continental giants by far. In Scandinavia, non–euro bloc Sweden awoke from a slumber that has lasted a generation, growing nearly 4 percent in 1999, more than double the rate of the Teutonic giant to the south, Germany. Meanwhile, in supposedly poor and backward Eastern Europe, some decidedly non–European Union nations, such as Poland and Hungary, began to show impressive, even explosive growth. In the Baltic countries, the transition to vibrant capitalism seemed to be proceeding at breathtaking speed. For example, Estonia by some accounts was showing double-digit output growth amid a supply-side revolution more in the tradition of Ronald Reagan or Margaret Thatcher than Jean Monnet.

All this shows that the road to economic unity in Europe does not proceed with some precise linearity, that there is more to economic progress than currency union, and that the remaining political obstacles to greater unification are far from trivial. It reminds us that the history of political and economic integration in Europe suggests that unification is neither inevitable nor a form of Manifest Destiny. Even if unity of sorts prevails, history tells us that it may not last terribly long.

Economic unification in Europe has taken two forms, which might be called hegemonic and voluntary. The great Roman conquests of two millennia ago were hegemonic attempts to unify much of what now comprises the European Union. The motives were power, glory, and economic gain. Yet economic gain in that zero-sum world was viewed more as an act of theft than of increasing output. The Roman Empire was arguably a "kleptocracy." Through seizing of treasures and the exacting of tribute, the generals of Rome and the city itself achieved a considerable measure of wealth. To be sure, Rome did some things that the latest efforts at integration are trying to emulate. It created a large free-trade area and removed bureaucratic constraints on the movement of goods, services, people, and ideas. Roman coins circulated throughout the realm, anticipating the euro by 2,000 years. It is perhaps appropriate that the Treaty of Rome of 1957, setting in motion the integration that has given us the euro and European Union, was signed within walking distance of the site where earlier that great proponent of European integration Julius Caesar was assassinated in 44 B.C.

The Roman kleptocracy was part of a rich European tradition. Even in the mid-twentieth century, would-be hegemonic integrators in Europe looked at unification as a path to wealth and power. Some would argue that the New Imperialism of the nineteenth century, when European nations colonized much of the Third World, was a similar manifestation of kleptocracy, and that the European exploiters benefited from the cheap raw materials of lands under their political control. Later, in the middle of the twentieth century, Joseph Stalin presided over the figurative and literal rape of Eastern Europe, hauling factories back to the Soviet Union in much the same way that Roman generals took back gold and slaves to Rome for their triumphs. Yet, as Paul Kennedy told us a decade or so ago, it may well be that in search of empire, capitalist and communist nations inevitably overextended themselves, and their very hegemony became more burden than benefit.

The economic decline in Europe in the middle centuries of the first millennium probably reflected the decline in economic integration that the EU is now restoring, as Henri Pirenne told us many decades ago. While during the Dark Ages political unification was more nominal than real, and the lack of trade was indeed as much a cause as a consequence of the economic stagnation that prevailed, Europe slowly began to develop new trading alliances that combined some aspects of military protection with something akin to a free-trade area. Perhaps the most famous was the Hanseatic League, a grouping of dozens of northern European (primarily Germanic) trading towns that formally began around 1358, although trading between the towns had gone on for years. The league was formed to remove obstacles to trade, such as pirates, and to achieve some sense of unity regarding currency, shipping rules, and the like. The league settled commercial disputes between its eighty members, and had a diet that met at Lübeck at least every three years to decide matters of policy. By the seventeenth century, when it dissolved, the league had lost influence. New, more efficient Dutch traders eroded the league's commercial supremacy. Wars, especially the Thirty Years' War, sapped the military strength and economic vitality of these Germanic towns. Yet the league was a step in the modernization of Europe that was the hallmark of the second millennium of the Christian era.

The Nobel Prize–winning economic historian Douglass North attributed the end of feudalism and the rise of the modern nation state to several factors, but most importantly to declining transaction costs. As the cost of trading declined, the gains from trade provided some economic growth, providing the momentum that ultimately led to the Industrial Revolution. The euro is only the latest, and perhaps the ultimate, step in a process that has lasted for several hundred years.

The move toward economic integration that probably most closely resembles the efforts of the late twentieth century was the Zollverein, a customs union of German states begun in 1834. Like the European Common Market of the 1950s, the Zollverein was a form of voluntary integration designed to reduce barriers to trade. By eliminating tariffs and other barriers, the Germanic states, aided by new railways, began to expand trade enormously, leading to what Walt Rostow terms a takeoff into sustained economic growth. By adopting the Prussian tariff of 1818 against non-Zollverein members, the union further developed European trade, since the Prussian tariff was moderate, believing low rates would enhance governmental revenues more than high ones (an early application of the Laffer Curve). Certainly the Zollverein aided Germany's Industrial Revolution. By increasing contacts between individual German states, it also aided the process of political unification that was ultimately achieved thirty-seven years after the beginning of the customs union.

Other nineteenth-century efforts anticipated both the euro and the creation of the European Central Bank. Thus in both Italy and in Germany the path to political unification was accompanied, and arguably preceded, by moves toward monetary union. The importance of economic factors in unification were revealed again in Germany, when in 1990 East Germany adopted the West German deutsche mark as its currency months before the formal reunification of the country.

The interesting question is whether the current exercise in economic integration parallels that of the Zollverein and other earlier efforts, and whether it will lead to the same political solution, namely integrating Europe into a European supernation. Will the economic benefits, imperatives if you will, that propel Europeans toward greater cooperation and unification in economic affairs ultimately dissolve political barriers as well? Or will Europe remain "an economic giant, but a political dwarf," as Norbert Walter, the chief economist at the Deutsche Bank, queried at the beginning of 1999 on the eve of the launching of the euro?

There are, to be sure, many similarities in the two situations. In both instances, the early efforts at reducing customs barriers were followed by high rates of economic growth—the Germanic states in the

1840s, 1850s, and 1860s; Western Europe in the late 1950s and 1960s. (In both cases, economic growth proceeded before the customs union was completed, although in both instances tariff reduction is believed to have had positive effects.) It may well be that in both instances concerns about nearby giant rivals may have been an impetus to the development of the union. The Zollverein came in the second decade after the Napoleonic Wars, while the Treaty of Rome came in the second decade after World War II. The Germanic states were worried about British economic hegemony and perhaps French and Habsburg economic and military strength. The Common Market evolved in the midst of the Cold War, and was viewed as a way of strengthening Western Europe against the threat of Soviet Communism. Both unions were probably seen as a means of increasing prospects for peace, providing economic incentives for peoples to maintain peaceful relations with neighbors.

Yet for all the similarities, there are profound differences, perhaps of a magnitude to prevent the political unification that may seem inevitable to some. Whereas the Zollverein was created in a relatively homogeneous culture of persons speaking the same language, the European Union and the euro exist in a world of different cultures and religions. While the people of, say, Saxony or even Bavaria might be willing to subordinate their regional loyalties to a bigger polity, it does not necessary follow that the French, British, Germans, and Italians will agree to a similar subordination more than a century later. At a time when nations as old and stable as the United Kingdom, or Italy, or Spain have trouble maintaining complete national sovereignty over their own peoples, it is not surprising that the move to fuller political union within Europe is somewhat rocky and perhaps even untenable. It may well be that the optimal-size political unit in Europe may deviate from the optimal-size free-trade area. It may be that a partial surrender of sovereignty to allow economic efficiency to reign (having common tariffs and possibly a common currency) may be possible without a complete merging of say, foreign policy or even the welfare state.

The 1999 winner of the Nobel Prize in economics, Robert Mundell, showed how nations sometimes have to surrender sovereignty over economic policies in order to accommodate the monetary regime in place. He also argued that the efficiencies of a single currency, the euro in this case, are sufficiently great to have a positive impact equal perhaps to the gains arising from free trade in goods and services. Yet the gains from the reduction in transactions costs implicit in more efficient monetary arrangements can be offset by costs imposed by excessive centralization of economic decisions and the reduction in governmental competition. For example, there is considerable pressure from the Germans and some other members of the EU to "harmonize" taxes, which to the Germans means set tax rates within the Union at uniformly high rates. Yet the very success of some European nations has come from offering lower tax "prices" for public services; Ireland is the best example. Estonia's double-digit growth coincides with the adoption of top marginal tax rates on income of around 26 percent, or about half the levels prevailing in most European countries. If the price of admission into the EU for Estonians is doubling their tax rates, then perhaps the country would be better off if they stayed out.

The 1999 Baker Peace Conference on the European Union was dedicated to Jean Monnet's vision of peace through commerce, at the urging of one of Ohio University's former presidents and benefactors. The late John C. Baker was a business leader and educator who believed that the mutual gains to people from trade and economic intercourse could help reduce cultural, social, and historic antagonisms that often led to war. Nations are less likely to attack other nations if they themselves have already profited from the prosperity of those nations (e.g., from investment in businesses there). Baker was of that great internationalist tradition in post–World War II America, a moderately conservative individual who saw commercial prosperity as a tool to promote peace. On the other side of the Atlantic, Jean Monnet was much in the same tradition. The European Union does have the power to reduce tensions. For example, Franco-German animosity has shrunk dramatically since 1945 with the growth in trade between those former rivals.

The 1999 Baker Peace Conference, which produced the essays in this collection, took place on the twentieth anniversary of Jean Monnet's death in 1979—the man who is usually credited (and occasionally criticized) for setting in motion, following World War II, what is now the European Union. Monnet has been referred to as Mr. Europe of the postwar period, the "first statesman of [European] interdependence," and the "architect of the European Economic Community" by most who have written about him. As early as 1943, Monnet, an official in the exiled French liberation movement, wrote to Charles de Gaulle urging the establishment of a European "federation" or some from of "European entity," as he said, "encompassing a common economic unit." In dedicating a plaque to Monnet on Europe Day in Washington, D.C., in May 1997, Hugo Paeman, ambassador from the European Commission, stated that although Monnet is best remembered as the Father of Europe, he could just as well be known as "the Father of transatlantic partnership . . . [because] he recognized that Europe's future required American ability to embrace new concepts" about the importance of economic integration among the Western allies of the United States.

When Monnet broached the subject of European unity to de Gaulle, he could have anticipated neither the long-term opposition he was to face from the general nor that a French-German alliance, not a French-English one, would become the core around which the European Economic Community ultimately evolved. The fact that de Gaulle did not respect Monnet made it all the more difficult to realize his vision of a unified Europe, as the essays by Stephen A. Schuker, Irene Finel-Honigman, and Henry Remak in this collection point out. Monnet's background as a cognac salesman, his lack of formal education, and his friendly contacts with officials of the United States government aroused de Gaulle's suspicion; the general thought Monnet favored European unity over past French glory and de Gaulle's own attempts to restore French leadership during the early years of the Cold War. Had de Gaulle remained in power through the early and mid-1950s, probably the European Coal and Steel Community, known initially as the Robert Schuman Plan, would not have come into existence as the first step toward European economic cooperation.

Despite de Gaulle's formidable opposition, Monnet characteristically worked doggedly behind the scenes with second-tier bureaucrats in both the United States and France to set in motion what remains a curiously antidemocratic, supranational institutional structure for European integration. Currently the European Commission consists of sixteen thousand professionals divided into twenty-four departments based on the French bureaucratic model. Its Council of Ministers, the European Union's intergovernmental governing body, consists of ministers from fifteen nations. Finally there is the European Parliament (EP), the only elected body of the EU. Until the beginning of 1999, the EP failed to exercise much democratic control over the twenty-member commission. Then, with its scathing report about "recent examples of fraud, mismanagement, or nepotism" and the threat of a vote of censure, the EP forced the resignation of the entire commission in March of that year.

In September 1999 the European Parliament approved the new commission, with Romano Prodi as its president, but not before it imposed a series of restrictions. The reforms include the provision that the commission will, in general, appear before the parliament whenever requested; the commission will take "utmost account" of new legislative proposals called for by the EP; it will examine seriously any EP request for individual commissioners to resign; it will consult and inform the EP on the commission's ongoing administrative reforms; and it is committed to a substantial agenda of institutional reform in the next Intergovernmental Conference that is "an essential prerequisite to enlargement" of the European Monetary Union.

It remains to be seen whether President Prodi and Vice President of Administrative Reform Neil Kinnock will be able to carry out all the complicated aspects of the reorganization package, which involve major staffing changes, including the appointment of more women to senior management positions, and a reduction of departments and posts, before the new commissioners' appointments expire in January 2005. For their part, Euro-MPs are not likely in the near future to compel another mass resignation by threatening a censure vote because the former commission remained in a caretaker role for almost six months.

However, even this first forced resignation did not affect the foreign-exchange markets as some had predicted.

These reforms further downgrade the commission's power in keeping with the 1997 Amsterdam Treaty. At that time EU nations decided that provisions for a minimal foreign-policy apparatus should be attached to the Council of Ministers, not to the commission. This means that if and when the EU begins to develop a "defence identity," this military arm of the EU will most likely amend its treaties to incorporate the Western European Union, a separate body that consists of associate members outside the EU. While the EU is far from achieving a political or military integration, its total population slightly exceeds that of the United States and so does its combined GNP of $8 trillion. These figures will increase dramatically as the Eastern European nations emerge from the fall of communism and meet the terms for EU membership.

To date, however, the European Union citizens have had little, if anything, to say about how further economic integration will take place. There has been almost no public questioning of the "democratic deficit" that still exists in the commission's structure based on Monnet's technocratic executive model, except during the debates over the Maastricht Treaty in 1992 and the resignation of the commission in 1999. Even then, such criticism surfaced primarily only in Britain, Denmark, and, curiously, in Monnet's own France. Thus, the European Monetary Union represents an undermining of national sovereignty of the current member countries rather than a reinforcement of "intergovernmentalism" urged by its critics at the beginning of the 1990s. This is in keeping with the bypassing of national parliaments that is represented by the supranational corporations at the heart of the current globalization of world trade.

The shift away from state control and national economic management and away from democratic supervision of corporations began in the West in the 1980s. Instead, "privatization, a market-driven approach to currency management, and dismantling of the welfare systems which had been erected in previous decades became the new orthodoxy," with the United Kingdom under Thatcher leading the way, has prevailed. Multinational corporations increasingly escaped national control as they became transnational (TNCs). The name of the game became foreign direct investment (FDI) flows, which the United States dominated until the 1980s. By 1989 the EU had caught up with American FDI flows, and Japan was not far behind. Although this profound change in the function of the world economy affected primarily developed Western nations, it spread to Third World countries, forcing them to compete for investment and to adopt market-driven policies.

The phrase "democratic markets" has become a euphemism in the 1990s for deregulation, privatization, and free trade. But when one considers that fifty-one of the world's hundred largest economies are corporations that are not organized along democratic lines, the connection between democratic nation-states and capitalism becomes problematic. Instead of nations amassing economic power and becoming more stable and democratic, multinational corporations are engaging in massive mergers with the blessings of the very states whose power is declining along with their democratic supervision over decisions affecting the material condition of average citizens all over the world. For example, according to Tony Judt, Belgium is often "held up as a postmodern model for the twenty-first century: a virtually stateless society . . . [and yet it is also] the first advanced country truly at the mercy of globalization in all its forms . . . exposed to unprecedented and unregulated pressures beyond local control," where fragmentation of politics has resulted in high-level crime, graft, and corruption running rampant throughout the government, business, and dozens of "communal" police forces.

While the reasons for this decline in the central power of even prosperous nation-states like Belgium are complex, all are related to unregulated global capitalism made possible through advances in information technology. Greater economic interdependence has been developing for most of this century, but the 1990s mark the first time that international markets actually began to create a borderless world. Technology in the form of global communications networks has become the driving force behind the world's economy. When capital transfers can exceed a trillion dollars per day, national exchange controls cannot be applied effectively. Belgium's franc, one of its last lingering tokens of nationality, is doomed to disappear with the advent of the euro.

It is doubtful that Monnet's vision, far-sighted as it was in the 1940s, could have anticipated the type of supranational globalization that was evolving when the twentieth century ended. Just as obviously, whether peace and democracy will prevail with globalization remains to be determined in the course of this, the third millennium. The essays in this collection provide the necessary background and speculation for understanding the role that European Monetary Union and the euro are likely to play in the world's economy in first decade of the twenty-first century.

One of the Contemporary History Institute's benefactors is a former president of Ohio University, John C. Baker, who died in 1999 at the age of 103. As the fourteenth president of Ohio University from 1945 until 1961, Baker saw the student body grow from 1,500 to 8,000. He started his career as a researcher, instructor, assistant dean, and professor of business administration in the Harvard Business School. From 1939 to 1945 he was associate dean of Harvard University. Baker long admired Jean Monnet. It is in his memory and that of his wife, Elizabeth Evans Baker, and their generosity to Ohio University in the form of the John and Elizabeth Baker Peace Studies Endowment, that we dedicate this book.

Part I

An Overview of the European Union

 The European Union

From Jean Monnet to the Euro

STEPHEN A. SCHUKER

Many members of this audience have savored the pleasure of a trip to the Fondation Jean Monnet on a lovely university campus just west of Lausanne. They have enjoyed the serene atmosphere, not to speak of the art bargains, in the picturesque towns on the borders of Lac Léman. On those special occasions when the sun breaks through the mist, they have thrilled to the spectacle of mountains rising to the sky along the further shore. One cannot help thinking of Baudelaire's verses:

> Là, tout n'est qu'ordre et beauté,
> Luxe, calme et volupté.

In such agreeable surroundings, everything seems possible. No wonder we prove unusually susceptible to the message conveyed in those many red-covered books with which the Fondation staff plies us as we leave off work each evening. It is hard to break intellectually free from that massive production of monographs and occasional papers purveying the Gospel according to Saint Jean.

There is indeed much to celebrate. In 1945 Europe lay in ruins, devastated by round two of the most destructive civil war in history. Half a century later, a largely peaceful and prosperous continent has reached a stage of integration that few would have thought possible in that span of time. The cumulative changes in economy, governance, society, and attitudes are overwhelming. With the adoption of the Single

European Act in 1986 and the initiation of a common currency starting in 1999, further progress toward national harmonization and closer integration now seems in the cards. It is tempting to attribute some teleological design to that process. It is seductive to perceive in the creation of a new Europe a stunning confirmation of the Whig view of history. Some of the true believers who have crafted the "red books" strongly embrace that view. And it is right that we honor the vision of the founders and of those who labored for "the European idea."

But it would be historically inaccurate to focus exclusively on the hopes and aspirations of the founding generation of Europeanists. Jean Monnet, Robert Schuman, Paul-Henri Spaak, Alcide de Gaspari, and Konrad Adenauer are not comparable to the founding fathers of the American Constitution—a coterie of men with a common ideology endeavoring to build a framework for the ages. We cannot seek through an exegesis of Monnet's vision a blueprint for the developments of fifty years. Rather, the European Union as it exists today derives from thousands of political bargains, large and small. Those deals, by nation-states above all, take place also among regional lobbies, private pressure groups, industrial and agricultural interests, strong-willed individuals, and an expert bureaucracy growing in esprit de corps, acting through a dense thicket of informal relations as well as through a byzantine structure of formal governance. In a paradoxical turn of phrase, Alan Milward has called the European Union "the rescuer of the nation-state." Yet it is in fact the amorphous and flexible nature of European institutions that have accommodated a multiplicity of self-seeking political interests, calculations of advantage, and provincial subcultures. All this makes for a messy descriptive history, but perhaps for a more stable process of mutual adjustment in the end.

Despite the voluminous biographies by François Duchêne and Eric Roussel, Jean Monnet remains for our generation an enigma wrapped in a self-generated mystique. He was not highly educated, nor an intellectual or political philosopher; he exhibited no special eloquence as a writer or public speaker; he had too little tolerance for detail to make a model bureaucrat. He possessed, however, extraordinarily shrewd judgments about politics and economics, combined with an uncommon gift for networking and for friendship. He had, we would say today, the best Rolodex on three continents. Monnet also boasted an exquisite sense of timing. He possessed an unusual knack for appropriating an idea whose time had come, talking it through the successive stages of acceptability and adoptability, identifying the effective decision makers both in and outside the relevant bureaucracies, and selling ideas across national boundaries like a preternaturally gifted salesman.

Looking back, it seems that Monnet's whole life served as a preparation for launching the European idea in 1950. Monnet is commonly thought of as the heir to a large brandy fortune, and he certainly lubricated social relations with cases of the stuff. In fact, he stood but two generations away from the peasant growers of his native Cognac; his father had worn wooden clogs as a boy and, far from starting as a merchant aristocrat, had worked himself up by founding a smallholder cooperative to compete with the Hennesseys and the Martells. All his life Monnet despised the hard-hearted captains of industry, be they in liquor, steel, or coal. He retained a romantic sympathy for the working man. That proved a key to his ideological compatibility with New Dealers like Harry Hopkins during the war and with the socialist ideologues of the Fourth Republic afterward. If truth be told, Monnet also cultivated communist leaders like François Billoux and Benoît Frachon of the Confédération Général du Travail (CGT) until the attempted revolution of November 1947 diminished his lingering innocence. Monnet could not have succeeded either at the Commissariat du Plan or in the Schuman Plan negotiations if he had not enjoyed the confidence of the working class and if he had not believed in a European union that would defend the interests of the common man.

Monnet's brandy business had taken him often to North America. He made many fast friends in the London. During World War I, he became a representative in England to Minister of Commerce Etienne Clémentel. In the Allied Maritime Transport Council he developed both a faith in international cooperation and the high-level inter-Allied contacts that would afford him access to governing circles over the next generation. Curiously, Monnet had no early exposure to Germany. Indeed, the plans that he and the Clémentel circle drew up for the 1916 Paris Conference foresaw an economic war after the war in which Germany would remain a permanent pariah. Monnet subsequently accepted appointment as deputy secretary-general of the League of Nations and after 1920 carved out a reputation as a progenitor of the accommodationist "Briand line" toward postwar reconstruction. But he wearied of the league routine and what he called its "little solutions to big problems." He turned to merchant banking instead. Unable land a post at J. P. Morgan's firm, he accepted a job as the European representative of Blair and Company, a Chase National Bank affiliate, and placed loans in Eastern Europe. Monnet never rose to the pinnacle in high finance, however, and he moved to New York in 1935 to run a third-tier boutique specializing in the China market, largely so that his wife could escape the long arm of the law. Having lost custody of her daughter to a prior husband in patriarchal Italy, Silvia Giannini Monnet acquired Soviet citizenship and absconded with the child so that she could obtain an outcome more in line with feminist precepts from the New York family court.

The 1930s did not figure as Monnet's finest hour. Thomas Lamont of J. P. Morgan described him as "very narrowly removed from [an] adventurer pure and simple because his sole motive is the 'rake-off' to Monnet which must come from the importation of capital to China." At the tail end of the decade Monnet helped to arrange the sale of Jewish assets in Eastern Europe to the Nazis at fire-sale prices and to facilitate the more profitable liquidation of German assets in America. Monnet later professed to have only a "sketchy recollection" of those activities, and the U.S. Treasury continued to investigate him for alleged income tax violations through 1942. The coming of war, however, provided enlarged opportunities for someone with such wide contacts. Monnet helped the Daladier government to negotiate the purchase of airplanes in the United States; he acted as chairman of the Anglo-French Coordinating Committee and served as a prime mover behind the abortive proposal for Anglo-French union in 1940. Following the Allied landings in North Africa, he masterminded the flow of Lend-

Lease material to the Free French and sought to keep a shaky truce going between Generals Henri Giraud and Charles de Gaulle. The latter assignment was not devoid of danger. De Gaulle did not conceive of politics as beanbag. He denounced Monnet as "the mouthpiece of the foreigner," and on at least two occasions the latter narrowly escaped from most suspicious accidents.

In 1943, de Gaulle and Monnet also confronted each other for the first time about the shape of postwar Europe. As a general idea, European union figured as a hoary chestnut. As early as the fourteenth century, visionaries had dreamed of creating a united Christian Europe on the model of the Roman Empire, the better to organize military defense of the Occident against the Turk. William Penn, Jean-Jacques Rousseau, Henri Saint-Simon, and Jeremy Bentham had all elaborated schemes for a European parliament, and the success of the Zollverein after 1834 suggested to free-traders in Western industrial states that the notion of lowering tariffs should be capable of further expansion.

In the interwar period, the idea of regional trading blocs made significant progress outside Europe. The Ottawa Agreement for the British Empire, the American scheme of reciprocal trade in the Western hemisphere, and the Japanese Co-Prosperity Sphere showed that the idea could take both benign and malign forms. In Europe, the Hapsburg aristocrat Count Richard Coudenhove-Kalergi founded a Pan-European Union with a view to preserving peace and organizing the Continent for effective competition. A number of statesmen later prominent in European integration lent their names to the Coudenhove-Kalergi movement, but it achieved no practical results outside of evanescent press notices. By contrast, after the Locarno settlement of 1925 had cleared away political problems, European steelmakers managed to reach an accord on a private basis to regulate the export markets of Lorraine, Luxembourg, Belgium, the Ruhr, and the Saar. The British and even the sanctimonious Americans surreptitiously joined that cartel, and similar arrangements evolved to control overproduction in chemicals, potash, and other industries. Industrial coordination became a buzzword. But, like the stipulations for central-bank cooperation under the gold-exchange standard, the industrial cartels failed to withstand the pressures of the Depression. Nor did such arrangements prevent political conflicts from erupting again. In 1927, as the Franco-German tariff negotiations moved wearily toward conclusion, Louis Loucheur and like-minded compatriots engineered a World Economic Conference. The gathering examined tariff levels and nontariff barriers, commercial-policy rules, the extension of production quotas, and the eventual creation of a European front against American export supremacy in the high-tech industries. Given the persistence of unresolved conflicts over reparations, war debts, and monetary regimes, the 1927 negotiators made no headway even toward a common customs system. In May 1930, finally, after the shaky European tariff truce collapsed, Foreign Minister Aristide Briand of France offered a broad scheme for a European Federal Union and common market. Whether Briand and his inspirers aimed to shore up the Young Plan, to head off a German drive for Anschluss with Austria in the wake of Gustav Stresemann's death, to bind Britain closer to the Continent, or to tweak Uncle Sam's beard remained unfathomable: the scheme fell everywhere on unreceptive ears. In any case, the real political and economic unification of Europe was subsequently achieved by Adolf Hitler. Although national resistance movements objected violently to Hitler's methods and goals, it was in resistance circles themselves that the notion of post-Nazi European integration first took concrete shape.

But what form precisely should the postwar European order assume? De Gaulle, Monnet, René Mayer, and the economist-bureaucrat Hervé Alphand debated the matter in October 1943 in Algiers. Monnet had earlier conceived of a supranational political entity that could control the key steel and coal areas of Western Europe. But his deputy, Etienne Hirsch, considered it utopian to think of "gouging areas . . . out of sovereign states and, after a gap of a thousand years, dream up a new Lotharingia." Eventually, Monnet retreated to a more modest idea—the division of Germany into several states, but then equality among all European countries to form a single economic entity, with international control of basic industries. De Gaulle thought more expansively.

France was aligned with no one in this war. The United States, he reckoned, had entered an era of imperialism and colonial expansion, and Churchill, with incredible stupidity and malice, had turned Britain into an American dominion. De Gaulle sought to conjure a Western federation grouped around France, Benelux, Italy, and Austria, possibly drawing in Spain and Switzerland, and certainly embracing the western and southern provinces of Germany, including the resource-rich Rhineland and Ruhr. Such an organized bloc, with a population exceeding 100 million, could defend the values of European civilization against the Americans, and if necessary the Russians. The areas east of a line down the middle of Germany would of course be reduced to Russian conditions, but that could not be helped. The protagonists would rehearse the issues repeatedly and in various contexts over the next seven years, but gradually the circumstances of the Cold War and France's slow recovery from the last conflict would push the nation toward the Monnet solution rather than that of de Gaulle.

In the immediate postwar period, de Gaulle lobbied vigorously for his unique approach to European integration, one based squarely on the restored power of France. In the fall of 1945, de Gaulle sent Couve de Murville to London and Washington to elaborate his plan for an international Ruhr state dominated by France, with two or three buffer states for security purposes tacked on in the Rhineland as well. Significantly, the French Foreign Ministry file on the subject begins with General Charles Mangin's scheme of 1923, not even redated for the occasion. Yet de Gaulle faced an insurmountable obstacle: outside his perfervid imagination, France enjoyed no restored power. The United States and Britain, already involved in bitter disputes with Russia in Germany and elsewhere, tacitly opposed French schemes and postponed the problems of setting German borders.

Meanwhile, the Nazis had run French industry into the ground; the Resistance had made improvident promises that could not be redeemed on the basis of French workers' and peasants' reduced productive powers; and the weak French state had no way to compel the return of private deposits in the United States. Monnet came to the rescue with one of his familiar conjuring tricks. France needed to modernize and reduce production costs, but with Lend-Lease over and the French people declining to tighten their belts, the necessary investment capital could only come from American pockets. Monnet did not really have a detailed plan in mind, but he could use the postwar fashionability of planning in general to win public support and American backing for industrial restructuring, inevitable nationalizations, and modest monetary reform. It made little economic sense for Monnet to privilege the public sectors of energy and transport and to leave capital markets to look after the private sector. But that strategy made good political sense and brought socialists and communists around to tolerating industrial restructuring.

By spring 1947, nevertheless, the French and other European economies had run into trouble. Lacking the necessary fuel, food, and fiber (primarily coal, fertilizer, and shipping), France and other countries ran a widening payments deficit with the United States. The Anglo-Saxons did not want the Russians in the Ruhr and had blocked an international settlement there; meanwhile, German productivity remained so low that the Ruhr could not provide coal for France and for German industrial revival as well. The Americans offered the Marshall Plan to break the key bottlenecks in Europe. But they insisted that the Europeans develop a common plan to foster intraregional trade and to take pressure off the dollar; they likewise required that France accept German revival as an integral part of the plan. The Marshall Plan proved a bitter pill for both France and Britain to swallow. Alphand and other Gaullist hangovers at the Quai d'Orsay opposed lifting the limits on German industry before a settlement on the Ruhr. The British would have preferred bilateral aid and complained that they should not have to recast domestic socialization schemes just because the Continentals chose to run payments deficits with Afro-Asian lands in the sterling bloc. Most all of the Europeans thought that American insistence on diminished trade barriers represented Hullian-Claytonian prejudice and would prove beside the point. Nevertheless, American money talked. The Europeans made an outward show of cooperation in such agencies as the Organization for European Economic Cooperation

(OEEC) and the European Payments Union. Even so, the continental trading partners reduced tariffs and quotas on a strictly business basis. De facto currency convertibility did not return until the mid-1950s. Schemes for bolder free-trade areas such as Finabel and Fritalux foundered on the details. And the British, still riveted on trading links with the Commonwealth and the special relationship with America, saw no economic advantage in tying up promiscuously with the continent. After their unilateral devaluation in 1949, the British made clear in OEEC talks that they might liberalize trade with the Netherlands and Scandinavia, but would link their fate with other Continentals only so far as the Americans forced their hand.

Far from wishing to depend exclusively on the United States, Monnet and other progressive Frenchmen still hankered for restoration of the Entente Cordiale in a form that would help keep Germany down. In March 1949, Monnet made a pitch for solidarity to Sir Edward Plowden of H.M. Treasury: "Western Europe was a vacuum, on either side of which were the two great dynamic forces of communism and American capitalism. . . . This vacuum could be filled either by one of these two outside forces or by the development of a Western European 'way of life.' . . . The only dynamic force in Western Europe was in the United Kingdom, which had in the past few years carried out a redistribution of wealth on a massive scale while at the same time retaining the freedom of the individual." The OEEC, Monnet went on, consisted of nineteen sovereign nations and could not consider European problems in a European way. Yet if England and France were to consider their problems "as if they were one nation," they could address the relationship of a resurgent Germany to Western Europe and develop a common line. Despite this and similar overtures, the British Treasury and Foreign Office rejected the proposition that "political considerations should compel us to go further in the way of integration with the French than seemed wise from the economic point of view. . . . We should obviously not agree . . . to anything which would render us incapable of sustaining an independent resistance if France were overrun."

The Schuman Plan that Monnet drew up in May 1950 and that the

French foreign minister honored with his name derived both from inspiration and desperation. At the 1948 London Conference, the British and Americans made plans to restore a West German state with full sovereignty over the Rhineland and Ruhr. Couve de Murville and Michel Debré, the archetypal Gaullists, maintained that France should ignore the blather about economic constraints and just say no. In the end, less impassioned heads prevailed. The French received some modest sops for public opinion—an International Ruhr Authority and the promise of a Mutual Security Board—but by the spring of 1950 it became evident that those frail institutions would fail to restrain the recovery of German steel production and the preemption of German coal supplies for domestic use. The Schuman Plan figured as a "hail Mary pass," a final attempt by creative Europeanists to bypass the sterile negativism of the Quai d'Orsay and to invent a formula that would contain the former Reich within a voluntary international architecture while paving the way for political rapprochement. In that objective, it succeeded. At the conference to confirm adoption of the Schuman Plan in April 1951, the atmosphere had so far improved that a boisterous Walter Hallstein could ease into a parody of the "Horst Wessel Lied":

> Die Preise hoch, Kartelle fest geschlossen,
> Monnet marchiert, mit ruhigem festen Schritt!

In theory, the European Coal and Steel Community (ECSC), as it came into effect in July 1952, aimed to utilize a supranational authority in order to rationalize the production and sale of coal and steel, break the power of the German coal sales organization, decartelize Ruhr steel into French-size units, and foster labor rights in the six participating nations. But as an economic institution, the ECSC never worked smoothly. Monnet and his allies imposed the scheme over the vociferous objections of technical experts both in the French and the German steel industries; the rise in raw-material prices during the Korean War upset all material projections; the supranational bureaucrats never developed the competence to overcome trade distortions and discriminatory practices by fiat; within a few years the main German firms expanded back to an economically rational size; yet paradoxically the availability of oil resources ended the dependence of European industry on Ruhr coal.

Politically, however, the Schuman Plan proved a stunning success. The Germans accepted the temporary economic disadvantages because the plan presaged their reacceptance into the community of democratic nations. The plan gave Chancellor Adenauer the requisite maneuvering room to anchor the Federal Republic firmly in the West and to resist the siren lure of reunification on Russian terms; it allowed him to outmaneuver Economics Minister Ludwig Erhard, who would have preferred a return to the world market rather than the deepening of European commercial ties; and it permitted him to place the Saar problem on ice until mutual passions had cooled. Above all it provided a framework for the initiation of Franco-German reconciliation on every level from state visits to the exchange of academics and schoolchildren.

Monnet's next proposal, the European Defense Community (EDC), can also be categorized as a practical failure but a potent lever for influencing hearts and minds. In 1949 the Council of Europe opened its first assembly in Strasbourg. It rapidly became manifest that the British would use the council of ministers to obstruct political integration. Paul Reynaud quipped acidulously that the Council of Europe consisted of two bodies, "one of them for Europe, the other against it." In the summer of 1950, despite the presence of a European-minded West German delegation, the British dug in their heels against any supranational authority. Concomitantly, the Americans put mounting pressure on the French to endorse German rearmament. Everyone knew that there could be no defense of continental Europe without German troops. The French were preoccupied with Indochina, the British fixated on the Middle East; and as Field Marshal Bernard Law Montgomery said of the Dutch in that politically incorrect era, they "couldn't hold their own against a field of naked savages." Yet French public opinion was not ready for a rearmed Germany. In those delicate circumstances, Monnet persuaded Premier René Pleven to propose a

European Defense Community—a true supranational army that would integrate German troops in manageable units of battalion size. The EDC made little sense militarily; in August 1954 the French themselves refused to ratify it. The Germans were eventually integrated into NATO, which had constituted the sensible military plan all along. In the meantime, the EDC had served as a useful agent for advancing the agenda of integration.

The next step, the Treaty of Rome (1957), also emerged as the by-product of a fortuitous political process. The indifferent success of the European Coal and Steel Community dampened hopes for sectoral unification. Monnet's next scheme, a joint European program for the peaceful use of atomic energy called Euratom, foundered first on the hesitation of the United States to share its uranium and then on the desire of France to keep its military options open. Nor did the Beyen Plan for creation of a customs union over twelve years win much support outside Benelux. Even within Benelux, skeptics feared that a Common Market might simply resuscitate Napoleon's Continental system through the back door. Grass, said one chamber of commerce official, would "grow on the quais of Rotterdam." Here again, a concatenation of political accidents led to a convergence of interests and the signing of the Treaty of Rome. A Socialist coalition under Guy Mollet, stung by the failure of the Suez invasion and a collapse of the British alliance by which Pierre Mendès-France had set such store, cast around for a public-relations success. Adenauer was happy to play up in order to strengthen bilateral ties, while the German Socialists under Ollenhauer moderated their heretofore fierce resistance to a Western orientation. Fearful that de Gaulle might return to power and end all supranational experiments, the other countries gladly paid the baksheesh demanded by France—acceptance by its partners of expensive social legislation, and lucrative subsidies for grains, sugar beets, and other French farm products under the Common Agricultural Policy.

Subsequent steps toward European union have generally followed the early pattern. Specific political problems or exogenous forces require a search for compromise. Practical men, usually cultivated members of the elites with a general disposition toward European cooperation but with a primary responsibility toward the bureaucracy they serve, look for pragmatic solutions. The solutions themselves may prove satisfactory or not. But slowly, in an incremental way, often interrupted by long periods without notable progress, the institutions of Europe solidify and deepen.

The return to power of Charles de Gaulle in 1958 opened a characteristic period of stagnation for European institutions. With a new wind blowing, Edward Heath, Macmillan's Lord Privy Seal, initiated a reappraisal of Britain's place in Europe. Recognizing that the mix of British commerce was changing, Heath and his team offered to reconsider long-held positions on Commonwealth trade, the European Free Trade Association (EFTA), and British agriculture. In 1963, however, de Gaulle vetoed British entry, not really on technical grounds, but rather because he viewed Britain and its Scandinavian partners as a Trojan horse for American dominance. Instead, without meaning to abate French sovereignty, de Gaulle maneuvered on political grounds for closer political integration of the original Six. This led to the Franco-German treaty of 1963 and the strengthening of what David Calleo has called Europe's "Franco-German engine." It also inclined de Gaulle, notwithstanding his inclinations and ideology, to allow acceleration of the agreed pace for dismantling internal tariffs, which ended two years ahead of schedule in 1968. Trade within the EEC rose more than sixfold from 1958 to 1971, belatedly justifying the prediction of Will Clayton in 1947 that Europe could meet a greater proportion of its needs through intraregional exchanges.

A further impetus toward integration derived from the problems of the U.S. dollar in the 1960s. Economists from Robert Triffin to Jacques Rueff observed that the United States was using its seignorage over the world monetary system to run a chronic payments deficit and in effect to oblige European central banks to finance the Great Society as well as American military programs. A series of monetary disturbances in 1968 and 1969—the collapse of sterling, the creation of a two-tier gold market, the devaluation of the franc, and the revaluation of the mark—impelled a search for regional solutions and the eventual formation of the Economic and Monetary Union (EMU). Meanwhile, the shift of power from de Gaulle to Pompidou allowed the French to reconsider Community enlargement. Britain, Denmark, and Iceland won entry to the EC in 1973. Free-trade arrangements with the other EFTA states followed. The missed opportunities of the 1950s, when Britain had stood aside, were apparently to be made good.

Despite those auspicious signs, 1973 ushered in another decade of stagnation in European integration. The first oil crisis marked the start of a deep depression in the Western world. The felicitous economic conditions of the previous generation—rapid technological innovation, full employment, a successful incomes policy, the apparent success of Keynesian fiscal management—rapidly disappeared as commodity prices spiraled upward relative to industrial prices. The next decade signaled the start of Eurosclerosis. It compelled the agonizing recognition that the profligate welfare state, which had kept the social peace in Europe, had also become a drag on economic growth.

The leading countries in the European Community met that challenge in different ways. The British turned to the free market under Margaret Thatcher in order to remove bottlenecks to labor and capital mobility that had built up like barnacles through a generation of heavy-handed socialism. France, meanwhile, as from a time capsule, revived the nostrums of the prewar Popular Front between 1980 and 1983, while Germany muddled along under a more moderate brand of social market economy. The partner countries failed to maintain the monetary "snake" intact until West German Chancellor Helmut Schmidt permitted the deutsche mark to serve as the anchor currency in 1978; and the EC could not agree on a common energy policy despite the severity of the second oil crisis. Few striking innovations originated from the top down. Yet the proliferating Brussels bureaucracy made progress in modest ways—through the harmonization of social action programs, the creation of a fund for regional development, the reform of the Community budget, an attack on sectoral problems in declining industries, and a renewed focus on north-south issues after the admission of

Greece, Portugal, and Spain. There was frequent talk of malaise in the elegant restaurants off the Avenue Louise, and yet in a hundred small ways Brussels became the locus of a pan-European administrative state and of a European-wide jurisprudence, symbolized by the increasing role of the European Court of Justice in settling antitrust disputes.

Building on those modest advances, the European Community got a second wind as national economies turned up after 1983. With Helmut Kohl's accession to power and acceptance by a sobered François Mitterand of a stable price level and a pro-European policy, the Franco-German engine went into high gear again. This time the leaders aspired to proceed beyond a customs union to a true internal EC market that would allow free flow of labor and capital. Implied in a single market were the fostering of technological progress, arrangements for regional development, and subsidized sectoral adjustment. The Single European Act of 1986 thus embodied ambitious objectives—the cementing of the Franco-German core of the EC, the further refinement of the Exchange Rate Mechanism, and an industrial policy that would allow European firms to compete effectually with U.S. multinationals and East Asian tigers. Although the so-called "relaunch" of the EC and the assault on internal barriers owed much to a Thatcher appointee, Lord Arthur Cockfield, Britain and other peripheral nations proved unwilling to swallow the panoply of measures reified in the Single Act. Once again, exogenous events—this time the reunification of Germany and the collapse of communism in Eastern Europe—mandated another effort to reequilibrate the Franco-German relationship.

It is far from surprising that the Maastricht summit of 1992 has led to a "Europe with variable geometry" rather than to the hoped-for "Europe without frontiers." As German unification became inevitable, Mitterand and EC President Jacques Delors came to perceive the adoption of a social charter and a common currency not as mere ends in themselves, but as mechanisms to reanchor the greater Germany in an institutional architecture designed by France. This is a plausible interpretation that we can give to Jacques Delors's 1989 address to the European Parliament: "It will not be enough to create a large frontier-free market nor . . . a vast economic area. It is for us . . . to put some flesh on the Community's bones and to give it a little more soul." The reaffirmation of the Schengen Agreement for open borders among the inner Five, the creation of a Franco-German military corps, and the initiation of a Common Foreign and Security Policy (however embryonic it remains to date) form part of an ongoing effort to make Europe the common project of Franco-German reconciliation.

American economists have voiced numerous technical criticisms of the Economic and Monetary Union. The pessimists claim that one cannot maintain a unified monetary policy without a common fiscal policy and a comparable willingness to tolerate unemployment for the sake of labor market flexibility. The optimists, mostly European, counter that one cannot achieve a true single market without exchange rate stability, that a common currency and central bank will generate pressures toward fiscal convergence, and that a financial market in euros will facilitate a reduction of dollar reserves and buy time for such convergence. A common currency will also make trade in goods and services increasingly transparent, tie wage rates closer to productivity, make capital more available, and promote lower interest rates. But technical controversies largely miss the point. As Hervé de Charette, the former foreign minister, has observed, "La monnaie, c'est bien entendu un projet politique." The common currency is meant to render European integration irreversible. It confirms the choice for deepening Europe as it is and for postponing a widening to the east until the former communist states can meet the economic criteria for entry.

That process may take a very long time. In the more immediate future, there remains an urgent need for reconfiguring the relationship between Europe and the United States. We must elaborate a new transatlantic bargain that takes into account both economics and strategy. The Clinton administration has neglected that task. The solid bonds across the Atlantic so laboriously forged in Jean Monnet's generation have snapped and are no more. Historians, wisely, do not predict the future. I close by noting that Jean Monnet kept in his office a model of the raft *Kon-Tiki*, on which Thor Heyerdahl crossed the South

Pacific. Monnet would surely welcome the challenges to come in the twenty-first century, confident of his ultimate direction, yet ever alert to the pragmatic opportunities of the hour.

BIBLIOGRAPHY

Apel, Emmanuel. *European Monetary Integration, 1958–2002.* London, 1998.

Boyce, Robert. *British Capitalism at the Crossroads, 1919–1932.* Cambridge, 1987.

Brinkley, Douglas, and Clifford Hackett, eds. *Jean Monnet: The Path to European Unity.* London, 1991.

Bromberger, Merry, and Serge Bromberger. *Jean Monnet and the United States of Europe.* New York, 1968.

Calleo, David, ed. *Europe's Franco-German Engine.* Washington, D.C., 1998.

Duchêne, François. *Jean Monnet: The First Statesman of Interdependence.* New York, 1994.

George, Stephen. *An Awkward Partner: Britain in the European Community.* Oxford, 1990.

———. *Politics and Policy in the European Community.* Oxford, 1996.

Gillingham, John. *Coal, Steel, and the Rebirth of Europe, 1945–1955.* Cambridge, 1991.

Glaser, Elisabeth. "European Integration between the Wars: The World Economic Conference of 1927." Working Paper of the American Institute for Contemporary German Studies, Washington, D.C., 1996.

Hirsch, Etienne. *Ainsi va la vie.* Lausanne, 1988.

Lodge, Juliet, ed. *The European Community and the Challenge of the Future.* London, 1989.

Mauriac, Claude. *The Other de Gaulle, 1944–1954.* London, 1973.

Mazzucelli, Colette. *France and Germany at Maastricht.* New York, 1997.

Middlemas, Keith, et al. *Orchestrating Europe: The Informal Politics of European Union, 1973–95.* London, 1995.

Milward, Alan S. *The European Rescue of the Nation State.* London, 1992.

———. *The Reconstruction of Western Europe, 1945–1951.* London, 1984.

Milward, Alan S., et al. *The Frontier of Sovereignty: History and Theory, 1945–1992.* London, 1993.

Mioche, Philippe. *Le Plan Monnet, genèse et élaboration, 1941–1947.* Paris, 1987.

Monnet, Jean. *Memoirs.* London, 1978.

Pedersen, Thomas. *Germany, France, and the Integration of Europe: A Realist Interpretation.* London, 1998.

Pegg, Carl. *Evolution of the European Idea, 1914–1932.* Chapel Hill, 1983.

Roussel, Eric. *Jean Monnet.* Paris, 1996.

Urwin, Derek W. *The Community of Europe: A History of European Integration since 1945.* London, 1991.

Musings on the European Economic and Monetary Union

HUGO M. KAUFMANN

It is a great honor, and a major challenge, to be the after-dinner speaker at the close of a long day of EMU exercises—exercises that started the prior day with a seminar in the economics department, followed by a dinner with a major address, proceeding today since the early morning hours, and continuing in a different setting and with a larger audience way into the evening. For more than twenty-four hours we have breathed EMU [the European Economic and Monetary Union]. Even security implications of EMU—that is, national security, not the security or securities of national and international financial markets and the banking industry, have been examined. This tour de force has not been for the faint of heart. In light of the late hour, I shall take an eclectic approach addressing potential problems that ought not be ignored, despite the successful, smooth introduction of the euro as a unit of account and its behavior in the first ten months since its birth.

Holding the EMU conference this weekend has been fortuitous: the German presidency was—as most of us expected it would be—unsuccessful in its effort to push the budgetary issue well along before the March meeting on budget reform, which was to include major and much-needed reform of the Common Agricultural Policy (CAP), the European Economic Union's golden calf. At the time of preparation for the next round of the World Trade Organization (WTO) negotiations, it was then still doubtful that progress on agricultural subsidies would be reached in time. But the extreme reluctance to touch CAP and reduce farm support is about to change.

The discussions have confirmed that the 1999-model EMU can—unlike its predecessor—indeed fly. For some, the big surprise may have come in May 1998, when the EMU charter membership was determined. The big EMU debate in 1996 and 1997 had been over the number and composition of founding-member countries. There were, however, several undisputed aspects: EMU, without its heavyweights, Germany and France (the prime movers), would not make much sense. Nor would a Luxembourg membership without Belgium's, since the two countries were already in a monetary union. One country, Luxembourg (one of the few countries that met the Maastricht criteria), without Belgium (which had a debt-to-GDP ratio twice the permissible one) would have meant a disengagement of that union. In the run-up to the initiation of EMU most observers had speculated about an EMU with five to seven charter members rather than the eleven that made it to the December 31, 1998, finish line.

Others had argued, more fundamentally and radically, that the time for EMU had not yet come; that for various rational economic reasons, it would be wise to ignore the fact that the Maastricht Treaty had set the clock ticking on automatic. The start of EMU should be postponed for a more opportune time—if not scuttled altogether. This being the British position especially. But then, probably no time would have been opportune, let alone ideal; and that having set target dates, as with the Single European Act's Project 1992, which was to complete the European Community's internal market, creates its own dynamics and concentrates one's mind.

We can safely state that a few issues stand out with the creation of the European Economic and Monetary Union:

For one, we have been witness to a most unusual development in the annals of national and international political economy. Sovereign nations have voluntarily decided to forgo one of their most important and ancient symbols of national political and economic autonomy: the right and authority to issue legal tender independently, where the legal-tender status of the means of payments in most instances coincided with the geographic boundaries of the nation-state. On the other hand, economic and monetary union abolishes those boundaries in the area of national economic policy, especially monetary policy. That finds its expression partly in irrevocably fixing their exchange rates or, even better, replacing national currencies with a single currency and the centralization of economic decision making for the union—in this particular instance in the hands of the European Central Bank (ECB). Historically speaking, irrevocability has been tampered with time and again and the suspicion of a conceivable break-up remains. The risk factor connected with the existence of different national currencies is, thus, completely removable.

Second, we might immediately ask ourselves, And what about fiscal policy? So far, fiscal policy remains in the hands of the national governments. Then the question arises as to how one can reconcile the fact that one of the two main macroeconomic policy instruments, monetary policy, will be administered at the center of the Union through the ECB, while the other fiscal policy will remain, albeit with limitations, in the hands of the national governments. The Stability and Growth Pact requires the nations to pursue and maintain the medium-term objective of a budget that is close to balance or in surplus.

Third, EMU substantially alters the international monetary and financial structure of post–World War II international arrangements—at least in Europe—and is, among others, a renewed expression of the belief that the monetary system on which one is not, happens to be the better arrangement. It is yet another link in the alternation between flexible and fixed exchange rates with managed (or dirty float) rates occupying a middle ground—all in an attempt to devise a well-functioning, efficient international monetary structure.

For the longest time, France has expressed great interest for the Group of Seven Industrialized Countries (G7) to institutionalize greater exchange rate stability, not only among themselves, as then expressed in the creation of the European Monetary System, but also between the dollar, the euro, and the yen through the establishment of exchange rate target zones for those currencies. More on that later.

EXPECTATIONS FROM ECONOMIC AND MONETARY UNION

European countries, intent on forming an Economic and Monetary Union, have pinned great hopes on EMU, as they did before on the

European Community's Project 1992, as if they were *dei ex machina*—which they distinctly are not. How high the expectations have been of EMU can be gleaned from the furious pace with which the Mediterranean laggards had moved to meet the Maastricht Convergence Criteria in order to become acceptable and be accepted as charter members in the elite club. I must add, however, that restrictive fiscal and anti-inflation policies were needed; EMU or no EMU, the necessary incentives for engaging these policies had been missing, as had the courage to introduce and administer unpopular policies before the Maastricht Treaty.

Greece's effort to join the club before the introduction of the euro as currency must not be underrated, and the most recent indications (fall 1999) are that Greece might be ready by 2002. Its projected inflation is down to 2.5 percent, its projected budget-deficit-to-GDP ratio at 1.5 is well within the Maastricht convergence criterion of below 3 percent when the economy is expanding, and its debt-to-GDP ratio has steadily declined to 105 percent, from 112 percent (1996).[1]

It seems entirely feasible that none of the PIGS (Portugal, Italy, Greece, and Spain), will be left behind come January 2002. Of course, it is the political prestige attached to entering EMU as a charter member, as much as the expected economic advantage, that propelled countries to partake in the endgame. Moreover, the larger the number countries joining from the inception, the greater the disadvantage from being excluded—or even staying behind, even if voluntarily.

With the grouping of the eleven initial members, EMU will have a population exceeding that of the United States, and its 16 percent share of world output (GDP) is about four percentage points less than that of the United States. As more countries join EMU, the gap will narrow and the United States will encounter a serious competitor in the not-too-distant future, especially in the monetary field.

Some Main Characteristics of EMU

Perhaps the most prominent characteristic of a monetary union and arguably its major cost is the loss of policy control in the member states, certainly in the monetary field, which includes exchange rate changes. Loss of national economic and possibly political sovereignty as well, further down the road, is a by-product of monetary union, irrespective of whether EMU comes with "irrevocably fixed" exchange rates or the ultimate in irrevocability, the elimination of different currencies. With the resultant monetary policy of one size fits all, monetary policy will be conducted no longer by the individual central banks, but will be determined at the center; in this case by the European Central Bank in Frankfurt am Main—for the entire Economic and Monetary Union—while fiscal policy will remain, however with strict limitations, in the hands of nation-state governments.

Expected Benefits from Monetary Union

A brief sketch ought to highlight the purported costs and benefits of membership in EMU and what countries might and might not expect for themselves and from their membership. These will then be held against the costs of membership that have to be expected. The question is not whether there will be a free lunch—there will be none—but who is going to bear the cost, and how the cost is going to be distributed among members and between the members and the nonmembers of the Economic and Monetary Union. We must assume that, as rational players (if, indeed, they are rational), the actors would expect the benefits to outweigh the costs—at least for the prime movers, even if, perhaps, not for the Community as a whole. A form of burden shifting might accompany the exercise. Additionally, we can rely on the advocates of new programs, including the EMU, to lean toward overstating projected benefits from the undertaking and underestimating its costs; otherwise there would be no takers. Indeed, leaders of doubting people might abhor the idea of giving citizens referenda, having learned a lesson from the experiences of Denmark, which in its first referendum on the Maastricht Treaty rejected it; of Norway and of Switzerland, both countries having rejected EU membership thus far. And since benefits have never come without costs, what matters is their relative magnitude and the net gains (losses).

Probably the major apparent benefit is the elimination of the exchange rate risk among the countries that participate in a monetary union. This in itself reduces not only the costs associated with exchange rate fluctuations, but it eliminates speculative attacks against currencies from within the Union and probably reduces the attack from the outside, since fluctuations for the Union might be smaller. What had been external imbalances before economic union become internal ones, reducing the demand for foreign-exchange reserves, while at the same time the pooling of Union reserves leaves the ECB with a much greater war chest to intervene in the market for foreign exchange— making attacks potentially costlier, thus less attractive.

The constellation was particularly unfortunate for the members of the Exchange Rate Mechanism (ERM) of the European Monetary System (EMS) in the summer of 1992 and led to speculative attacks in September, ultimately forcing the United Kingdom and Italy to abandon the pegged-rate system of the ERM. Europe suffered from widespread recession, as the unemployment rate climbed to 10 percent. Lowering interest rates in some high-unemployment countries would have led to massive capital outflows. Germany resisted concerted monetary policy of lower interest rates, as the Deutsche Bundesbank (DBB) feared the inflationary impact it would have exerted on top of the inflation already imparted on Germany from its unification. Quite to the contrary, the Bundesbank saw itself forced to conduct a tight-money policy even though it had an upward pull on interest rates in other countries. Turmoil in foreign-exchange markets developed expectations that at least three countries— France, the United Kingdom, and Italy—would succumb to internal political pressures and abandon a Germany-induced tight-money policy.

Experiences in the 1930s' worldwide depression and competitive devaluations, and fear of a repetition of such a scene in the wake of the 1998 Asian crisis, strengthened the desire to reintroduce an international monetary system that would be more stable through introducing target zones for exchange rates and even reimposition of capital controls to stem the speculative capital movements. Speculative capital flows have génerally been blamed for the international financial turmoil.

Clearly, within EMU, intra-EMU speculative capital flows in anticipation of exchange rate changes were no longer conceivable. With the lowering of potential for speculative attacks on an individual currency, and the greater expected stability of the aggregate of European currencies, the risk premium associated with holding foreign exchange—by both insiders and outsiders—will be lower. With it, the cost of borrowing will also decline.

This, in turn, will transmit a stimulus for investment activity as interest rates fall owing to lower risk, as exchange rate volatility is reduced and members' exchange rate changes are eliminated. An added benefit is that lower interest rates make it also somewhat easier for governments to satisfy the requirements of the Stability and Growth Pact that puts a ceiling on government deficit at three percent of GDP. A higher level of economic activity will also help, keeping debt within the prescribed limits and reducing the government debt. Yet, in spite of the convergence that took place in the real sector and the reduced risk, the yield spreads on non-German eurozone benchmark bonds have increased slightly over the level they had reached six months before the start of the monetary union.[2]

An obvious benefit of currency unification is a reduction of transaction costs from no longer having to convert domestic currencies into foreign exchange or vice versa, an estimated saving of about 0.4 percent of GDP. On the other hand, banks will have to forgo the income they derived from currency conversion. But this loss cannot be considered a loss to society, since the cost of those transactions has been deadweight cost, and as such was of no benefit to society. With a single currency, hedging operations against exchange rate movements will also fall by the wayside, and with them, the costs of those transactions.

The Costs of Monetary Unification

As mentioned earlier, the most obvious cost of monetary union is the loss of autonomy in conducting monetary policy. But for the smaller countries this has been the case for quite some time, as it has also been for the larger ones—with the exception of Germany. Also, as a result of the liberalization of capital flows since 1992, interest rate differentials when adjusted for inflation differentials have been shrinking over the years. However, with EMU, the smaller countries will have greater influence than before, owing to their ability to vote when setting the direction of monetary policy, even though it is the task of the ECB to conduct a policy of price stability.

What many consider an advantage—the absence of speculative exchange rate changes and exchange rate uncertainty—has also eliminated what might be much needed: real effective exchange rate changes in response to shocks, especially asymmetric ones. These shocks affect different countries differently as a result of their unequal endowments or economic structures—which generally are more dissimilar than are regional differences within countries. A long literature has been spawned, analyzing the question of how a single monetary policy in the EU will, and whether it actually can, handle asymmetric shocks. Also the question is raised in this context, whether the EU, and especially the completion of the Single European Market as well as monetary unification, will lead to greater country specialization or whether the countries will become more similar. The impact of further country integration on a European scale on similarities or dissimilarities in economic structure will greatly affect the degree of ease or difficulty with which the ECB can conduct a single EMU-wide monetary policy.

The euro will fluctuate against the other currencies, as it should. There is continuous discussion in some circles (French, German, and Japanese) of setting up an international monetary system that will reintroduce target zones, as if that were a way to assure greater exchange rate stability between the major currencies. Such anticipations ignore past lessons: international monetary arrangements with exchange rate target zones did not exhibit great stability, nor did they prevent major currency crises. Markets will test the ability and determination of central banks to lean against the wind and stay within the agreed-upon target zones, and if they are not revealed, the markets will test the waters and set out to find them. Possibly worse, target zones might actually increase exchange rate volatility as they reintroduce the one-way bets, which were so detrimental to pegged rates under both the Bretton Woods and the ERM arrangements.

EMU has been blamed for many unpleasant economic policies that preceded the membership in EMU and the introduction of the euro, in particular high interest rates, and high unemployment. They were seen, at least partly, to be the consequence of the change in governments' fiscal policies to achieve rapid reductions in the budget deficits and the national debts, as required by the Maastricht Convergence Criteria.

EMU members, by accepting the Stability and Growth Pact, have agreed to limit the use of fiscal policy through multilateral surveillance. Members are expected not only to reduce their budget deficits and debt-to-GDP ratios to *meet* the Maastricht Convergence Criteria, but also to *maintain* budgetary discipline according to the Stability and Growth Pact. Strict limitations as to how far deficit spending is permitted in a particular period have been set, and member states' budgetary strategies are examined by the European Council. Consequently, adjustments against recessions or overheating of economic activity will have to be made primarily through wages and prices or labor migration from one country to another.

Inflation and Performance at the End of 1998

As of December 1998, EU inflation was about half of what it was in the previous year—having fallen to an annualized average of 0.8 percent—in France 0.3 percent and in Germany 0.4 percent. Only Ireland's and Portugal's were above 2 percent. According to EuroStat, annual inflation in the EU member states had fallen to 1 percent on average in December 1998, compared with 1.6 percent in December 1997. In the meantime, Spain joined the ranks of the higher-inflation countries, and while the initial stance of the ECB was to lower interest rates, its latest move (November 4, 1999) was a much-anticipated fifty-basis-point increase in its lending rate.

Interestingly, in the context of ECB policy and national autonomy, the Bank of England, an outsider, also raised its repo rate (by twenty-five basis points); the Swiss National Bank, on the other hand, did not follow the lead of the ECB, although it had done so in the past.

What We May Not Expect from EMU and the Euro

Full employment: Many have believed that EMU, by its very nature of currency unification, would make the unemployment problem tractable and solvable. This expectation was overly optimistic, and if proof be needed, it could be found in Germany: the unemployment differences in the two Germanies, where the unemployment rate in the East is twice that of Western Germany—a decade after its unification and a fiscal transfer of over a trillion deutsche marks (DM) during that decade—amply demonstrates that a single currency does not bring forth convergence in the real sector automatically.

The major handicap in finding a solution to the unemployment problem has been that it was interpreted as almost exclusively a demand instead of a supply problem. Consequently, the approach to the solution was from the macroeconomic rather than from the microeconomic side. As has been pointed out, especially here in the United States and in Great Britain, and by some international organizations, Europe would have to introduce greater flexibility in the labor market and employment laws. To this date, the European Union seems to have moved, if anything, in the opposite direction, introducing cost-increasing labor regulation, resisting greater flexibility, and rejecting it as representative of the Anglo-Saxon model—not exactly a complimentary term on the European Continent.

Possible Effects of EMU on the EU Banking System

First, and most obvious: we expect a reduction in foreign-exchange transactions and income from those transactions to soften the impact on employment. This may lead to greater banking activity in other markets, especially in securities transactions. With the introduction of the euro and the elimination of exchange rate risk, we may expect deeper and more liquid integrated capital markets, generating growth but also increased competition in this area. There may also be a reduction in government debt owing to fiscal consolidation, freeing funds for the private sector, so that the private capital market takes over some of the reduction of transactions in the government bond market.

With the introduction of the euro, a single money in Euroland and with it greater transparency, competition in the financial sector is bound to increase as customers search for higher-yielding investments as bank deposits are expected to yield lower interest returns than before. One might expect further market liberalization, intensification of competition, pressure on bank profitability, transnational mergers, and geographical diversification in the financial industry. Some major transnational and even transatlantic mergers have already taken place, as well as strategic alliances and cooperation arrangements. Together with the merger movement and increased competitive pressures on the banking industry, services will improve and variety of products will likely increase.

The ECB expects reduced credit risk in the euro area resulting from positive macroeconomic developments and from the elimination of intra-EMU exchange rate losses and interest rate risks.

▓ THE EUROSYSTEM

The European Central Bank and the European System of Central Banks

The overarching consideration of the central bank position is that it not be beholden to the political powers—neither the member countries nor any of the institutions of the EU, including the European Parliament. While this seems unambiguous enough, there are some peculiarities in the structure which deserve mention. Such independence is seen as indispensable if the central bank is to achieve the goal of price stability, as there is an established negative correlation between inflation and central bank independence.

The Eurosystem comprises the ECB and the EMU member states' central banks. If and when all fifteen member states participate in the euro area, the term *Eurosystem* will be synonymous with the European System of Central Banks (ESCB); the latter includes EU member states that have not yet adopted the euro. The Governing Council of the ECB consists of members of the executive board and the governors of the national central banks (NCBs) of the member states that have adopted the euro. The Executive Board is composed of the president, vice president, and four members appointed by the heads of state or government of the member states that have adopted the euro. The ESCB is governed by the Governing Council and the Executive Board of the ECB and, as a third decision-making body of the ECB, by the General Council, comprising the president, vice president, and the governors of all fifteen NCBs. While the members of the ECB council come from the member countries, they must conduct monetary policy for the entire EU.[3] Quite a quilt this is.

Central Bank Independence—Concept and Rationale

Great confusion reigns concerning the meaning of central bank independence (CBI) and the distinction between independence within the government versus independence of the government. Governments not only determine the budget but also try to finance it as cheaply as possible. The primary task of central banks ought to be preserving price stability by controlling the noninflationary growth of the money supply—the central banks' comparative advantage. This division of responsibility benefits the governments since the central bank, as guarantor of price stability, serves, in addition to everything else and at low cost to governments, as whipping boy during times when tough monetary policy decisions have to be made. Such a situation existed, for instance, when inflation rates in many countries had to be brought down rapidly and persistently in the mid-1990s in order to meet the Maastricht Convergence Criteria. There is a safeguard against the possibility of abuse of independence: to preserve CBI, central banks ultimately need the support of their citizens.

Several criteria have to be fulfilled to consider a central bank independent. Among the most significant is the duration for serving as central bank governor, generally considered to be between five and eight years, and the nonrenewability of a contract. In light of this, Willem Duisenberg, the choice of ten of the eleven euro countries to serve as Euroland's first central bank, rightly resisted French pressures to have Jean-Claude Trichet, president of the Bank of France, replace him after four years and to split his term of service with Trichet. Such an arrangement would have given Trichet the chance to serve for twelve years—Duisenberg's unexpired term plus his own. This splitting of Duisenberg's term was a concession to the French, who wanted their man to serve as ECB president from the beginning. Quite an assault on the principle of central bank *independence,* and this at a time when there was no track record of the ECB and when confidence would have to be earned. It would not have been an overt attack on the central bank pursuing the goal of price stability, at least not initially, since Trichet was known as a staunch inflation fighter, earning him the nickname Trichemeier—combining his name with that of then Bundesbank president Hans Tietmeier. (Tietmeier was not amused.)

It may be of interest to point out, in this context, that independence of national central banks was made one of the prerequisites for accession to Euroland just at the time that the national central banks were about to lose their independence within the ESCB. Independence of national central banks was to guarantee the independence of the ECB, since the presidents of the national central banks serve on its governing board and participate in the formation of EMU monetary policy.

In a show of independence but yet as concerted action, ten of the eleven founding members of EMU lowered their benchmark rates by 0.25 percentage points on December 3, 1998, with Italy, the eleventh, following shortly thereafter. This occurred a few weeks before the ECB started its operations and was designed to make the beginning of ECB operations easier.

Speculation was rife in February with further lowering of the benchmark rate by another 0.25 percentage points, as the new German government let it be known that deflation can be as damaging as inflation. Because of political interference in the beginning of 1999, especially by former German finance minister Oskar Lafontaine, the ECB could not lower interest rates as early as it might have wanted to and as the economic indicators might have given justification to, in order not to give the impression the ECB had caved in to political demands. On April 8, 1999, it finally lowered interest rates by 0.5 percentage points—more than the 0.25 percentage points the markets had anticipated. It had done so as a clear signal that the ECB would not change interest rates so soon again. The Swiss National Bank and the Bank of England, nonmember countries both, lowered their interest rates in tandem,[4] and the Danish National Bank followed with a half-percentage-point cut the following day,[5] a clear indication of the tight interdependence of the European financial markets irrespective of membership in Euroland.

Quantification of Price Stability

Price stability as guidance for ECB monetary policy has been defined as an increase in the harmonized index of consumer prices (HICP) below 2 percent—thus clearly indicating the upper limit of price increases tolerated. However, there is agreement among the policy makers, including Willem Duisenberg, that price decreases were not reconcilable with the goal of price stability either.[6]

One is reminded of the suggestion: neither inflation nor deflation create, but flation? As mentioned earlier, in December 1998, EU inflation was about half of what it had been the previous year. According to EuroStat, annual inflation in the EU-15 had fallen to 1 percent on average in December 1998, compared with 1.6 percent a year earlier, and even the agreement on reducing oil production was not expected to produce substantial price increases.[7]

$1.18–$1.20–$1.25—or is it rather $1.18–$1.15–$1.10–$1.05—*parity?* Which of these dollar-euro exchange rates were we going to see? All numbers were produced as the euro was launched on January 1, 1999.

Whether the euro will be weak or strong, either way the euro will change Europe and its relationship with the trading partners economically and politically—perhaps even culturally; the euro will change Europe's financial position in the world, and it will change the international financial system. However, neither a strong nor a weak euro will come without its benefits—but also its costs.

The euro is slated to be a challenge to the international reserve distribution. Some, among them C. Fred Bergsten, have estimated that the reserve distribution might evolve to be dollar: 40, euro: 40, yen: 20. Since no one can know for sure, this is as good a guess as any.

Exchange Rate Movements

The deutsche mark (DM) and the euro: It had been a mantra and a promise for a long time preceding the introduction of the euro—primarily at the insistence of Germany and in the mouth of German politicians—the euro will doubtless be a strong a currency, as strong as the mark. This was to make the new currency palatable to the German citizens, who had gotten to see the DM as symbol for stability and postwar achievement. But it was also designed to instill confidence in a new currency with which the world had no experience. Only trouble was that by the time the euro was introduced on January 1, 1999, the DM had lost over 20 percent against the dollar. Also ignored in the mantra was that a strong currency has both its advantages and drawbacks for the different sectors of the economy and the population. A strong euro is not advantageous for a Europe suffering from high unemployment.

Meanwhile, euro exchange rate movements have ignored prophecies of both strength and doom, and after having receded almost to parity with the U.S. dollar, seem to settle in a fairly narrow range. The misguided question of whether the euro will be strong or weak has now and then been replaced by what I fear might be an attempt to develop target zones for the dollar-euro-yen triangle.

Some Recent and Not-So-Recent Developments

Some eclectic references to recent developments that might, directly or indirectly, affect the international position of the euro: On the European continent, Norway appears to have had second thoughts on staying out of Euroland—with the Norwegians changing their minds several times. For the first time, polls taken in early in 1999 indicate that in a new referendum a majority of Norwegians would now favor membership—favorable assessment that has since been reversed. Similar mood swings could be observed in Sweden, all related to the sometimes less-than-stellar performance of both the European Union and the euro.

Switzerland might find it too costly to stay outside the European Union and may join the group sooner or later with the enormous disadvantage of having to accept all the rules and regulations of the EU without having had any say in the shaping of the agreements. Owing to the *acquis communautaire* and the Amsterdam Treaty, any new member country will have to accept also the Schengen Agreement, according to which there is free mobility of people among the signatory countries. I would not be surprised to see the euro become initially a parallel currency to the Swiss franc, even before Switzerland's entry into EMU. But no one can refuse Switzerland to shadow the euro. And the latest developments have been mostly a clear indication that no matter how the Swiss population is going to vote concerning EMU membership, the reality of a close link is already there. With trade links and exports to EU of 61 percent, and 70 percent of imports from EU countries, Switzerland is adapting laws and regulations to meet EU standards.[8] Coutts Bank (Switzerland), in a report on Economic and Monetary Union, notes that if the euro stimulates economic growth in the EMU area, Swiss companies will be able to export more. If the euro increases competitiveness, Swiss consumers will benefit from cheaper imports. The euro will be adopted as currency in trade and especially in the financial sector, where Swiss banks have a tradition of carrying deposits in foreign exchange. And the Swiss stock exchange is scheduled to permit parallel trading of shares in Swiss francs and euros.

In England, the Bank of England lowered its benchmark interest rate five times in as many months, most recently February 4, the last time by an unexpectedly large 0.5 percentage points [this key lending rate stood at 7.5 percent on October 8, when the Bank of England started its course of lowering the rate]—bringing it closer to the ECB's, but still leaving it 2 percentage points above Euroland's—and, incidentally, also closer to the Fed's. What happened is that the three "independent" central banks had to calibrate their actions in light of economic and financial developments within EMU, but also considering developments in other part of the world. On November 4, 1999, there was the first increase in interest rates set by the ECB, which was quickly followed by some non-EMU countries, a continuing testimony to the integration of financial markets.

Finally, EMU has not only become a magnet for the European countries, but might be used as an example that finds possible imitators in the Western Hemisphere. Some countries—Argentina and Mexico, for instance—have expressed varying degrees of interest to create a monetary union with the United States—even adopting the U.S. dollar as their currency. And Montenegro announced at the beginning of November 1999 that it would use the DM as a parallel currency partly to demonstrate its independence from Serbia.

Concealed Problems with Agreements

A complicating factor with many agreements and arrangements is that circumstances often change drastically between the time when plans are hammered out and agreed upon and the time when they become effective.

Two examples from recent developments should amply clarify this point:

The European Community's Project 1992 starting period was set for January 1, 1993, but the Single European Act of 1986, the base of Europe 1992, was introduced when the boundaries of Europe were well defined; Europe was Europe—i.e., Western Europe and the EC was a community of twelve members. By the time the Single European Market was to become effective, the Berlin Wall, dividing Germany, was no longer.

Germany had insisted on tough convergence criteria as prerequisite for membership in EMU, with its single currency. But there was a hidden agenda: keep some countries out without naming them. At the time the convergence criteria were set, West Germany had been in excellent financial/fiscal condition and fulfilling the criteria, it seemed, was no problem; but no such luck as the deadline for meeting the criteria approached: inflation rates were higher than even in Italy; deficits had climbed and the debt-to-GDP ratio came precariously close to the limit—even exceeded it. What a few years and unification could do to the impeccable situation.

EMU and the United States

In the end we have to ask, If there have been so many hurdles to get to the beginning of EMU, *cui bono?* We have seen at the beginning of tonight's presentation what the expected benefits are for on the member countries. The EMU might not, and has not been designed to, benefit the United States; on the other hand, irrespective of the benediction, U.S. officials might give and have done so in the past. It is a *fait accompli,* and we have no choice but to adjust to it.

One of the major, and most likely not unintended, implications of EMU and the introduction of a single currency, have been that the dollar will get a serious competitor in countries' selection of their international reserves. So far the dollar has occupied a practically unrivaled position as the international reserve, key, intervention, and vehicle currency par excellence.

One of the consequences will be that the United States might be deprived in future of the luxury of what Charles de Gaulle called the exorbitant privilege of conducting its policies, especially its balance of payments policy, with benign or malign neglect—with a trade deficit for 1998 of $170 billion, up from $110 billion in 1997, and still rising.

Whether the international reserve distribution will be 40-40-20, as Fred Bergsten once intimated, remains to be seen, but the dollar will have a serious competitor. Of course, there are those who argue, *au contraire,* that the dollar will be in even higher demand, since with the merger of Euroland currencies, fewer contenders for reserve-currency status will be available, and currency diversification will enhance the demand for dollars. The same considerations are applicable to the intervention, investment, and key-currency aspects.

EMU countries have a population exceeding that of the United States by about 100 million. Their GDP is $1.5 trillion smaller than that of the United States ($6.5 trillion versus $8 trillion) while each continent's share of world trade is almost the same (18 percent), with both exporting about 11 percent of GDP—most of it to Canada, Mexico, and the EU. Financial markets in Europe have gained in liquidity and depth, and will gradually catch up with U.S. markets. The absence of exchange rate risk for the current eleven members will make the sum of financial resources greater than its parts.

THE UNEMPLOYMENT ISSUE

The European unemployment problem has remained as stubborn and intractable as ever—at least until now. Anyone who still harbors the illusion that eliminating foreign-exchange fluctuations, with all the promised benefits associated with that, would automatically solve one of Europe's main problem—unemployment—is believing futilely in a false god. You need not look farther than Germany, where eastern Germany still suffers from an unemployment rate that is nearly twice as high as western Germany's—a relationship that has remained almost unchanged since the currency unification (incidentally also preceding the political one, as is the case with EMU). And this, after nearly a decade and annual transfers from western to eastern Germany, exceeding 100 billion deutsche marks per annum—over one trillion DM during the last decade.

Europeans' latest attempt at solving the unemployment problem is the left-of-center, socialists' manifesto for jobs, which they planned to use in the June elections for the European Parliament. Rudolf Sharping, Germany's defense minister and president of the Party of European Socialists (PES), talked about special support for small- and medium-size enterprises (SMEs), who in many countries have been the main sources of employment growth. Of course, not all legislation is a guarantee for a desired outcome, especially not if the legislation is fundamentally flawed, increasing cost of production and reducing instead of increasing flexibility in the labor market and thus violating basic economic principles—and common sense.

The manifesto states the support for a market economy but said "no to market society."[9]

Reading manifestos and proposals by the commission and other organizations leaves little doubt that everyone is well-meaning and wishes to accommodate everyone and thinks that one can achieve conflicting goals simultaneously by just legislating them. Few are willing to go beyond paying lip service to the fact that Europe's unemployment is primarily not a macroeconomic—lack of demand that could be tackled through deficit spending and expansionary monetary policy—but a microeconomic problem.

Having stated that, one of the implications is that the ECB alone cannot be held responsible for creating and prolonging high unemployment. At best, the ECB can foster an environment which is consistent with other policy instruments. Microeconomic policy response to the unemployment issue requires the political courage and perseverance to engage in deep structural adjustments—like it or not—patterned in one form or other after the much maligned (by the French) Anglo-Saxon model. I am not advocating exact imitation, but I am at least taking a close and more positive look at some of its undeniable advantages and benefits. Germany's hallowed Social Market Economy has over the years put ever-increasing emphasis on the "social" part. There may be a redirection in the making.

CONCLUSION

Projections about the future are always risky, and the same holds for venturing those about the EMU. The likely enormous expansion of the European Union during the next decade by twelve additional members, might make anyone who dares producing even educated guesses look not only daring but foolish. Thus, I will conclude with a sober assessment: EMU will most likely function less well than the optimists promise themselves, but better than the pessimists expect, with the caveat that the system not be burdened with tasks it cannot handle.

Let us hope the policy makers in all countries as well as those of the European Commission and the European Parliament will adhere to the oath of Hippocrates: Do no harm.

NOTES

I have kept the tenor of this after-dinner speech intact, but have taken the liberty of slightly updating it here and there, where I thought new developments might illustrate points I made.

1. *Financial Times*, November 4, 1999, 25.

2. Federal Reserve Bank of St. Louis, *Monetary Trends*, October 1999, 1.

3. Based on ECB, *Monthly Bulletin*, January 1999.

4. As has been pointed out on other occasions, nonmembership in the EMU does not rule out shadowing ECB policy.

5. *New York Times*, April 10, 1999, C2.

6. Willem F. Duisenberg, "Die 'einheitliche europäische Geldpolitik,'" speech at the University of Hohenheim, February 9, 1999.

7. Willem F. Duisenberg, press conference, April 8, 1999, www.ecb.int/key/st990408.

8. William Hall, "Euro: Switzerland Races against Clock," *Financial Times*, October 22, 1998.

9. Peter Norman, "Europe's Left Backs Manifesto for Jobs," *Financial Times*, January 30/31, 1999, 2. The draft manifesto devoted the first six of "21 commitments for the 21st century" to a "Europe of jobs and growth."

Part II

Jean Monnet: Personality,
Vision, and Legacy

The Man from Cognac

Jean Monnet and the Anglo-American Mindset

HENRY H. H. REMAK

> J'avais la vue d'ensemble.
>
> A une œuvre collective, il faut une organisation collective et une consultation collective constantes.
>
> Pour moi, tout n'est qu'un moyen, même l'obstacle.
>
> Rien n'est efficace autant que la persuasion.
>
> —Jean Monnet

This essay is not—and is not intended to be—a traditional research paper (which would have no negative connotations for me, on the contrary) but the condensed result of my fascination with the singular gestalt of Jean Monnet (1888–1979) for well over thirty years. During that period I have repeatedly visited and worked in the rich archives of the Fondation Jean Monnet pour l'Europe of the Centre de Recherches Européennes at the University of Lausanne, perused its distinguished *Cahiers rouges,* talked to many collaborators of Monnet, from associates, friends, and scholars to his secretaries and his chauffeur, interviewed a number of them (French, American, British), and read additional interviews with European and American statesmen, scholars, and associates harbored in the archives. Basically, what intrigued me, coming from the direction of comparative (particularly West European) literature and culture and, inevitably, its relation to North America, was and is how this unlikely person with an unlikely education from an unlikely corner of France was able to achieve, against all odds, what nobody else has been able to do since Charlemagne: the functioning structure of a European Community (EC). Not alone, certainly, but without him it would not have happened. And the longer I plunged into this (I believe) unique phenomenon, the more surprised (but, to tell the truth, not displeased) I have been to discover how instrumental (but by no means exclusive) the Anglo-American model and reality have been for Monnet in laying the groundwork for a federated Europe. Due to his intervention and his ability to motivate crucial allies and implementers, this is no longer a vision, a dream, let alone an illusion, but a reality, if only the first though crucial step toward a more fully integrated United States of Europe.

This paper is simply a distillation of my total Monnet experience of many years. It has been done, frankly, not to impress but to be read, and possibly to be enjoyed. I do not see why historical-humanistic scholarship needs to encapsulate itself in a hermetically impenetrable language. Monnet certainly did not. His memoirs, in addition to my total Monnet experience and readings, have been my most immediate, crystallizing source. But I have not adorned my essay with numerous footnotes. The main, serialized source of Monnet studies, the *Cahiers rouges*, have few footnotes—and little lingo—but they are widely (not only in academia) read with pleasure as well as profit. I limit my few footnotes, then, in French (since I think it is essential to catch the flavor of the original text) to direct quotations from his recollections.

First, a confession. I am the odd man out in this august assembly. I have never taken a course in political science or economics, much less taught them. When I first went to the equivalents of college, "political science" had not yet been invented. To this day I believe that politics is, ultimately, an art and a high-stake game demanding a total personality of self-confidence, intelligence, eloquence, intuition, sangfroid, stamina, charisma—and luck. Jean Monnet had all of these but especially stamina, exasperating stamina for those whom he badgered for over sixty years with his—not *vision*, not *dream*, he disdained these flaky terms—blueprint, prosaic in form, dramatic in content, of a federated

Europe. If my lack of academically professional credentials in the social sciences renders me suspect in the eyes of my colleagues from that bailiwick, it brings me, in another way, closer to Jean Monnet himself. Not only did he never take advantage of the touted blessings of a university —he did not even finish high school! It bored him, as it has many great minds. It made him nervous. He could not sit still—for the rest of his life. He wanted to get things done. Horror of horrors, he had little respect for intellectuals as such (a Frenchman!), let alone professors *tels quels*. He was not interested in problems but in solutions to problems. Nor did he have any interest in history itself unless it was directly relevant to the prevention of a third world war—likely the last war Europe might ever experience, for after it little of Europe would be left worth saving. Monnet had no political ambitions of his own—none. Even though he was a prominent international banker for much of the 1920s and 1930s, his personal prosperity was secondary to his wider goal of solving economic problems that might otherwise lead to national and international crises and conflicts of major proportions. He was, however, smart and realistic enough to know that without the instrumentation and implementation of his designs by industrialists, labor leaders, and politicians in office (the higher the better), his ideas would remain—ideas.

And he was extra smart in always giving the politicians, not himself, credit for passing "his" legislation and in rarely criticizing them if they failed—because there was always a next time! Yet he detested the lethargy, the stifling of imagination, of calculated risk endemic to ensconced bureaucracy so dominant on the European continent. How could this outsider get so far with the implementation of his ideas without ever entering French government service except when on special assignment giving him wide latitude to achieve his mission in his own way? The only regular "office job" he held was deputy secretary-general of the League of Nations from 1919 to 1923, although we have it on good authority that he hardly kept regular office hours. The constrictions of *Beamtentum*, *fonctionnarisme* never suited his style. He literally could not sit still.

How could a cognac salesman working for his family's relatively small firm turn out to shape—more decisively, if unobtrusively, than perhaps any peacemaking European leader of the twentieth century—world politics, coordinate the industrial procurement of France and Great Britain during the First World War, of Great Britain and the United States during the Second World War, maneuver in crucial Algeria (1942–43) between Vichy's Admiral Jean Darlan (assassinated December 25, 1942) and his honest, patriotic, but politically inept successor, General Henri Giraud, be entrusted by President Charles de Gaulle, who spoke of him condescendingly and disliked him personally, with the reinvention of the French economy in the immediate post–World War II period? Design, with French Foreign Minister Robert Schuman, the groundbreaking European Coal and Steel Community (ECSC) (1949) and be named its first president (1950–55)? Secure the agreement of the French government for a bold European Defense Community Plan in 1952, only to be defeated by an exasperating procedural vote in the French National Assembly (August 30, 1952)—and yet finally see the achievement, in his lifetime, of the reality (if not formality) of this concept in spite of the intransigence of President de Gaulle? Lay the foundation for Euratom and the European Economic Community (EEC) at the Messina meeting (1955) and seal the formal reality of the Organization for European Economic Cooperation (OEEC) in the Treaty of Rome (1957)? Spearhead the Action Committee for a United States of Europe (1955–75) and dissolve it, with measured confidence, after having established, four years before his death, at age eighty-seven, the ground floor for its goal through the European Council of Heads of State and Government (meeting, it was expected, at regular intervals, but no less than three times a year)? And here we are, despite the inevitability of temporary reverses such as British and sporadic Scandinavian reluctance to endorse all of Maastricht, with the euro, not only an officially imposed but, as I have been able to convince myself *sur place*, already natural and familiar common currency on the old continent so deeply marked by historical cleavages, by the residues of collective memories, by history that is not just about the past!

How did he do it in France, of all lands, a culture so markedly conscious of its unique, glorious heritage, when by all French logic he could not and should not? A Frenchman who, from his first two-year-long stay in England (1904–6) as a cognac salesman, made no bones about his admiration for British step-by-step evolutionary pragmatism in lieu of grandiose rhetoric (à la de Gaulle) more at home in his own country? And who relegated England to second place in his inspiration only to substitute the United States, even better than the United Kingdom in "getting it done," as number one? Who admired the American constitution as one of the greatest documents of all time and whose favorite bedside reading was the Federalist papers? Who shocked even some of his American, let alone European, friends by proclaiming his admiration for the Continental uniformity of American fast-food chains, thus putting the continental European obsession with a highly calibrated hierarchy of menus into critical perspective? What a treasonous sell-out for a Frenchman, denizen of the proudest gastronomic culture on our globe!

These pronounced American proclivities surely hurt him with de Gaulle and at least initially with many other compatriots, but they also helped him in the long run, since twice in this lifetime the fate of France hinged on its wartime alliance with Great Britain as well as the United States, and Monnet understood their approach to businesslike action in all spheres of life better than any other Frenchman of his time. France, twice in half a century on the brink of defeat, needed him, if somewhat *contre cœur,* and the two Anglo-Saxon countries needed him also as they had to confront the direst existential emergency of Western civilization in modern times: Adolf Hitler.

What extraordinary combination of personality and circumstances drove this singular, inconspicuous and ultimately, against all odds, so productive provincial French cognac salesman with his Anglo-Saxon propensities to become the progenitor of the European Community?

Actually, Monnet's home environment furnished him with the roots of his productive empathy for the Calvinist work credo fundamental to the operation of the Anglo-Saxon world: the originally ascetic, self-demanding, self-critical soul searching based on voluntary renunciation or deferral of self-gratification in the hope but by no means certainty of ultimate grace. This dour, religious self-discipline turned out to be the very source of the secular success of long-term investment-based Western capitalism.

Historically, the links with the Calvinist Anglo-Saxon work ethic of the Kingdom of Aquitaine, the old identity of the larger domain of which Monnet's ancestral province, the Charente, is a part, are unusually strong: geographically, dynastically, politically, culturally, commercially, personally. The Charente, in which Monnet's hometown, Cognac, is located has, to this day, the reputation of producing a special kind of people: canny, crafty, earthy, smart, stick-to-it-and-don't-be-fooled, patient, tenacious—appropriate to the slow, at its best about seven-year-long maturing, in venerable oaken barrels, of its world-famous cognac product. The Charente—not surprisingly also the home of François Mitterand—is about the equivalent of our Show Me State, Missouri. The British presence in the history of southwestern France's viticultural commerce has been distinct and enduring: witness the names of such famous cognac firms as Hennessy, Hine, Martell, etc. What would, under different constellations, have been provincial, small-town, self-sufficient Frenchmen, had continuous commercial and very personal contacts with Great Britain. Monnet himself, leaving high school before graduation, started selling his paternal product, J.-G. Monnet cognac, from age sixteen, first in England, then all over Europe, the United States, and Canada. This gave him a direct, down-to-earth insight into Anglo-American psychology in depth—not just of the thin upper layers of society—that proved to be exceptionally productive in understanding the hinterland of the bankers, economists, businessmen, industrialists, politicians, and statesmen in English-speaking cultures with whom he had to deal to get things done. It was precisely one of the rare, long-term strengths of Monnet that he did not limit himself to the dogged pursuit of persuading top players in highly differentiated cultures of the substantive, logical, and pragmatic rightness of his ideas—he was even able to tell them that he had already probed, in many cases up and down, representatives, voters, and other regional interest groups—that is, domestic constituencies which, let us not forget, are at least as important in the foreign- or continental-policy decisions of elected politicians (looking to their and their party's reelection) as the necessities of the world outside their bread and butter.

Along the same line, Monnet understood, early for his time, the crucial intermediary role played by journalists between legislators / government leaders and their electorate, especially in predominantly Protestant nations such as, in his case, the pivotal United Kingdom and the United States. So he also sounded them out, consulted them, and took their advice seriously. Naturally, having had a stake in the genesis of his projects, these journalists were inclined to view them sympathetically once they were submitted to the public at large.

A further, for a Frenchman, exceptional factor prepared Monnet for his unusual empathy for the Protestant, result-minded, feel right (not just feel good)–oriented work ethic. Monnet, like the overwhelming majority of his compatriots, was born and died a Catholic, but there is little indication that he practiced his religion to any extent. Familial fidelity considerations likely were instrumental in his formal adherence. France has never recovered from the suppression of its indigenous Protestantism, the revocation by Louis XIV, in 1685, of Henri IV's wise Edict of Nantes (1598) that had given French Protestants, at least officially, equal citizenship and religious practice rights. The annulment of the Edict of Nantes left French Protestants with the dismal choice of converting to Catholicism, leaving their country, or the official conversion to Catholicism but often with the secret practice of Protestantism, liable to extreme penalties. But in certain regions of the country, particularly southern and southwestern France, Monnet's own, Protestantism (presently about 2 percent of the French population) has survived or regrouped, and Cognac in particular has been a stronghold of it. One of the incisive early recollections in Monnet's memoirs is of his mother's—a "religious" and "very tolerant" Catholic—admiration for a Protestant family friend, Monsieur Barrault, who—a Biblical picture—"abandoned his plow" every Sunday to officiate at services in the Protestant temple in Segonzac. "He is a man of the Bible," she would say respectfully.

Most of Monnet's business life in the 1920s and 1930s was in banking and financial advising all over the globe. It is not irrelevant to note that to this day French Protestants are prominent in banking and industry (as well as in the diplomatic service) far beyond their low percentage of the French population. Not only was Monnet interacting with these constituencies in France but also as an international banker and financial adviser in the United States, working in a sector dominated to this day by Protestants or Protestant work habits. Furthermore, his favorite manner of graphically delineating vast economic procurement and political integration problems was the balance sheet: credits to one side, debits to the other, with the aim of coming out in the black rather than the red. It was not only a consanguineous way to control the pragmatic accuracy of, or correct, his own thinking but a graphic teaching and persuasion device for those he wanted to convince. To think in terms of credits and debits beyond existential necessities, beyond making ends meet, may seem very secular, but for both practicing Catholics and Protestants, and most acutely for Calvinists, the day of reckoning is precisely that: the externally, divinely decided balance sheet and, for Calvinists especially, a lifelong self-reckoning, the obligation of constant soul searching from a long-term spiritual perspective which, oddly enough, paid off by its transfer to financial, long-range, delayed self-gratification (capitalism in business) and the hope, engendered by worldly success achieved with a good conscience, that it might be the harbinger of eternal grace. Monnet fits that pattern minus, however, a concern about eternal life.

Whatever the wider roots and ramifications of his evolution, the closer one looks at Monnet's recollections of his childhood and adolescence in his memoirs ("Une enfance à Cognac") the more one is astonished to what extent the fundamental culture of provincial Cognac provided a fertile soil for his subsequent international convictions as well as strategies. Jean Monnet's practical imagination, to the extent one can attribute individual character traits to heredity and immediate environment, was also derived from a viable fusion of the imagination of his father with the practicality of his mother as well as from the ethics of both, and from his contacts in depth and duration with indigenous as well as Anglo-Saxon practical visions.

Long distance advertising did not sell J.-G. Monnet cognac in Hudson Bay or in the Canadian West, only the direct, spoken word, personal confidence between salesman and potential buyer—the instrumentation of Monnet's later, unique international style relying on direct persuasion, not manifestos.

You had to be there yourself to get it done. That provides the key, I submit, to Monnet's very unorthodox, persistent (and, to some, *agaçant* [annoying], perhaps even obnoxious) pursuit of direct contacts with the power brokers, if not (preferably) in body, then by phone. Buttonholing was, for Monnet, as many photographs attest to, not a metaphor but a political as well as emotional necessity. The cognac trade was, Monnet notes in his memoirs, helped in this direct approach to its Anglo-Saxon and other foreign customers because, unlike much of French commerce (and culture), it did not have to go through (or end in) Paris—and again this also turned out to be the pattern for much of Monnet the diplomat's strategy and its dividends. In the cognac trade, confidence had to be backed up by the continuing quality of the product, by the tangible satisfaction each bottle gave to the client—just like building, later on, step by step, patiently, doggedly, on the confidence of the leaders of the West bound to be skeptical of Jean Monnet, the purveyor of such radical, but actually very sensible ideas. Then and later, words did not sell cognac, words did not sell the European community, action did: one sale at a time, one step at a time. Not a promise, only a sale assured the Monnet enterprise and family of making a living, and that's what Jean Monnet the cognac salesman was up to in Germany, Scandinavia, England, the United States, and Canada, and that's what Jean Monnet the salesman of the European community, and ultimately federated union, was up to later on: give the often hard-nosed potential customer the experience of one substantive taste or step, and then another, and then another, in order to reach a goal which the seller has always had in mind: become your client, your collaborator, your ally, and, last not least, your friend.

Another unusual Cognac experience left, I submit, a deep mark on Monnet's subsequent values. In his memoirs, he notes that the "grandes maisons" of the Cognac business, such as Hennessy and Martell, did not try to put the smaller cognac manufacturers, such as J.-G. Monnet, out of business. Here I see the seed of Monnet's subsequent, courageous, and principled insistence that large and small nations must have equality in the decisions of the European Community. That did not and could not mean that vital, especially economic and legal interests of a nation could and should not be taken into account—but that there must be unanimous agreement to them by the member states, large and small, if a political unit wanted to be a full member of the community.

Just as good cognac takes many years to mature in solid-oak barrels and demands long-term planning and patience until the right moment has come to sell it—and resell it, because there will always be competitors trying to beat the customer to it—Monnet, the European-unity salesman, had a long-term excellent but short-term problematic product. He faced daunting obstacles, whether selling fine, aged cognac to settlers in primitive Manitoba or structured European solidarity to the functionally oriented British, challenges leading to redoubling his efforts and fine-tuning the quality of his product and getting ready to seize the right moment to act—which also happens to be what Monnet admired in American business dynamics and political imagination at their best.

Monnet's first deep immersion in the Anglo-Saxon world did not occur on the American continent but when he went to England, at the age of sixteen, in 1905—having happily ditched dry (to him) French school learning—to live there for two years with a wine merchant family to learn what was to be his trade. For the rest of his life, he went back to visit the British Isles at least once every year until he was in his eighties, an inclination and need not characteristic of too many of his compatriots.

What attracted him so early and so long to the British? Basically, it was and remained their unique, deep-seated combination of liberal discipline and disciplined liberty emerging since habeas corpus days, tested and ultimately integrated into a unique combination of formality and informality. Firmly believing that individuals perish but institutions persist—the key to his entire life's work—he admired their soft-spokenness that comes with relaxed self-confidence, the quiet elegance of their manners, exemplified by the City of London, their common sense, the balance between their insularity and the cosmopolitanism inherent in their empire, and equally its orderly, evolutionary relaxation and ultimate dissolution replaced by an informal, voluntary association: the Commonwealth of Nations. Above all—and perhaps with a regretful eye to France—he admired their daily practices, their steady, natural, inner commitment to their public values: as he put it, not just part of their brains but of their bones and their blood. He marveled—who did not?—at their calm resolve after Dunkirk and during the devastating air blitz, truly their finest hour.

His Anglophilia was not shattered by his encounter with the double-strength resistance of Britain's insular steadiness to the unpredictable Continent, reinforced by their ancestral and institutional overseas ties with the Commonwealth and the United States—an enduring phenomenon, as we know. But what for most other people would have been frustrating obstacles were, for Monnet, challenges and opportunities to perfect his act, part of the long-duration perspective of his task. He took them in stride. For anyone who had to cope with the intransigence of a de Gaulle on matters affecting the grandeur of France and the inviolability of the sovereign state, the British were manageable. Monnet was convinced that they were weary of hypotheses, theories, grand design, but respected accomplished facts, ideas of merit that had, initially, proved workable. Monnet relates, for example, that despite earlier and weighty objections to the newly created European Coal and Steel Community, headed by Monnet, the first telegram of cordial congratulations when he arrived in the City of Luxembourg (August 10, 1952) to assume his function came—from Her Majesty's government!

Much as he wanted them to join, Monnet opposed offering particular privileges to the British in hopes of inducing them to join the European enterprise: he knew that once they committed themselves they would be excellent partners. He handled pragmatists much more willingly than visionaries.

Over and over again, with a linear consistency throughout his entire life, work, and strategy that is as rare as it is, in this case, admirable, Monnet's lodestone was necessity, the inescapable reality of a specific situation, a particular circumstance that transformed long-standing hesitations, external and internal, public and personal blockages of all kinds—endemic passivity—into the inevitability of bold action because self-interest finally coincided with other-interest. It is not idealism but pragmatism, dire necessity, that catapulted the twenty-six-year-old Monnet, in 1914, without any political, professional, or administrative credentials except having sold cognac throughout the Western world, to be entrusted by both the French and British governments with the coordination of previously unproductive British and French war procurement during World War I. Without, except for a three-year stint as deputy secretary-general of the League of Nations (1919–1923), any other political or administrative credentials than a very active (and, to some, suspect) international banking career, Monnet became, analogously, in the late 1930s, the principal procurement agent for the British government and, subsequently, the Free French in Washington, D.C., and finally, in 1943, the emissary of President Roosevelt in mediating first between Vichy's collaborationist governor of Algeria, Admiral Jean Darlan, and Algeria's military commander, General Henri Giraud, a fine officer and gentleman but politically not at ease. Monnet's mission was to protect the flanks of the Allies' North African offensive and ultimate landing in Italy.

Healthy unorthodoxy does not have a chance until a dire emergency leaves little choice: witness the long and frustrating wait of Winston Churchill until, when it was almost too late, he got into Great Britain's prime ministership. It is, similarly, Monnet's enlightened pragmatism combined with perseverance that, finally, got Monnet the decisive break; it was those qualities profiled in British and American culture that coincided with and gave a chance to the expansion of Jean Monnet's Cognac core.

Although never relinquishing his respect and affection for British ways, Monnet, working and living off and on in the United States, turned, as his life progressed, steadily in the direction of the United States, involved in major national and international high-risk banking and financial advising ventures throughout the 1920s and 1930s, long before he left for the United States in August 1940 from England, where he had once again coordinated the combined war effort of the French and the British. His mission as head of the joint British–Free French purchasing commission in the United States was to mobilize, urgently, the armament industry of the United States, to have them, in effect, become British military partners while still not officially at war with Germany and its allies (until December 11, 1941). From then on, to the formal end of his official activities as president of the Comité d'Action pour les Etats-Unis d'Europe (1955–1975), Monnet was an unflinching admirer of the "American way." What were the foundations of this astonishing empathy?

Early in his life, in the United States and Canada, as a salesman for J.-G. Monnet cognac, the young man from small Cognac, far from being turned off by the forbidding vastness of this sparsely settled continent, was fired by its unparalleled opportunity for expansion—not only purely geographical but as a chance for the human spirit, honed by European culture but hamstrung by European precedents and occupied land, to expand, to start from scratch. Sent to the solitudes of Manitoba at the age of eighteen to sell cognac ("Don't take books, look through the windows. Talk to the people," his father admonished him—he hardly needed the advice), he was impressed, for the rest of his long life of ninety-one years, by watching, disembarking from trains, waves of immigrants neither from the margins of society nor starved, not speculators but entrepreneurs ready to make nature productive, to give down-to-earth, solid people a better life. "On ne pensait pas aux limites, on ne savait pas où était la frontière."[1]

The British were empirical but their pragmatism was also shaped by the cosmopolitanism of an empire permeated by a self-conscious tradition of insular singularity. America was not and needed not to be a colonial power: it had a whole world to conquer right at home. American pragmatism had a freedom from bygones, an elasticity of thought constantly adjusting to reality (but—and what was important to Monnet—firmly anchored in the American constitution, the Bill of Rights, the Federalist papers, all of which owed a lot to British thought and practice) that produced an imaginative realism, not only outer but inner expansion fed by experience (not ideology or theory, for which Monnet had little regard). Monnet's own goal: a federated, continental Europe liberating itself gradually from inhibiting precedents (particularly the sovereign-state obsession à la de Gaulle) required precisely the imaginative realism that had enabled the United States, after searching discussions, to organize its continent into a federal republic, a central government balancing out with states and individual rights. But British informality gracefully superimposed on time-honored ceremonial was attractive to Monnet throughout his life and work, and he tenaciously stuck to his persuasion that Europe not only needs, but must want Great Britain, so that Great Britain will see that it, too, requires and, ultimately, wants Europe.

The disadvantage in dealing with the United States—that it was far enough from Europe so it could, if need be, act independently from it, its constant and understandable concern with avoiding foreign entanglements that threaten the cherished virginal credo of the American dream—had to be overcome, gradually and perhaps never entirely, by the valid argument that washing its hands of Europe (as in the post-–World War I, persistently isolationist period: witness the enormous difficulties Roosevelt encountered before he "got into the war," forced by Pearl Harbor, for that matter) precisely created, twice in the first half of our century, situations that ultimately forced the New World, at a perilously late hour, to "return" to the Old World and the, perhaps avoidable, loss of life of some of America's finest manhood.

Another conspicuous feature of American culture corresponded to as well as reinforced "the man from Cognac's" own salient drive: accessibility. Basic to the personal-approach principle of Monnet was his conviction that "les oppositions de caractère échappent à la rationalité"[2] and that therefore it was imperative to face and to know them directly. This axiom was quasi-bred into him as a must from adolescence on. To compete with its big-shot rivals in the cognac trade, the Hennessys, Martells, etc., the need for the smaller J.-G. Monnet firm to deal face to face with its clients throughout the world was existential, but it so happened that, fortunately for humanity, Monnet's own impatience with abstractions (leading to his premature departure from school) was in consonance with it. Early in his endeavors, Monnet faced, in France (and elsewhere in Europe), a Napoleonic structure preserving, even in a republican form, a highly stratified and ubiquitous administrative architecture with almost mathematically precise lines of responsibility and therefore of controlled access. Such an major obstacle hindered his antitraditional, pragmatic ideas which stood a much better chance when exposed, face to face, and especially when coupled with the tenacity of this driven salesman of a European confederation.

Monnet's political baptism by fire came early during World War I. Hardly had the fighting commenced when France, reeling under the apparently irresistible drive of the German army toward Paris, relocated its government to Bordeaux, not far from Cognac. The young salesman of twenty-five persisted, against the seasoned reservations of the family, in seeking a personal interview (via family connections, the legendary way of circumventing the inert official hierarchy in traditional cultures) with the French prime minister, René Viviani, and managed to persuade him, despite prohibitive odds, to give him a chance to engineer a collaborative effort between France and England to coordinate their military procurement needs. It was not a glamorous breakthrough likely to catch the headlines, then and later, but, characteristic of and for Monnet, basic, in the long run, for victory.

In his subsequent activities, Monnet maintained and refined his uncanny, determined ability to have direct access to the top: Millerand, Clémenceau, de Gaulle, Churchill, and Roosevelt. Direct accessibility of U.S. public servants and public service agencies to individual Americans is part of the unwritten constitution and certainly of the deep-down expectations of the citizens of the United States. It is historically rooted in the populist direction American politics took under Andrew Jackson in the 1830s. Many subsequent American sources have fed it: the growth of literacy, the ultimate accessibility of the vote to geographically isolated, disenfranchised, or otherwise impeded groups of the population, the spectacular surge of technological communications (trains, telegraph, telephone, cars, planes, etc.) demanded by a continental nation of rapid growth, but also the psychological need for Americans finding themselves alone (and even bored) in their (compared to Western Europe) vast spaces and yearning for what I call numerous gregariousness to have a say in, be a part of the implementation of the American dream. In particular, economic entrepreneurship —the prime cause of American power—the organized exploitation of natural resources, human and terrestrial, to serve a potential market scattered all over the continent, was and is a driving force in this need or urge to this day.

As Monnet saw it, the American genius was nourished not only by the urge of conquering wide-open spaces at home but of organizing them—and in general, not only by its drive for innovation as such but for organizing it, often in imaginative and yet, at its best, pragmatically promising ways. This urge, this talent, corresponded, in turn, to the leitmotif of Monnet's life: Individuals perish, institutions persist. Motivation, effort, ideas, in the right direction, were essential, but not enough. Structure was indispensable for survival. Only the union of "effort and discipline" by "energetic and responsible men" could do it. "J'ai voulu vivre au milieu de ces hommes,"[3] wrote Monnet—and he did, for many years, or, when not, came to American shores every year. Thus, his, in Monnet's lifetime, extraordinary and, for Europe, shocking, combined, systematic use of one-to-one dialogue—body-to-body or by telephone—was likewise an indispensable weapon, honed in the United States, to obtain his aims.

Personal, informal accessibility to the power brokers, whether motivated by necessity or friendship or both, so essential to semi-instinctive, semi-premeditated drives, was greatly facilitated by the

British and, even more accentuated, American culture. That culture, at least initially, oral, one-by-one or small-group informality was much more likely to bring about ultimate consensus without hard feelings than early, "hard-on-hard," written standpoints more, at least formerly, in the continental European tradition. The latter tradition made it much harder for each side to give ground, especially if prematurely publicized by the media.

Another characteristic of the Anglo-American, unwritten, internalized—and, therefore, to him, more genuine—"constitution" that Monnet considered exemplary was the mobility between the public and the private sectors in situations involving the national interest rather than partisanship. Along the same lines, Monnet admired the Anglo-American tradition of government calling on willing members of the opposition party (often elder statesmen) to serve in government or on *ad hoc*, independent, nonpolitical blue-ribbon committees called for in emergencies to reach a nonpartisan consensus. This bone-and-blood rather than formalized phenomenon found a deep echo in him because it joined his profound sense of civic virtue with the pragmatic priorities of his personality. It proved his encompassing motivation: the absolute necessity to spare Europe another war that might be its last, the end of Western civilization. Armageddon could only be prevented by a genuine collaboration of all sectors of society, public and private. He himself was probably the most striking example of this. But he saw it quasi-institutionalized—and therefore surviving—in the coming and going into and out from government service, or as highly influential outside government advisers, of the foremost professional American talents, a custom likely inherited from British ways. Examples of such American public servants include William Bullitt, Henry Stimson, Robert Murphy, Harry Hopkins, Felix Frankfurter, George Marshall, Dwight Eisenhower, Dean Acheson, George Ball, Robert Bowie, Walter and Eugene Rostow, McGeorge Bundy, John McCloy, David Bruce, "Tommy" Tomlinson, Bill Clayton, Averell Harriman, and George Kennan.

Both American characteristics—the interaction between the private and public sectors as well as the strong inclination toward informality and flexibility—helped Monnet in the United States for another reason. In Western Europe (including, in this case, much of the British tradition, with the partial exception of the Labor Party), formal education, having a "respectable" immersion in "culture" (history, philosophy, language arts, in short, style), is a potent if unwritten prerequisite of public figures in high office. This has been, in American history, far less the case; indeed, too much patent, let alone ostentatious, literacy may deter, it is assumed, American voters, impede popularity, and be a handicap in practice, though certainly not set down in articulated codes. Monnet may have been vulnerable in Europe on this score, but, if at all, not in America, where his practical, analytic, precise, direct intelligence was, on the contrary, deemed an asset.

A combination of accessibility, opportunity, and flexibility reinforced Monnet's realization (and inherent conviction) that he would have to use unconventional means to overcome the inertia of officialdom. Americans, he knew, remained partial to youth, a natural mindset for a nation needing both physical strength and daring imagination to master a continent far from hospitable to civilization. He could be more certain in America that promising, innovative (to this day one of the most used and abused terms in the American vocabulary) ideas would be not just welcome but sought. Even in France, in his time much more seniority oriented than presently, Monnet had an extraordinary knack for picking young or younger collaborators, free of government control, at liberty to use their fullest enthusiasm, intelligence, and imagination to have a direct and profound influence on the future of their continent. And Monnet was certainly aware that preferably picking men who would very likely survive him, some by decades, and be somebody would guarantee the long duration of his pioneering work under changing circumstances—and that has certainly and happily happened.

A revealing leitmotif of Monnet's memoirs belongs in this delineation of the mainsprings of Monnet the doer: *amitié*. The American use, or rather abuse, of *friend* has so diluted and, frankly, cheapened it that I prefer to use the French term, which better reflects Monnet's concept, which he applied to his European and particularly his American confidants—people whom he, to be sure, needed but also trusted as well as liked. It is thanks to this deep mutual trust that Monnet was able to convey, via Supreme Court Associate Justice Felix Frankfurter, the famous phrase, which he had coined, of America as "the Arsenal of Democracy" to President Franklin D. Roosevelt, who used it as the beacon in his celebrated address to the nation of December 29, 1940. Contrary to the understandable impression of Monnet as a cold fish relentlessly pursuing his goal, acquiring and ditching "friends" as needed (and, let us admit it, he made no bones about making use, for the good cause, of more temporary "friends," too, of whatever connections got him direct access to the top), Monnet's (to some, prosaic) memoirs reveal genuine, discerning, and abiding human empathy for persons of character, and generosity toward those who delayed, opposed, or blocked him—including de Gaulle. Even targets getting annoyed by his persistence recognized that he was not interested in personal but in collective gain.

Personal *amitié* resting on mutual trust and respect, surviving initial or subsequent reciprocal hesitations and reservations but preserving openness and goodwill were also the key to Monnet's exceptional efforts to establish direct contacts with journalists. Journalism—especially in a balance of representative and popular democracy and a less entrenched and cohesive governmental structure such as, by Western standards, the huge territory of the United States—gained, in Monnet's lifetime, a formal and formidable place astride the communication and interpretation bridge. That bridge connected government, legislators, and officials in general with the public and, especially, the voters. The early establishment of schools of journalism in major American universities precedes, characteristically, the corresponding development in European higher education by a wide margin. Monnet was on intimate, trusting, and enduring terms—speaking only of Americans at this point—with such *grands journalistes* as Walter Lippmann, James Reston, Joseph Alsop, David Schoenbrun, and Robert Kleiman, and with the influential publishers of the *Washington Post*, Philip and Kay Graham.

Ironically, if you wish, America's intelligent and far-sighted generosity after World War II, concretized by the Marshall Plan, to build up not only the victors allied with it but also, for the sake of the future of Europe, the losers (Germany, Austria, Italy) also worried, for good reason, Monnet, since he feared that European states would separately compete against other European states in getting a maximum of help from America and lose the impetus for a unified European community able to vie, productively, with the United States. In itself, Monnet knew, the American postwar policy toward Europe was generally sound—combining ideological, military, strategic, economic, political, pragmatic but also substantive, future-oriented considerations. It was as essential for the United States as for democratic Europe to pull together against the communist military threat (NATO), although the Common Market would give concerted Europe an economic clout comparable to the United States. Competition has always been an integral part of the American drive, internal and external, though, of course, not without fears and internal challenges. Besides, a common market could be expected to simplify American exports to and imports from Europe.

It has certainly not been the intention of this précis to extol the Anglo-American paradigm at the expense of other cultures, nor to claim that the Anglo-Saxon heritage is the exclusive determinant of American culture, far from it. But it *is* the dominant basis of the religious, political, legal, and economic structure of the United States, and, beyond that, has been very influential in the way we live and deal with each other on this continent, day by day, regardless of our provenance. Most important, this is the way Monnet saw it, experienced it, and chose it, with all its imperfections, as a working model for the future of Europe. But the beauty of it is that this acquired predilection for the Anglo-American paradigm was a natural extension of his native Cognac heritage.

NOTES

I dedicate this essay to Clifford Hackett, Henri Rieben, and the late François Fontaine, with gratitude.

I wish to express my hearty thanks to Karen Boschker and Ken Adams (West European Studies, Indiana University) for their courageous and expeditious processing of my forbidding manuscript.

1. Jean Monnet, *Mémoires* (Paris: Fayard, 1976), 48.
2. Ibid., 251.
3. Ibid., 211.

Jean Monnet and the Origins of European Monetary Union

JOHN GILLINGHAM

Jean Monnet's attempt to promote a European monetary union in the late 1950s and early 1960s provides a convenient window through which to examine the most important process to have shaped the history of contemporary Europe since World War II. It is what the historian Daniel Yergin has depicted as the seizure of the "commanding heights" of state economic power by the mechanism of the market.[1] Yergin's metaphor, though powerful, is, unfortunately, not altogether apt. The transformation to which he refers does not involve the takeover of existing institutions—in this case the mighty control levers first described by Marx—so much as the replacement of one philosophy of economic and political management—statism—by another—neoliberalism—as well as the consequent adoption of new nongovernmental and market-based approaches to public problems, and a resultant change of historical setting.

The 1958 restoration of European currency convertibility is what set in motion Monnet's campaign to create a permanent monetary union for the nations of the Common Market. Circumstances were propitious, as for about four and a half years stable exchange rates prevailed. Soon thereafter, however, a spreading inflationary virus would produce convulsions that would rock, and eventually destroy, the Bretton Woods system. The days of smooth sailing had come to an end. Lifeboat drills were the order of the day. Monnet's various proposals called for institutions closely resembling the eventual European Monetary Union

(EMU). Their failure had less to do with intrinsic shortcomings than with prevailing political and economic realities. The intransigent General Charles de Gaulle was one of them. Another was the refusal of European Community (EC) member states to sacrifice monetary autonomy lest the loss of this vital Keynesian policy lever threaten full employment. The chief prerequisites for the eventual monetary union would be the restoration of international capital mobility and the development of a new consensus among decision makers that controls would slow economic growth unacceptably. This realization represented a break with a fundament of the Bretton Woods system and was, at the same time, a first step toward its replacement.

The argument made in this paper follows the arguments of the economists Robert Mundell and J. Marcus Fleming, who posit that an open economy can only maintain unrestricted capital mobility and fixed exchange rates by sacrificing monetary autonomy. The inescapable conclusion is that countries joining a monetary union (which presupposes either fixed rates or the use of a single currency), unless prepared to sacrifice growth, must give up monetary independence.[2] "In Mundell-Fleming terms," according to Lewis W. Pauly, "a successful monetary union depends inevitably upon a willingness by member governments to subordinate the independence of their monetary policies to the common goal of stability in prices and real exchange rates."[3] The Maastricht convergence criteria are meant to satisfy this condition.

If, as Barry Eichengreen has recently suggested, "the development of the international monetary system is fundamentally a historical process," one must situate events in a context and introduce a narrative.[4] This paper will thus describe the postwar international financial system as created at Bretton Woods and modified in the 1950s during the period of the European Payments Union, then introduce the personality and ideas of Monnet and his close associate Robert Triffin, suggest why they failed, and, in conclusion, cite some of the developments that led to the formation of eventual European monetary union.

The June 1944 Bretton Woods Agreement, which created both the International Monetary Fund (IMF) and the less important World

Bank, was to have provided a framework for the postwar international monetary system, a goal which, to a certain extent, has been achieved. Though signed by all important trading nations except the Soviet Union, the treaty was a compromise document of the two important reserve currency countries, the United States and Great Britain. It would consequently rest on less-than-solid foundations.

The United States and United Kingdom did agree on the overriding purpose of the organization: to maintain stable exchange rates in order to stave off beggar-thy-neighbor devaluations like those of the 1930s. Only thus—or so held the post-Depression policy consensus—could the authority of the state be restored and governments provide the long-deferred better life promised their citizens. Parities were therefore fixed relative to the one important currency that remained fully convertible, the U.S. dollar, which in turn was pegged to gold at $35 an ounce (dollar exchange standard). The maintenance of these parities presupposed channeling capital flows into government-sanctioned projects and discouraging the development of international securities and money markets. Capitalism would be tolerated to the extent that it served the needs of the state.

Serious Anglo-American disagreement arose over the issue of how to finance Europe's recovery from the war in a world where economic power resided disproportionately in the United States. The British delegate, Lord Keynes, advocated "automaticity"; in his plans for an "international clearing union," a nation's surplus on current account would be required to give unlimited access to the resulting balances to those in deficit. Such an arrangement would have shifted the burden of adjustment to postwar conditions to the United States from the national economies of Europe, which during a transitional period of unspecified length would be shielded from competitive pressure. The absence of such protection, it was clear to everyone concerned, would put at risk the British Empire, the role of sterling as a reserve currency, and above all Labour's plans for the new welfare state.

The U.S. Bretton Woods delegation, headed by Harry Dexter White, in the end managed to nullify those provisions of the treaty granting unrestricted access to dollar balances. The "scarce-currency clause" allowed borrowing of national accounts surpluses, but was so encumbered that it has never been invoked. The American subscription to the IMF, moreover, was sharply reduced from the amount sought by Keynes. The organization was, as remarked at the time, like a boy facing a man's work. It simply lacked the means to deal with the dollar shortage.[5]

Enough nevertheless remained of the Bretton Woods settlement to keep the idea of fixed exchange rates alive as a guiding idea, because it rested on a substructure of national currency boards and other regulatory agencies that restricted capital movements and reduced the impact of foreign competition. IMF par values could thus be officially maintained. At the same time, the excess liquidity that overhung all European economies—largely a consequence of forced savings induced by war financing—grossly overvalued their currencies vis-à-vis the dollar. Within Europe itself, furthermore, wild—and due to a lack of price signals, often *unknown*—amounts of overvaluation existed from one currency to another. Under the circumstances foreign trade could only be conducted on a dollar basis or by means of barter conducted bilaterally, clothed in the fictive denominations of official exchange rates, and administratively adjusted to domestic price levels by elaborate compensation mechanisms.[6]

The Marshall Plan is what gave rise to the European Payments Union (EPU). The Organization of European Economic Cooperation (OEEC)—an agency of the Marshall Plan—set up the EPU in 1949 at American behest in order to bypass the largely moribund International Monetary Fund. The IMF had in fact already proved unable to protect pound parity in 1947, when an American-dictated decision to float resulted in abject devaluation. For its part, the EPU was a key transition mechanism; it superintended and guided the shift from the bilateral pattern of trade settlement characteristic of the immediate postwar period to multilateralization. The EPU owes its success to dollar loans, a 1949 devaluation of all European currencies vis-à-vis the dollar following a second collapse of sterling, and American acceptance of trade discrimination; but also to the dynamism of a liberalizing West German economy, which by the mid-1950s had become the hub of European trade and, finally, to the restoration and reinforcement of traditional European central-bank cooperation. Thanks to such things, and a timely devaluation of the French franc by the new government of the Fifth Republic, European currencies became convertible in 1958. For the first time, a Bretton Woods system of currency parities based on the dollar exchange standard can be said to have actually existed.[7]

Nineteen fifty-eight was also the inaugural year of the European Economic Community (EEC), or Common Market. The Treaty of Rome, which brought it into being, further established the goal of monetary union. Through his Action Committee for the United States of Europe, a high-level pressure group of statesmen and academics, Jean Monnet at once launched an intense campaign of lobbying for it on behalf of his overarching and overriding lifetime goal, European integration.

Monnet's public persona was that of financier. In his long and varied career he had been involved in, among other episodes: the post–World War I stabilization of the Austrian and Polish currencies; bond underwriting in the late 1920s as head of the Blair and Company office in Paris; the representation of creditor interests in the 1931 liquidation of the Krueger, Toll matchstick empire; and, following that, an abortive attempt to take over the Bank of America. As François Duchêne discloses in a recent biography, Monnet's close connections to the Hudson Bay Company, actually an investment bank, and the international financial house Lazard provided him with secret sources of power both on Wall Street and in government during much of his long career.[8]

Though at home in the world of big money, Monnet's real expertise was deal making, not finance or economics. Precisely how much he understood about the complexities of central-bank operations, the intricacies of trading in currency and securities, or the workings, permutations, and subtleties of the market process is difficult to determine. Monnet never completed the *bac* and generally felt uncomfortable in realms of theory. He was by nature a problem solver rather than a speculator. In issues of public finance he relied heavily on the expertise of others, and in those of monetary union on one man in particular, Robert Triffin. In this respect Triffin served, in the words of Gérard Bossuat, as "Monnet's essential resource." The relationship between them was so close, according to Bossuat, "one cannot say how the thoughts of these two men interacted and developed from one another."[9] Triffin was in any case the author of each important proposal made by Monnet's Action Committee during the critical transitions at the end of the 1950s and early 1960s—namely of August 1957, January 1958, September 1959, and December 1962.

The name Robert Triffin, a Belgian-born professor of economics at Yale, will be forever associated with the word *dilemma;* it was he who first presciently pointed out how the flow of dollars needed to finance European economic growth at the same time undermined the gold exchange standard adopted at Bretton Woods. Put simply, the danger was that the conversion of the increasing numbers of foreign-held dollars into gold would—as actually happened—eventually deplete U.S. reserves of the precious metal and open the door to a host of evils ranging from dollar devaluation to international financial collapse. His solution was, again, to co-opt the newly convertible European currencies into use as reserves. To this end Triffin developed numerous proposals for reforming the IMF, creating a clearing union for the OEEC nations including the U.K., and, most important, building a European monetary union.

Triffin recognized the path-breaking importance of the Treaty of Rome: the commitments spelled out in it—to eliminate tariffs and restrictions on trade and payments and to adopt a common commercial policy toward nonmembers—would, if enforced, subject national economies of the EEC to market discipline, weaken the trade and payments controls built or extended after the war, and—as deficit nations would be obliged to move toward equilibrium in order to maintain parities while surplus nations lacked similar constraints—have a deflationary impact. He also appreciated the fact that integration, as conceived by Monnet and written into the Treaty of Rome, foresaw the assumption of sovereign powers by the EEC, which alone could develop the necessary political muscle to exercise control over national monetary policies.

There was little difference, in Triffin's view, between a full currency merger and a system of free and stable exchange rates; the limitations and discipline imposed on national economies would be similar. However, a real merger, would, he noted, be at the same time irreversible. Perhaps unwisely, he counseled gradualism. "Rueffians," followers of the French monetarist Jacques Rueff, would, however, later argue that a powerful exogenous shock induced by the adoption of a single European exchange rate or a common currency would be required to work the rigidified structures of protected economies into flexible markets. According to Triffin's scenario, in any case, a European unit of account should first be created, then be made convertible into national monetary units, allowing circulation of the national currencies at par within the community. A new European Monetary Authority would then take over the assets and liabilities of the national banks, one organized like the U.S. Federal Reserve System, with the former central banks serving as regional affiliates. A single currency was, finally, to have become the sole circulating medium within the new union.[10]

Monnet's persistent submission of successive revisions of "Triffin plans" to Brussels, Bonn, Paris, and other European capitals may well have contributed something to the adoption of the Werner Report of 1970, in which the European Commission set out plans for the realization of a monetary union as the next great step in the integration process. As Bossuat nonetheless sadly concludes, in the 1960s neither "the Six, nor more specifically France and Germany, had the determination to coordinate monetary and economic policy in any serious way."[11]

The Bretton Woods system presupposed the limitation, by controls, of capital mobility. In light of the immense increase in the size of both markets and flows beginning in the 1960s, the survival, not collapse, of the dollar exchange standard is worth remarking. Without the intense, unprecedented cooperation of world monetary authorities it would have disappeared much earlier. Central bankers and treasury officials would act increasingly on the premise that international currency stability required the coordination of national fiscal and especially monetary policies and that to provide economic discipline capital had to be allowed to flow to places offering generous and secure yields. Once this recognition became general, the stage was set for full employment to cede primacy to economic growth, controls to give way to open markets, and national monetary policies to be sacrificed for the sake of union. A new monetary regime had, in short, replaced an old one. As Douglas Forsyth put it, a sea change in economic governance had taken place across Europe.[12]

NOTES

1. Daniel Yergin and Joseph Stanislaw, *The Commanding Heights: The Battle between Government and the Marketplace That Is Remaking the Modern World* (New York: Simon and Schuster, 1998).

2. Robert Mundell, "Capital Mobility and Stabilization Policy under Fixed and Flexible Exchange Rates," *Canadian Journal of Economics* 29 (November 1963): 475–85; J. Marcus Fleming, "Domestic Financial Policies under Fixed and Flexible Exchange Rates," *International Monetary Fund Staff Papers* 9 (November 3, 1962): 369–80.

3. Louis W. Pauly, *Who Elected the Bankers? Surveillance and Control in the World Economy* (Ithaca: Cornell University Press, 1996), 27.

4. Barry Eichengreen, *Globalizing Capital: A History of the International Monetary System,* (Princeton, N.J.: Princeton University Press, 1996), 6.

5. Ibid., 93–95.

6. Ibid., 100.

7. Barry Eichengreen, *Reconstructing Europe's Trade and Payments: The European Payments Union* (Ann Arbor: University of Michigan Press, 1993).

8. François Duchêne, *Jean Monnet: The First Statesman of Interdependence* (New York: Norton, 1994), 43–63.

9. Gérard Bossuat, "Monnet et l'identité monétaire européenne," manuscript, 19.

10. Robert Triffin, *Gold and the Dollar Crisis: Yesterday and Tomorrow,* Essays in International Finance 132 (Princeton: Princeton University, 1978); *Gold and the Dollar Crisis: The Future of Convertibility,* rev. ed. (New Haven: Yale University Press, 1961), 131–45.

11. Bossuat, "Monnet et l'identité," 18.

12. Douglas J. Forsyth and Ton Notermans, "Macroeconomic Policy Regimes and Financial Regulation in Europe, 1931–1944," in *Regime Changes: Macroeconomic Policy and Financial Regulation in Europe from the 1930s to the 1990s,* ed. Forsyth and Notermans (Providence: Berghahn Books, 1997), 17–69.

 Monnet and de Gaulle

The French Paradigm in the Competitiveness
between the United States and the European Union
IRENE FINEL-HONIGMAN

A discussion of Jean Monnet's role and position as emissary between France and the United States is part of a larger discourse on the issues of sovereignty versus integration and enlargement, the continuation and reevaluation of the core French-German relationship once its architects and visionaries are gone, and the dichotomy between economic and political priorities and the larger and constant role of institutional development, its contingencies and responsibilities within a global framework.

In *C'était de Gaulle* (1994), Alain Peyrefitte, press secretary and adviser to President Charles de Gaulle, recalled that in 1963, the general had claimed that "the Americans have favored Jean Monnet's Europe insofar as it was for them a means of maintaining or developing their hegemony."[1] Today, after the Cold War, within the framework of a new monetary union, Monnet's concept of unification based on large regional blocs built upon cross-border institutional pillars and relationships is viewed as far more viable and stabilizing than de Gaulle's autocratic view of a Europe "from the Atlantic to the Urals" dependent on a confederation of a Europe of nations.[2]

However, when Felix Rohatyn, U.S. ambassador to France, was asked in a recent interview whether the euro would presuppose a United States of Europe, he diplomatically deflected the question: "I do not know what the political outcome will be. . . . I cannot predict the end result, whether it will be an American-style federation, a confederation, or an entirely different European solution. But I know one thing: if the Euro succeeds, the rest will follow."[3]

Since 1946, the question of how Europe should be defined and what direction its slow but steady evolution from the European Economic Community (EEC) to the European Community (EC) to the European Union (EU) to the Economic and Monetary Union (EMU) should take, has been at the heart of the U.S.-EU relationship. But most often, for better or worse, it has been articulated, interpreted, and deconstructed within the context and subtext of the U.S.-French relationship. France, since Monnet and in large part because of Monnet, has taken on the role of formulating the key issues in both U.S.-EU competitiveness and partnership. From the end of the Cold War and more vocally since 1993, in the General Agreement on Tariffs and Trade (GATT) talks, in World Trade Organization (WTO) issues (from audiovisual to maritime to financial to bananas), in the Boeing debate with Airbus on state subsidies, in the challenge to U.S. sanctions on grounds of sovereignty in the Helms-Burton conflict on Cuba, and in the D'Amato bill on Iran and Iraq, France has directly or indirectly expressed its views on its own behalf and, as spokesperson, on behalf of the European Union. In 1999, during President Jacques Chirac's last visit to Washington, as representative of the EU's defense position on the Kosovo crisis in Albania, France no longer projected its perspective in a David-and-Goliath context, but as lead member and spokesperson of a vast, powerful monetary and commercial rival and equal. In fact, part of France's ability to accept the euro since 1997, and therefore to relinquish a portion of its sovereignty, has depended on France's transferring its own ambitions and agenda to a larger stage in which it can be an equal among equals, but just a bit more equal, as defined in the original Gaullist vision of three international realities, the United States, Russia, and France.[4]

Several ironies have shaped the U.S.-France, U.S.-EU paradigm. Chirac (although considered in 1995 to be fervently pro-American, based on his record of American-style reforms instituted during his tenure as prime minister in 1986–1988), needed a Socialist prime minister to soften the tone for a more conciliatory dialogue and to help launch a new French American Business Council. Although French-American linkages remain extremely strong in direct investment, in two-way trade, and in a presence in each other's markets, where French companies employ nearly 400,000 Americans in the United States, and more than fifty high-technology U.S. companies with 2,500 workers are now located in Sophia Antipolis, the tone remains often prickly and nervous. When Régis Debray in 1993 spoke of the dangers of American monocultural-ism and the French foreign minister, Hubert Védrine, recently charac-terized the United States as a "hyperpower," they reiterate and reinforce the Gaullist perception of the United States as a threat to French culture and political identity within Europe.

Without a Jean Monnet to smooth the path, the Clinton adminis-tration's first exposure to the European Union under French tutelage was negative. The EU appeared between 1993 and 1995, as it went through its post–currency crisis recession, to be arrogant in the scope of its ambitions and incapable of achieving its goals, including EMU. Without a Dean Acheson, Paul Nitze, or Henry Kissinger in charge, the United States came across as bullying and reactive, ignoring EU progress and denigrating the significance of its policy goals. EMU was ignored in Washington until the deputy secretary of the treasury, Larry Sum-mers, issued the first U.S. position statement in October 1997.

As Craig Whitney wrote in his charming piece in the New York Times, "The French Aren't Alone in Having Gall," although the British have been far more critical of U.S. policies from Truman to Bush than is usu-ally assumed, the Roosevelt-Churchill camaraderie set the tone where "Americans tend to think the world of the British and the worst of the French." In turn, "French leaders tend to see the United States in Stein-beckian terms, as a strong, friendly but unsophisticated giant whose full embrace might be fatal."[5] It is important to note that despite the strong friendship which has bound French and German leaders from de Gaulle and Adenauer to Valéry Giscard d'Estaing and Helmut Schmidt to François Mitterand and Helmut Kohl, EU partners, even when agreeing and cooperating with the French, have seen them as overbearing and reverting to Gaullist paternalism, in cases such as the naming of the European currency unit (ECU), French dominance of major financial and multilateral institutions[6] and the Duisenberg-Trichet arrangement on the European Central Bank presidency. One French suggestion for naming the new currency in 1991 was the monnet, in honor of Jean Monnet's seminal role and also as a homonym for *monnaie:* money.

To understand the nature of France's role in U.S.-EU competitiveness, it is necessary to return to U.S.-French competition in the period of the creation of a European Union. Raymond Aron, de Gaulle's economic adviser, wrote in his memoirs that if, in 1946, the general had remained in power, "I doubt that under his rule Jean Monnet would have had the opportunity to persuade the government and with its help to launch the coal-and-steel agreement and obtain the assembly's vote in favor of the Treaty of Rome. The French of today have forgotten that Jean Monnet and Robert Schuman prepared the way for Franco-German reconciliation through institutions that the general and the Gaullists fought against."[7] As late as 1960, de Gaulle railed against what he contemptuously named le Systeme Monnet and its "virtualités supranationales": "Supranationality, it's absurd. Nothing is above the nation-state. Unless it is what their governments decide together. The pretensions of commissioners in Brussels to want to give orders to governments, it's a mockery, a mockery."[8]

Adamantly opposed to what he called apatriate technocrats, de Gaulle felt, justifiably within the context of the ideological dichotomy of the Cold War, that only nation-states, working in cooperation, could maintain the balance of power and control the delicate shifts between Bonn, Washington, and Moscow. In today's environment, where financial frontiers and an information revolution are the dominant criteria for political influence, Monnet's view of a Europe based on coalitions and compromise without great leaders is far more realistic and relevant. The issues of sovereignty and integration still need to be resolved, but they are part of a different discourse in which both nationhood and statehood have to be redefined. Just as tension between Roosevelt and de Gaulle would characterize future U.S.-French relations and set a pattern of reciprocal wariness and reversion to stereotypes, the Monnet–de Gaulle relationship established the lines of demarcation between a United States of Europe and a European Union.

De Gaulle and Monnet each had his interpretation, bringing his own *Weltanschauung*—Monnet's pragmatism and de Gaulle's moral and political absolutism—all the while knowing that the ultimate goal was the same, to forge a new and stronger identity for the continent. Both were necessary, in fact essential. Similar in intent, they remained diametrically opposed in philosophy and tactics. Monnet was a statesman—shrewd, subtle, pragmatic, and willing to appear more malleable to the United States, as Charles Cogan described him, "more in the dimensions of a Frenchman seen through foreign eyes and more in keeping with the image of a complaisant France."[9] De Gaulle physically and morally never bent; emphatic and inflexible, he firmly believed that the United States neither would nor could appreciate France's history or national interest. Monnet, much more in the tradition of Voltaire, could assume a conciliatory stance in order to gain an advantage. De Gaulle remained the medieval monarch hero, Charlemagne of the *Chanson de Roland*.

France's careful maneuvering between the European Union's needs and the United States' demands and its slow but steady psychocultural adaptation toward what Alain Minc has called "une mondialisation heureuse" (a successful globalization) would have disgusted and shocked de Gaulle while it would have pleased Monnet immensely.[10] Monnet was willing to incorporate American viewpoints and to accept U.S. intervention in economic and security decisions. He set goals but sought to attain them by consensus rather than by a broad-stroke political agenda. After World War II, de Gaulle alone had the moral power to rebuild and heal France's identity, but Monnet understood how process could reconcile. De Gaulle's genius was to use Monnet as the perfect foil, as emissary to the United States in both official and unofficial functions. Monnet's wisdom was to gracefully accept his role and often explain de Gaulle to the Americans. In a 1946 letter to President Harry S. Truman, he wrote of de Gaulle: "his knowledge of this enormous country had previously been limited and imperfect."[11] As Alain Peyrefitte explained, the general never learned English, not because he couldn't but because he wouldn't on principle.

In the chronicle *Paris Journals,* which appeared in the *New Yorker* in 1964, the Francophile journalist Janet Flanner (Génet) best summarized the often paradoxical nature of Monnet's reputation in France: "Few republics in our time anywhere have had a public servant so intelligently used as M. Jean Monnet, father of the European Common Market, though the Fourth Republic and its young technocrats had little praise in France for their farsighted faith in him."[12]

For U.S. politicians and diplomats, Monnet was the best and often sole means of negotiating with France. Many of Monnet's American contacts went back to his days as deputy secretary-general of the League of Nations. When Monnet followed de Gaulle to London in 1940, he originally saw the new Europe as a French-British pact. Although he supported de Gaulle's stance, until 1943 he was more comfortable with General Giraud and thought that the main war effort should come from Giraud's offensive in North Africa. Monnet's position and influence crystallized the conflict in the United States among the exiled French community between the pro–de Gaulle and pro-Giraud factors. Once in Washington, Monnet met Roosevelt's trusted adviser Harry Hopkins, and became the liaison between Roosevelt's inner circle and the Free French. However, in his memoirs Monnet made clear that he felt "the sovereignty of France belongs to the French people. . . . No French political authority can exist or be authorized to be created outside of France." By 1943 he stated that "a European entity encompassing a common economic unit" had to be the basis for creating a community framework.[13]

By the end of 1943, once Monnet realized that de Gaulle's popular support made him the best representative of France, he worked hard on his behalf to persuade Roosevelt to recognize the French Committee for National Liberation and finally invite de Gaulle to Washington in July 1944. In 1945, Monnet was instrumental in extending Lend-Lease aid and granting France a $550 million Eximbank credit. But Monnet could never overcome the tense and antagonistic relationship between de Gaulle and Roosevelt. De Gaulle never forgave Roosevelt's isolationist stance toward Europe from 1933 to 1940, seeing the U.S. president as manipulative and opportunistic; in turn Roosevelt saw de Gaulle as dictatorial and megalomaniacal.

Monnet's greatest achievements for which history honors him took place in the interim Fourth Republic years, between 1950 and 1958, when far more pliable French presidents allowed Robert Schuman and Monnet to create the European Coal and Steel Community (ECSC), to set out a blueprint in the Monnet-Pleven plan for a European Defense Community, and to establish the principles of the Treaty of Rome and the Common Market.

For both de Gaulle and Monnet, the core relationship after 1945 had to be the construction of a French-German alliance; but for Monnet, U.S. approval and involvement were positive and necessary. For de Gaulle they always remained a threat to French and European sovereignty and to France's ability to control the balance of power. During the Cold War, this attitude was not merely de Gaulle's arrogance or mythomania. As described by Kissinger in *Diplomacy,* the de Gaulle vision of a European Community based on "West Germany for economic preponderance, French political dominance of the EC and American nuclear protection as a form of insurance," made sense as, in fact, France alone could maintain and speak for an EC equilibrium.[14] The idea that the United States would appear if and when necessary has been the prevalent European view throughout the 1990s, demonstrated by its role in the Bosnia conflict and the EU's inability and unwillingness to take charge of its own security issues. Only since 1999, with a Gaullist and a Socialist in power, has France taken on a stronger and clearer position on European conflict issues in the quest for a resolution in Kosovo. The latest Chirac-Clinton meeting on NATO issues and Kosovo in fact was a vindication of both the Monnet and de Gaulle positions' with France representing European NATO interests, engaging the United States intervention, and yet, remaining ensconced in its own non-NATO membership position.

When John F. Kennedy entered the White House in 1961, Monnet again became the conciliatory force behind a new stronger alliance between Europe and the United States. By 1962 his close friend Dean Acheson brought him to Kennedy's attention, concerned that de Gaulle was isolating the United States out of Europe. Monnet and Acheson helped to launch the Atlantic Partnership which led to Kennedy's speech on July 4, 1962, in which the president endorsed for the first time "a concrete Atlantic partnership, a mutually beneficial partnership between the new union now emerging in Europe and the old American Union founded here 173 years ago." In 1963, Kennedy awarded Monnet the Freedom Medal as founder of the ECSC.

But de Gaulle, incensed by Monnet's version of a Common Market and his slant toward Britain, vetoed Britain's entry in January 1963 and accused Monnet of conceiving of a structure which would give the impression that France no longer was a world power.[15] Despite the ensuing tensions, the Transatlantic Partnership led to the Bush-Baker Transatlantic Declaration in 1990 and has been the basis of all subsequent U.S.-EU accords and agreements. De Gaulle believed that Europe would become a confederation but only within a long-term historical and political framework: "I don't exclude, far later, a confederation which would be the crowning point of a patient effort to bring forth a common policy, common diplomacy, common security at the end of a long period when the six nations have become accustomed to living together."[16]

It was Monnet's vision of a steady evolutionary process of economic coordination and institutional cooperation which set the stage for Jacques Delors's creation of a European government and monetary structure. Delors, as first EC president and architect of the Maastricht Treaty, followed the Monnet philosophy of reaffirming institutional linkages, of working through coalitions, of slowly moving the project behind the scenes. Delors, like Monnet, understood that grand gestures were needed to inspire but that the building blocks had to be set in place before there could be concrete, lasting results. Fundamentally the greatest challenge to creating the European Union has been to depoliticize post–World War II Europe through economic necessity and reciprocity, yet to achieve economic and monetary unifications through political and national will. For Monnet, economic and political priorities had to be reconciled in order to guarantee France's position. Monnet would have appreciated the nuances of Dominique Strauss Kahn's positioning of the euro not against the dollar, but as a means of further strengthening the international financial system.[17] He would have understood that assimilation and national cultural specificity are both needed to articulate and define the French-EU and the French-U.S. dialogue.

For de Gaulle, who hated any reference to money, French economic diplomacy was only justifiable in the name of France's prestige. De Gaulle understood that American capitalism was the leading force behind American power. He could never find a genuine affinity with Jean Monnet, his merchant diplomat who always remained a salesman —first for cognac, then for Europe. It was at a state dinner at the Elysée Palace in former President Dwight D. Eisenhower's honor on August 8, 1962, that in response to Eisenhower's praise (delivered inadvertently or on purpose) for Monnet's achievements, de Gaulle uttered the famous rejoinder: "Il fait un très bon cognac. Malheureusement cette occupation ne lui suffit pas!"[18]

NOTES

1. "Les Américains ont favorisé l'Europe de Jean Monnet tant qu'elle était pour eux un moyen de maintenir ou de développer leur hégémonie." Alain Peyrefitte, *C'était de Gaulle* (Paris: Fayard, 1994), 366.

2. Ibid., 282.

3. Felix Rohatyn, "Un entretien avec l'ambassadeur des États Unis en France, Felix Rohatyn: Vive l'euro!" interview with Charles Lambroschini, *France-Amérique*, January 30–February 5, 1999.

4. Alain Peyrefitte, *C'était de Gaulle*, 283.

5. Craig Whitney, "The French Aren't Alone in Having Gall," *New York Times*, December 6, 1998.

6. Klaus C. Engelen, "French Fried," *International Economy*, May–June 1992.

7. Raymond Aron, *Memoirs: Fifty Years of Political Reflection*, trans. George Holoch (London: Holmes and Meier, 1990), 166.

8. "Supra nationalité, c'est absurde! Rien n'est au-dessus des nations, sinon ce que leurs États decident ensemble! Les prétentions des Commissaires de Bruxelles à vouloir donner des ordres aux gouvernements dont dérisoires! Dérisoires!" Alain Peyrefitte, *C'était de Gaulle*, 66.

9. Charles Cogan, *Oldest Allies, Guarded Friends. The United States and France since 1940* (New York: Praeger, 1994), 5.

10. Alain Minc, *La mondialisation heureuse* (Paris: Plon, 1997).

11. Cogan, *Oldest Allies*, 7.

12. Janet Flanner (Génet), *Paris Journal, 1944–1965* (London: Harcourt Brace Jovanovich, 1965), 594.

13. Douglas Brinkley, *Dean Acheson: The Cold War Years, 1953–1971* (New Haven: Yale University Press, 1992), 189–93.

14. Quoted in Henry Kissinger, *Diplomacy* (New York: Simon and Schuster, 1994), 603.

15. Alain Peyrefitte, personal communication, December 6, 1963.

16. "Je n'exclus pas, pour plus tard, une confédération, qui serait le couronnement d'un patient effort pour dégager une politique commune, une diplomatie commune, une sécurité commune, au bout d'une longue période où les six États auraient pris l'habitude de vivre ensemble." Quoted in Alain Peyrefitte, *C'était de Gaulle*, 69.

17. "Mr. Euro Zone," *Financial Times*, February 12, 1999.

18. Quoted in Alain Peyrefitte, *C'était de Gaulle*, 309.

Part III

The European Union:
Social Dimension

The Euro and
European Social Policies

GEORGE ROSS

The euro came on January 1, 1999—at least for bankers and account-
ants. And there is no denying how important this is. What are the
euro's implications for European societies? This is a topic that is both
important and complicated. It is complicated because the eurozone is
composed of eleven very different societies with very different social
policies, each facing the new situation differently. Moreover, uncover-
ing the actual causal significance of Economic and Monetary Union
(EMU) and the euro is, like any serious social science problem, very
difficult to do. It is important because Europe has long been distinctive
because of its "social model." European societies generally have much
more generous social programs (health care, income supports, pensions), more employment security, and much more bargaining over key
social issues than the U.S.A. Indeed, it has been common in recent
years, with the U.S. economy in a long, low-unemployment economic
boom, to point to the contrasts between American flexibility and European rigidity, the latter behind Europe's sluggishness and high unemployment levels. Will the euro change this?

Complexity dictates a historical approach. The euro needs to be
put into contexts if we are to understand its social implications. First
of all, it is important to understand the euro as part, and only part, of
a much broader package of changes in Europe connected to broader
European integration. Next, the euro did not begin from a standing
start on January 1, 1999. Rather it has been in the making for the last

decade and more and its effects have been felt already in significant ways before the euro officially existed. Third, if the euro's effects on social matters stretch back into the recent past, they must be projected forward into the near future.

◈ THE EURO'S BACKGROUND

EMU—the euro program—is the ultimate stage in a very long process. In the background of European integration, after World War II, there were independent nations and independent economies that had been in conflict, often brutal and bloody, for centuries. After a number of false starts the process of integration began in earnest with the 1957 Treaty of Rome. Rome saw the six Continental partners of the European Coal and Steel Community, Jean Monnet's greatest invention, create a customs-free zone and a common external tariff. This European Economic Community (EEC), or Common Market, as it was called, promoted enhanced trade among the still quite separated national economies which belonged to it. The next major building block came in the 1970s, after the Bretton Woods financial system, based on U.S. international monetary stewardship, had broken down into a system of internationally floating exchange rates. Europeans, disadvantaged by such floating tried and failed to find a better one with the "snake in the tunnel," a complex way of packaging European Union (EU) currencies to gain greater stability. Their second try worked better. The European Monetary System (EMS) in 1979 linked different European currencies in a scheme where their values would fluctuate against each other within designated limits. The goal of the EMS was to create predictable monetary interaction within the EEC, which had grown to ten members by the early 1980s, to prevent monetary fluctuations from destroying the Common Market. The third step—in many ways the biggest one— began in 1985 with the "1992" program. The official title of the program was Completing the Single Market. It aimed at eliminating remaining internal barriers to trade within the EU, particularly the nontariff barriers that had emerged as EU member states tried to cope with the new economic problems of inflation, lower growth, and rising unemployment in the 1970s. The purpose of "1992" was to create a single market and single economy out of Europe's existing national economies.

EMU and the euro, first proposed in 1970 in the quickly shelved Werner Report, reemerged on the EU agenda in the second half of the 1980s. EMU could not have happened without the earlier steps I have described, and it was also the logical conclusion to those steps. Without a common currency backed by a coherent common monetary system it might have become extremely difficult to sustain the Single Market, and without the Single Market, European integration was a nonstarter. The introduction of the euro is thus part of a larger and longer-term program to shift the location of monetary policy from the national to the European level and to create one monetary zone in the EU to complement the single European market.

European integration, including EMU, is at bottom rapid economic liberalization to create a single economy in a context of the multiple nations who belong to the EU. Europe started with a discreet number of protected, stand-alone economies (and societies) which then dismantled many of their means of protecting themselves economically and sought conditions to make their economic outlooks more cooperative and transnational. Ultimately the very ambitious goal of this is— for it is not yet achieved—to create a situation in which very little specifically national remains, at least in economic terms. In particular, through EMU and other changes, EU member states stand to lose most of their national policy levers to control economic flows.

If European integration has very rapidly turned the EU area into a single market out of fifteen national markets, and it is rapidly creating a single European economy with a single currency, European integration has so far touched social policy very little. One of the most significant constitutional specificities of European integration is that the industrial relations and welfare state areas have been excluded from what European integration can effect directly. For the most part European integration has been about market building—trade and economic matters. Social matters have been left to member states. Of course, those who promoted this division of competencies knew what they were about. Redistributional issues within nation-states lie at the heart of modern democratic politics. They are central in the minds of voters and interest groups and, for this reason, they are very difficult to change. If one feels that national social policy arrangements present barriers to necessary economic modernization—and many European leaders came to believe this in the past two decades—then changing the market structures around them, as European integration has done, is one way to promote the evolution of social policy.

The effects of the single currency and EMU, on social matters, are indirect. This should not be taken to mean insignificant, however. Many of these effects began well before the euro came into existence on January 1, 1999. EMU and the euro reemerged as live proposals in the mid-1980s. The French, the main innovators, had a number of objectives, the most important of which was to create structures which would allow others—i.e., themselves—greater influence over European monetary policy. The German deutsche mark (DM) had become the strongest currency in the EMS. This gave the Germans, particularly the Bundesbank (the German central bank), the final call on EMS policies. Thus they consistently used their monetary power to promote their definition of price stability. On more than one occasion in the 1980s and early 1990s the effects of this on other European countries tied to the mark through EMS were overly restrictive. The French understood that success at making the euro happen would have certain shorter-run costs. There would have to be a convergence of monetary policies and, to a degree, macroeconomic policies, of key EU member states, and everyone initially would pretty much have to converge around German —Bundesbank—standards. For other currencies this would involve achieving stability against the deutsche mark, bringing inflation down to German levels, lowering national budget deficits and debt levels, and eliminating controls on the free movement of capital.

These paths to convergence had important social policy implications. In most of Europe in the mid-1980s deflation had already begun and unemployment had begun to rise toward Great Depression levels.

Pre-EMU policies in these circumstances made it much more difficult for governments to stimulate demand in their economy and counteract the business cycle when it was down. They also tended to increase unemployment. These processes, in their turn, played a significant role in softening and changing regulations in European labor markets. It became easier for employers to hire and fire, to employ people in part-time and in short-term contract work, and to insist on more flexible workweek schedules. Increased unemployment weakened unions and gave employers a much stronger bargaining position. There was variation in these matters across Europe, however. For those countries whose currencies were already tied directly to the DM the challenges were much gentler. The Netherlands was one such, tied to the DM beginning in 1982, and the Belgians followed a bit later. For countries not tied to the DM things were much more difficult. This was particularly true for southern Europe. The French themselves, who sought to use EMU eventually to constrain the Germans, had to work very hard to catch up.

Coping initially cost many countries additional unemployment compensation, provisions for early retirement, work programs for unemployed young people, and other such emergency social policy measures. Eventually short-term coping began to spill over into a slow rethinking of labor market policies. Policy makers started to seek new active measures to replace the passive ones in place. This usually involved getting people into training, developing new incentives (including cutbacks in benefit replacement rates and eligibility) to get the unemployed back into the labor market, giving employers tax breaks for new hiring and reflecting in general about how to equip people to compete in more changeable job markets. Behind this was growing understanding that long-term unemployment, a serious problem across the continent, created long-term poverty and social exclusion. People who were kept out of the labor market for long periods had tremendous difficulty reentering. Social exclusion—what the French called the new poor—had not been a major issue in the relatively full-employment economies of the three decades after World War II. But in the 1980s, the pre-EMU period, poverty became a new focus of attention, with new discussion of ways to provide income support and dignity to those who were in danger of such exclusion. In more general labor market terms, early moves toward EMU clearly encouraged greater flexibility and as such they complemented similar effects caused by the single-market policy.

In terms of classic welfare-state programs pre-EMU economic policies of the later 1980s also promoted indirect changes. The basic problems of welfare-state programs—with pensions and health care systems the big ticket items, with family assistance policies a distant third—had little to do with pre-EMU convergence. There would have been big issues to face with or without EMU. Partly because of aging, but also because of the cost of scientific progress and of built-in inefficiencies in programs, health care costs were rising more rapidly than national product, sometimes dramatically. Demographic pressures threatened the financial bases of the pay-as-you go pension insurance programs. Still, preparing for EMU put greater pressures on national budgets. This, indirectly, instilled a greater sense of urgency in governments to find solutions to the pension problems and to control costs in health care.

THE 1990S: FROM MAASTRICHT TO THE MILLENNIUM

Programmed movement toward EMU was officially agreed on at Maastricht in December 1991, after a full year of hard negotiations among EU members. Maastricht amended the EU treaties to place EMU and the euro officially on the table, with a timetable for transition set out and a target date of January 1, 1999, when EMU would become irreversible for those eligible. This officialization of EMU and the detailed processes of transition then set into motion accentuated the indirect changes in social policy that had already begun in the 1980s. They also introduced some new problems.

The Maastricht Treaty specified stringent convergence criteria to be met by potential EMU members before they would be eligible to join. These criteria, which represented German priorities enacted into law because of German political and economic power in the EU, involved low inflation levels, interest rates, currency stability, general debt levels, and, most important, annual budget deficit levels (3 percent or less). These criteria were subsequently extended well beyond 1999 by the "stability and growth pact" negotiated at the Dublin EU Summit in December 1996. From 1992 to 1997, EU member nations experienced the worst recession since the 1930s, also largely a result of German political and financial power, and this complicated movement to EMU. German unification was worked out in 1990 by a currency exchange policy with the former German Democratic Republic (GDR) that created a brief inflationary boom in Germany that the German Bundesbank then choked off with harsh austerity then communicated throughout the EMS. Unemployment shot through the roof, to more than 11 percent across the EU, the highest levels since 1945.

How did these two things impact—albeit indirectly, again—on social policy? The recession vastly increased unemployment and the costs of coping with it. It also decreased tax revenues. Most aspirant EMU members were compelled to worsen their debts and deficits in the mid-1990s. This was, of course, the threshold of the moment when they had to make their debt and budget accounts look better to join EMU. The actual decision about which countries would be eligible was scheduled for 1998 on the basis of comparisons between 1997 accounts and the convergence criteria. Put another way, the magnitude of the problems, in particular the social policy problems, that countries would have to solve to join EMU got exponentially worse just before they would absolutely have to solve them.

What were the social policy results? For the most part they involved an intensification of what had already been begun prior to Maastricht in 1991. More new unemployment made unions weaker, yet kept wages stable, led to greater pressures to "flexibilize" employment schedules and hiring and firing, and granted more power advantages to employers. There was also a continuing rise in part-time and temporary work. "New poverty," clustered among those who find it difficult to find work, spread. The search for more active labor market policies—more training, more education, changes in eligibility rules for unemployment insurance—pushed people back to training and work.

In welfare state programs the story was similar as tendencies already in place were accentuated. In the first big-ticket item, pension programs, there have been efforts to root out expensive anomalies (differential retirement ages for civil servants, for example). There also has been talk, and some action, about raising retirement ages (which had fallen to sixty and below in some places). Finally, contributions have been raised and replacement rates lowered. By the 1990s there was also much greater stress on the need for deeper reform, and in many places beginnings of significant reform. Serious discussion about the need for individually contracted, private-investment-based complementary pensions is also now on the table. This type of reform is seen as a way to lessen the burden on state pensions and to generate more investment capital. Here there is another indirect connection with EMU. The creation of a single-currency area is designed to nourish more energetic and larger European capital markets. These days capitalized pension funds are the single largest sources of investment capital. Serious action has yet to follow the discussion, however, except in the U.K. (for reasons having nothing to do with EMU, since pension changes in Great Britain have been driven by domestic politics). Moving from pay-as-you-go insurance-based pensions to some combination of public and private pension programs is a hugely complicated and politically difficult job, however. The timidity that one sees presently is understandable.

In health care, the second big-ticket item, serious cost control programs have been undertaken. User fees have been introduced, physician autonomy has been curtailed, and there have been many hospital closings and speedups. Universality remains a commitment, however, even if luxuries are being eliminated. In many places complementary private insurance programs have been beefed up—often to cover new-user fees and drug costs, and there are more private clinics—indicating the slow, perhaps inevitable, incursion of new inequalities. Change thus far, however, remains incremental. Like pensions, health care programs are political third rails. It is not difficult to foresee real change, however.

There has been action on the revenue side as well. Tax reform to change the revenue basis of social programs is being contemplated almost everywhere and has already begun in some places. This is often because the insurance structures of most Continental social protection programs have come, under EMU, to pose serious problems of economic effect and equity. Insurance-based programs usually cover those at work. Contributions to such programs most often come from employers and employees and are calculated as part of the costs of employment. This system raises the costs to employers of employing people. At a moment of high unemployment and competitive difficulty, this is clearly a problem. Moreover, the large number of those in a situation of mass unemployment who do not, or are unable to, earn wages and make insurance contributions has to be treated in different ways.

Here there is an important conflict between two different notions of social solidarity. The system as it stands is based on a redistribution of risks and revenues among workers. Providing coverage for people who cannot find work becomes a subsidiary system based on different principles, usually of citizenship entitlement. Citizenship entitlements are most often transfers financed out of tax revenues and not insurance contributions. France, for example, has recently decided to change the way it finances health care altogether, prodded by Maastricht convergence pressures. The old source of revenue was taxation on employment relationships, which is being replaced by revenues from general taxation—a special tax fund for social programs. Implied here is a slow, but general, movement away from insurance contributions based on employment relationships toward more general taxation, a very different form of solidarity. This is both a way to lower deficits because of EMU and a way to lower labor costs to employers who, under the Single Market and approaching EMU, have ever more choice where to locate, who and whether to hire, and whether to invest.

By 1996–97 governments throughout the EU had to find ways to cut and change social and labor market programs to get near membership in EMU. In some places, where finances were in order, things were easier—the case, for example, in the Netherlands and Austria. In general, however, the processes were painful and one heard new arguments for change. "We have to change because Europe and the coming of the euro oblige us to—we are all in this together and if we don't get into EMU we will suffer and even if we do get into EMU, if we are not more competitive we will suffer." Connected with this—or at least this is my contention—by 1997 a remarkable shift toward the election of center-left parties across the EU was underway—Italy, France, England, the Netherlands, Portugal, and ultimately Germany in 1998.

This sea change in the coalitional composition of European governments is clearly a direct electoral response to the austerity that preparing the euro has brought. It is also a signal that European electorates may be willing to accept reforms of social programs and labor markets, but they most definitely are unwilling to accept the degree of inequality, poverty, and individual lack of protection that one finds in the United States. In other words, the changes that moving to EMU have promoted directly and indirectly have led to warnings about the need to place some limits on the changes.

▨ AND NOW THAT THE EURO EXISTS?

It has taken a decade or more for the euro to come. The long process leading to its creation has in itself done a great deal to change the contexts and nature of European societies and social policies. Greater labor market flexibility has been achieved. European welfare states have not been dismantled, but the budgetary pressure on different programs, not caused, but certainly increased, by EMU has prodded different governments toward considerable reform. That these changes are not revolutionary is obvious. In some places they have been more extensive than in others. In a few, like Germany, there has been little change at all. Whether what has happened to this point will provide enough structural reform to make Europe more competitive is quite unclear, however.

Now we actually do have the euro, however. What will the new euro do, in and of itself, to push change forward in social policy? The first answer is that the euro will produce more of the same effects that we have just described. The euro will make wage and social benefit costs more transparent across the eurozone. It is important not to exaggerate how important this will be, however. Employers have for some time worked under conditions of reasonable transparency, and the new increment achieved by EMU will not create spectacular change. More transparency will encourage greater care in wage setting and budgeting. This should force organized labor to think more about transnational coordination, something that it needs desperately to do.

Next there is the problem of the asymmetric effects of the new single currency and their corollary, asymmetric shocks. In the new eurozone some regions and economic sectors will lag behind others, depending on their relative competitiveness. The EU has very little money to equalize regions or sectors and few automatic stabilizers—the EU is far from a strong federal system—to cushion shocks. The abilities of particular countries to cope will also be limited. Thus troubled areas will have to adjust more or less on their own within their national contexts. This means that in a situation of shock they will have to act to become more competitive or decline. There are not thousands of ways to become more competitive. It comes down to lowering wages or the costs of social programs, or both. There are other asymmetries implicit in EMU as well. The eurozone is set up as a one-size-fits-all currency zone. The European Central Bank (ECB, in which there are representatives from all eurozone central banks) sets one interest rate, targets monetary supplies in a uniform way, and seeks to influence exchange rates for the entire euro area. This means that national economies out of sync with the rest may be penalized. The first example of this occurred when the "shadow" ECB cut interest rates in December 1998. This was meant to stimulate Continental economies, where growth was lagging. It penalized Ireland, however, which was booming and risked inflationary tendencies with lower interest rates. Had the Irish economy then turned toward inflation the government would have had to act in ways that cut back on domestic employment. Asymmetries of different kinds are certain to be real issues with important social policy implications. And when they occur they are certain to become important political matters both for member states and for the EU more broadly.

On another plane, everyone predicts that the euro will stimulate the development of new, greatly expanded, and more efficient European financial markets. From the point of view of efficiency this should be a welcome development. Freer, larger, and more energetic capital markets ought to prove better able to allocate investment where it is needed than what exists now. Such capital markets should make companies much more responsive to shareholder interests as well, and for important parts of Europe this will be a big change. In many national contexts big companies, banks, and workforces have had cozy arrangements for obtaining capital in "sheltered ways." For the so-called Rhine (German) model of capitalism, to take but one example, many writers have argued that these arrangements have facilitated longer-term perspectives and successful corporate planning. No doubt this has been true in Germany and perhaps even elsewhere. But there are many counterexamples where capital has been provided for wasteful purposes in ways that undercut longer-term efficiency. In any event, the EMU's new capital markets, plus the EU's competition policies, are rapidly changing things. To the degree to which this makes labor markets more volatile and threatens employment arrangements, social trouble is conceivable here as well.

The euro is also likely to stimulate a degree of tax reform across Europe—"tax harmonization" is the phrase these days. This is because competition between EU members through manipulating tax systems is a danger. Some EU members have tax systems that impose serious burdens on their ability to compete—I spoke earlier of the French case, to take but one example. Tax harmonization will most likely be done by transnational cooperation and market effects rather than by European-level legislation. But its effects are likely to reinforce many of the labor market and social program processes already sketched out.

CONCLUSIONS AND FUTURES

What is likely to happen because of the euro? We should remember, first of all, that EMU is part, the biggest part, of a longer-term package of policies to liberalize Europe's erstwhile national economies through regional integration. The euro itself has been coming for a decade or more, and because of this many of its social effects, and the effects of the larger package, are already evident. One safe conclusion is that there will be more such effects. There will be increasing, although carefully controlled, reforms toward greater flexibility and more "active" policies in labor markets. There will be substantial changes in financing and more stringent cost controls in health care. There will be widespread movement toward two-tier pension systems, one tier more or less public and the second market based and complementary to it.

It is very important to add that the European Union itself has not been very active to this point in promoting *transnational* social policy. As noted earlier, the European treaties have by and large left social policy issues in the hands of the member states. This is not completely true, however. Article 119 of the Rome treaty, which enjoined equal pay for equal work between men and women, has been very important more generally in promoting equal rights in employment for women and men, leveling standards across the Union. The EU has also been very active since the Single European Act ratified in 1987 (the SEA brought a set of changes to the Rome treaty to allow the 1992 program to work) in legislating on workplace and product health and safety. Such regulation was justified because health and safety standards might be used by EU members as nontariff barriers in the Single Market. A substantial amount of health-and-safety legislation has been enacted, but it is as yet early to know how effective it is. The EU since 1988 has also been very active in regional economic development activities in poorer areas through its economic and social cohesion programs. In many ways this regional development activity has helped less developed regions of the EU to make considerable economic progress and, while so doing, it has prodded them to raise their social policy standards.

Perhaps most interesting, because of the 1989 Social Charter and the Social Chapter of the Maastricht Treaty, there have been a few pieces of significant social regulatory legislation passed at European level, often in innovative ways. There are European-level regulations on working time, for example, on plant closings, and on a number of other matters. The Social Chapter of Maastricht established new procedures which encouraged European-level union and employer organizations to negotiate and to make it possible for any deals reached to become EU law. The hidden agenda in this was to beef up collective discussion and bargaining at the European level. The results have been limited, but there have been some. The creation of European Works Councils—arrangements to create organizations for the information and consultation of workers in multinational companies operating in Europe were legislated after the "social partners" failed to agree. Negotiated legislation using the Social Chapter on parental leave and the regulation of part-time work and short-term work contracts stand out as achievements, but there are others.

The big picture, however, is that European integration, including the euro, has been about liberal market building and economics. Social policy arrangements have been left largely to EU member states. The Single Market and EMU have acted indirectly on these arrangements, creating constraining new market contexts which have obliged member states to respond and adapt by making changes in their labor market and welfare state policies. These changes have varied greatly because they are based in national politics and national traditions. There are some clear trends, however. Labor markets have become more flexible and welfare states are being updated and in some places seriously reformed. Such trends do not indicate that problems of inflexibility, inefficiency, and financing have been fully resolved. Consensus does seem to be emerging on a number of things, however. "Active" labor market policies, with consequent changes in educational systems and the structuring of social entitlements to keep people in the labor market, are on the table everywhere. Discussion about tax reforms to change the financing of social programs is lively. Health care costs are being scrutinized and squeezed across Europe. Pension reform, in particular the addition of "capitalized" pension funds to existing insurance-based and state minimum pensions, is presently a very hot issue. The presence of strong interest groups protecting what exists makes deep reform a difficult matter indeed. Much remains to be done, therefore. The most interesting question is whether it will be done proactively, by smart governments, or induced indirectly by the euro and market changes.

There is a twist in the narrative, however. The deeper logic of the story will continue. But there is a possibility that the particular shape of action may change in the years to come because of the new predominance of center-left governments. These governments were elected to do social policy differently from their predecessors on the center-right, in particular to find new solutions that avoid complete deregulation and liberalization. Whether they can find formulae that will conciliate Europe's social policy achievements with new needs for flexibility and competitiveness is the issue.

How will things shape up? First, let us focus on Euro-level change. I have mentioned tax reform many times already. It will have indirect but important effects on social policy. The taxes on employment customarily used in many countries as parts of insurance programs to finance health and pensions raise the cost of labor to employers. In a completely open market this cannot be allowed. This tax burden is likely to shift onto general taxation. This is very important, because it will change the principles underlying social policy from the insurance principle, in which individuals contribute to their own benefits, toward a system of broader general social solidarity. As this occurs social expenditures will become more transparent and the multiple transfers between different groups will become clearer. This could change political debate considerably.

The 1998 Amsterdam Treaty, the most recent EU treaty change, put into place a set of procedures for promoting national plans for employment policy and job creation and mandated European-level efforts for harmonizing these plans. The beginnings of this have been successful and the effort is likely to continue in the future. The thrust so far has been to set up targets for job creation and training and to promote the "active" labor market line. There is a possibility that center-left governments will try to coordinate this Euro-level employment policy coordinating exercise with Euro-level macroeconomic policy coordination. At present the two exercises are carried on separately. Combining them would, in part, put pressure on the new Central Bank to be more expansive. The policy buzzword of the day in Europe is that the danger of deflation has become more significant than that of inflation and that the new bank may not be sufficiently aware of this.

Finally there is new talk—coming from the German government in particular—about the need for minimum social policy standards at the European level. This is pitched in terms of continuing in the spirit of the 1989 Social Charter. How serious this talk actually is we do not yet know. The process of promoting such European standards would be difficult, but if it began it would be significant.

But there is also considerable new reflection on the effects of the euro and EMU on social matters at the national level. There is a significant tendency in many member states, for example, toward the striking of "social pacts"—time-limited agreements between employers, unions, governments, and others—about functioning with the euro and promoting national competitiveness. These pacts have elements of wage control, social program reform, labor market reform, and complicated tradeoffs in them. The prototypes are found in Italy, Austria, Ireland, Portugal, and the Netherlands. The Germans and Belgians are presently talking about a pact and the French are trying to approximate one through statist actions. The implications of this "pactism," if it continues, is that the social policy sides of the euro will be handled at the national level and coordinated at the Euro-level, not the other way around.

Finally, the European union movement has been making noise about transnational sectoral collective bargaining—beginning with the German IGMetall union in the metalworking industry. There has already been some action of this kind between German regional unions and those just across the Dutch and Belgian borders. Coordinated wage bargaining at the European level would be a big change, and it might well counteract some of the divisive propensities inherent in the euro. It will be very difficult to engineer, however.

Where does this leave things? There is much experimentation in social policy at both the national and European levels. There remains plenty of space for innovation, however. There may also be even more space for stalling. Innovation poses large problems of coordination both at the euro level and between EMU member states. The biggest issue—and mystery—however, is whether the euro will create more jobs for Europe. If not, trouble for the center-left, and perhaps for the euro and EU as well, will come quickly.

Equality in the European Union and the United States

ELIZABETH F. DEFEIS

The movement for European integration in the 1950s, spearheaded by Jean Monnet, primarily focused on economic integration. The 1957 Treaty of Rome (EEC Treaty), which established the European Economic Community (EEC), virtually ignored human rights and fundamental freedoms.[1] Instead, human rights were to be safeguarded by the European Convention for the Protection of Human Rights and Fundamental Freedoms, which each of the EEC member states had ratified and begun implementing through the so-called Strasbourg process.[2] Under the Strasbourg process, the European Court of Human Rights and the European Commission of Human Rights sit in Strasbourg and hear cases brought under the convention. Today, all members of the European Union (EU), as well as all potential members, such as Russia and Macedonia, have ratified the convention. The Strasbourg process and the European Court of Human Rights are separate and apart from the European Court of Justice (ECJ) and the mechanisms of the EU, such as the Commission and Council of Europe.

Although the EEC Treaty contains a social chapter that addresses human rights, it primarily focuses on workers' rights in an effort to improve working conditions and standards of living throughout the EU. Nevertheless, from its very inception, the EU has embodied the principle of gender equality, at least so far as equal pay for men and women in employment is concerned. The EEC Treaty, which functions as a constitution for the EU, provides in Article 119 "that men and women should receive equal pay for equal work."[3] This provision is, of

117

course, in stark contrast to the U.S. Constitution, which contains no textual commitment to gender equality.[4]

▨ THE EQUALITY PRINCIPLE

Article 119 is the articulated basis for all other EU legislation concerning gender equality. However, it was economic concerns rather than social concerns that led to the inclusion of Article 119 in the EEC Treaty.[5] At the time, France was the only country in the European Community in which workers were constitutionally entitled to equal pay.[6] France feared its businesses would be competitively underpriced by businesses in the other member states with no equal pay requirements, so it insisted that the EEC Treaty include an equal pay provision.[7]

Article 119

Article 119 has been the subject of voluminous EU legislation and litigation that has led to an extensive body of law on gender equality. Much of this litigation has emanated from Denmark, Germany, the Netherlands, and the United Kingdom due to more effective procedures for attacking discrimination and active women's rights groups in these states. Under the constitutional structure of the EU, any court or tribunal of a member state may refer a question to the ECJ for a preliminary ruling. Article 119 also allows individuals to refer questions to the ECJ. The constitutional structure thus has enabled individuals and organizations in member states to pursue test cases to develop the law, even when the outcome is doubtful. Consequently, EU law on gender discrimination in employment is constantly in flux, its meaning developing over time, and may be described as a mini-constitution.

Equal Pay Directive of 1975

The principle of equal pay for equal work in Article 119 of the EEC Treaty was implemented through the Equal Pay Directive of 1975 (EPD).[8] The EPD compliments the principle of equal pay, refines member states' obligations under Article 119, and introduces a comparable worth standard. The comparable worth standard requires equal pay "for the same work or for work to which equal value is attributed"[9] and demands "the elimination of all discrimination on grounds of sex with regard to all aspects and conditions of remuneration."[10] The incorporation of the comparable worth standard in the EPD satisfies international obligations set forth by the International Labor Organization.[11] The EPD further requires that a "job classification system" be nondiscriminatory.[12] The directive's strict enforcement requirements mandate member states to review their laws, regulations, and practices in order to eliminate discriminatory provisions. Member states must also assure that both collective bargaining agreements applicable to industry and private employment contracts abide by the equal pay principle. Finally, member states must generally "ensure that the principle of equal pay is applied,"[13] must establish judicial procedures to enable enforcement,[14] and must inform employees of their rights "at their place of employment."[15] Pay has been interpreted broadly to include retirement benefits, pension benefits, sick pay, and severance allowances.[16]

U.S. Equal Pay Act of 1963

Unlike the European approach, equal pay for work of comparable value is not specifically authorized by U.S. federal legislation, and indeed, the principle of comparable worth continues to be very controversial in the United States. The U.S. Equal Pay Act (EPA)[17] was enacted in 1963 to address the national and international problems caused by paying women less than men for identical work. The EPA demands equal pay for equal work that is performed under similar working conditions and that requires equal skill, effort, and responsibility. Although a claim for equal pay for work of comparable worth cannot be brought under the EPA, such a claim may be brought under common law. In 1981 the U.S. Supreme Court held in *County of Washington v Gunther*[18] that under some circumstances women who perform work not equal to, but comparable to, that performed by men, can bring a claim against their employer for sex-based wage discrimination.

In *Gunther,* female prison guards brought a claim under Title VII of the Civil Rights Act of 1964 against their county employer for wage discrimination, because male prison guards were paid higher wages. The plaintiffs argued that they were paid less for work that was substantially equal to that of male guards and, alternatively, that the county intentionally discriminated against the female guards because of their sex. The female guards based the latter claim on the fact that after conducting a survey of the market value of the job, the county increased the salary of male guards to reflect the survey but left the salary of female guards unchanged.

In upholding the claim, the Court was clear to point out that the claim was not based on what it called "the controversial concept of 'comparable worth'"[19] but rather on intentional discrimination. The intentional discrimination consisted of setting the female wage scale at a lower level than that set out in the county's own survey while at the same time adjusting the male guards' salary to the prevailing higher survey level. The Court did not explain how sex-based wage discrimination litigation under Title VII should be structured. It did, however, seem to open the door to claims of wage discrimination based on comparable worth.

Overall, asserting comparable worth as a litigation strategy has not been successful in the United States. When considering comparable worth claims, U.S. courts have focused on whether the employer was in fact paying market wages and have overlooked the fact that by paying such market wages, employers may be exploiting societal biases, stereotypes, and past discrimination.[20]

The ECJ, on the other hand, has been less receptive to the argument that market forces justify wage disparities.[21] Together with the commission, the ECJ has been forceful in regulating and providing guidance to implement the comparable worth standard throughout the EU. Despite such efforts, wage disparities continue to exist in the EU. One Eurostat survey conducted in four member states reveals that women's salaries are still lagging. Women's hourly earnings in relation to men's are only 84 percent in Sweden, 73 percent in France and Spain, and 64 percent in the United Kingdom (these figures are for full-time and part-time workers but do not include earnings for overtime).[22]

There are now efforts in the United States to address comparable worth that would bring equal pay issues more in line with the model of the EU. In 1997 the Fair Pay Act was introduced in the U.S. Congress to address comparable worth. It was designed to "provide for equal pay for work in jobs that are comparable in skill, effort, responsibility, and working conditions"[23] and to prohibit employers from paying wages to employees "at a rate less than the rate at which the employer pays wages to employees . . . in another job that is dominated by employees of the opposite sex . . . for work on equivalent jobs."[24] The bill was based on a congressional finding that "wage rate differentials exist between equivalent jobs segregated by sex, race, and national origin" and that "discrimination in hiring and promotion has played a role in maintaining a segregated work force."[25] The Fair Pay Act was reintroduced into Congress in 1998 and in March 1999.[26] If enacted, the act would bring the United States closer to the European model and to wage equity.

Equal Treatment Directive of 1976

The EPD of 1975 was limited to issues of equal pay and did not address other employment matters. As a result, the Council of Europe passed the Equal Treatment Directive of 1976 (ETD) one year later, expanding the scope of Article 119's equality principle.[27] The ETD addresses gender discrimination in access to employment. Article 1(1) states: "The purpose of this Directive is to put into effect in the Member States the principle of equal treatment for men and women as regards access to employment, including promotion, and to vocational training as regards working conditions."[28] The ETD sanctions positive action, also known as affirmative action, in certain situations. European social policy has always been sensitive to family and maternity issues. Consequently, the ETD also provides that "the principle of equal treatment shall mean that there shall be no discrimination whatsoever on grounds of sex either directly or indirectly by reference in particular to marital or family status."[29]

In an early case arising under the ETD, *Hofmann v Ersatzkasse*,[30] a man who remained at home to care for his child challenged the denial of certain child care benefits. The ECJ held that member states were not required to provide the same benefits for fathers and mothers of newborn children, regardless of who is actually responsible for rearing the child.[31] The ECJ reasoned that one of the legitimate intents of the ETD, particularly under Article 2(3), was to protect a woman's physical and mental health both during and after the pregnancy and to protect the relationship a mother forms with her child by keeping it unhampered by simultaneous employment constraints.[32] Additionally, the court noted that a woman is entitled to legal protection in order to avoid the conflicting duties of maintaining employment and raising a child.[33]

While the ETD expands the scope of Article 119, it also provides for several exceptions. First, the ETD permits protective treatment for pregnancy and maternity.[34] Second, employers can discriminate by gender if sex "constitutes a determining factor" in the nature or context of the job.[35] To warrant this exception, the employer must prove that the criteria used to determine whether gender is a determining factor are objective.[36] Thus, in an early decision, the ECJ held that Northern Ireland could not restrict the ability of women employees to carry guns and thereby limit women's employment opportunities as police officers.[37] For the ETD's second exception to apply, the ECJ explained that the risk faced by a woman must be higher than the risk faced by a man; mere public opinion that favors protection for women was not sufficient.[38] Furthermore, the ECJ ruled that the above exception must be strictly construed:

> Article 2(3) . . . must be interpreted strictly. It is clear from the express reference to pregnancy and maternity that the directive is intended to protect a woman's biological condition and the special relationship which exists between a woman and her child. . . . The directive does not therefore allow women to be excluded from a certain type of employment on the ground that public opinion demands that women be given a greater protection than men against risks which affect men and women in the same way.[39]

This approach is similar to the U.S. approach. While the EPA is limited to wage discrimination, Title VII of the Civil Rights Act of 1964 is much more expansive, and is the most comprehensive and effective legislation dealing with gender discrimination. It prohibits discrimination on the basis of race, color, religion, national origin, or sex in all terms and conditions of employment. Title VII protects the rights of persons to obtain and hold a job, as well as the right to equal treatment once the job has been obtained, and covers employers with fifteen or more workers. As the European ETD allows for discrimination based on sex if gender is a determining factor, so does the Civil Rights Act.[40] And like the ETD's Article 2 exception, the Bona Fide Occupational Qualification (BFOQ) exception has been narrowly construed.

POSITIVE ACTION

Kalanke v Freie Hansestadt Bremen

The ETD also addresses positive action. It states that the equality principle "shall be without prejudice to measures to promote equal opportunity for men and women, in particular by removing existing inequalities which affect women's opportunities."[41] In Kalanke v Freie Hansestadt Bremen, the ECJ gave a preliminary ruling on a quota system established pursuant to Article 2(4) of the ETD.[42] The male plaintiff, Kalanke, brought a suit claiming gender discrimination when he was passed over for employment in favor of an equally qualified female co-worker pursuant to a German law. The German law provided that in cases of appointments, "women who have the same qualifications as men applying for the same post are to be given priority if they are underrepresented."[43] In Kalanke, it was undisputed that both candidates possessed similar qualifications, but priority was given to the female candidate. Advocate General Tesauro described positive action programs as "a means of achieving equal opportunities for minority . . . or disadvantaged groups, which generally takes place through the granting of preferential treatment to the groups in question."[44]

Nonetheless, the advocate general read Article 2(4) of the ETD narrowly to permit positive action programs only when "directed at removing obstacles preventing women from having equal opportunities."[45] In adopting this reasoning, the ECJ ruled that "a national rule . . . where men and women who are candidates for the same promotion are equally qualified, women are automatically to be given priority in sectors where they are under-represented, involves discrimination on the grounds of sex."[46]

The *Kalanke* decision was met with much criticism throughout the EU. The European Commission issued an interpretative communication that stated, "it is crucial to reaffirm the need to use, where appropriate, positive action measures to promote equal opportunities for women and men."[47] Thus, the communication established that automatic preferences would not be allowed, but quota systems, which were not automatic, would remain unaffected by *Kalanke*.[48] The commission then set forth a list of affirmative action programs that were permissible, including "plans for promoting women including those that prescribe goals and time limits."[49]

Marschall v Land Nordrhein-Westfalen

In 1997 the ECJ took a slightly more generous view toward positive action programs in *Marschall v Land Nordrhein-Westfalen*.[50] In this case Marschall sued for gender discrimination, because a female candidate in his relevant career bracket was given priority for a promotion, pursuant to a German law. The law provided that "[w]here, in the sector of the authority responsible for promotion, there are fewer women than men in the particular higher grade post in the career bracket, women are to be given priority for promotion in the event of equal suitability, competence and professional performance, unless reasons specific to an individual [male] candidate tilt the balance in his favour."[51] The ECJ held that, although a national rule should be able to remedy discrimination, it cannot guarantee absolute priority to women over men.[52] Therefore, the inclusion of a savings clause that would enable male candidates, who are as qualified as female candidates, to be the subject of an objective assessment, would be sufficient to validate the statute.[53] The ECJ noted that "the mere fact that a male candidate and female candidate are equally qualified does not mean that they have the same chances."[54] *Marschall* marks a major departure from *Kalanke,* which held that the guarantee of an equal starting point was sufficient positive action.

The *Marschall* decision did much to revive positive action programs within the EU by dispelling some of the uncertainty created by the *Kalanke* decision. Nevertheless, commentators have mixed interpretations of the decision. Some are pleased with the outcome of *Marschall* and promote quotas favoring women where they are underrepresented in the job market.[55] Others contend that the *Marschall* ruling fails to resolve the conflict between the varied legislation of member states on equal treatment and is not sufficiently clear with respect to the permissible scope of positive action programs.[56] They argue that another ruling may be necessary to define what constitutes "nondiscriminatory employment criteria."[57]

AFFIRMATIVE ACTION IN THE UNITED STATES

In the United States, Title VII of the Civil Rights Act is silent with respect to the legality of affirmative action programs, and as in Europe, the issue of affirmative action has been a source of much controversy. The constitutionality, as well as the fairness, of affirmative action programs has been the focus of debate in the United States for almost half a century. While the debate has primarily centered on race-based affirmative action programs, gender-based programs also have been effected. Because the relevant constitutional provision is the equal protection clause of the U.S. Constitution, the same legal principles apply to both race-based and gender-based preferences, albeit in slightly different forms.

The U.S. Supreme Court's first substantive decision on affirmative action came in 1978 in *Regents of the University of California v Bakke.*[58] The case concerned the constitutionality of a program mandating that sixteen seats be set aside each year for minority applicants in the state medical school. The Court, although sharply divided, ruled that the state had a legitimate interest in achieving a diverse student body and could use race as a positive factor in the admissions process in order to achieve this end, but the rigid two-track approach, akin to a quota, was unconstitutional. While the Supreme Court invalidated quotas in *Bakke,* it approved goals and timetables for achieving equal representation in the workforce. More recently, however, the Court has severely limited the permissible scope of affirmative action programs. Of particular interest is *Taxman v Board of Education of Piscataway,*[59] which was scheduled to be decided by the Supreme Court in the 1997–98 term. The Court never rendered a decision in this case, because the litigants settled before oral argument. The Court, however, will surely resolve the issues presented in *Taxman* in the near future.

In *Taxman,* a white teacher who was dismissed because of a reduction in the workforce brought a claim for discrimination. The high school where he was employed was required to reduce the number of faculty in the business department for budgetary reasons. It was stipulated that the white teacher, Taxman, possessed qualifications equal to those of a black teacher, who was retained. The teachers were deemed "equal in that they were both hired on the same day and were of 'equal ability' with 'equal qualifications,'"[60] leaving the teachers' race the distinguishing factor. Because of the affirmative action plan previously adopted by the town, the white teacher was discharged. The Third Circuit Court of Appeals held that the white teacher's discharge violated Title VII of the Civil Rights Act of 1964, because such an affirmative action program was used solely to promote diversity within the school system. Diversity alone, the court explained, cannot be considered a compelling governmental interest.

At the federal level, the enforcement of affirmative action programs has been effectively vitiated, even though Executive Order 11246,[61] which first sanctioned affirmative action, technically continues to exist. In 1995 the Labor Department issued a policy stating that preferences and quotas will not be permitted in any government programs. Instead, the department encouraged efforts focused on outreach programs designed to broaden the pool of qualified candidates. Despite the fact that the U.S. Supreme Court sanctioned affirmative action programs more than thirty years ago, debate about the legitimacy and wisdom of such programs continues. Indeed, in attempting to evaluate the legality of specific programs, one is faced with an ever-changing legal landscape.

Along with the federal courts, state governments and citizen-initiated referenda have been attacking affirmative action programs. For example, California, Delaware, and Texas have implemented legislation that bans the use of preferences based on race, sex, and ethnicity or national origin in any state program.[62] The effective use of affirmative action programs in the United States, therefore, has been largely diminished.

▧ TREATY OF AMSTERDAM

While the United States appears to be retreating from its earlier commitment to affirmative action, the EU is developing its own jurisprudence of affirmative action through directives, decisions of the ECJ, and the new Treaty of Amsterdam.[63] The Treaty of Amsterdam, signed in 1997, is a major step toward implementing equality in the workforce throughout the EU. The treaty establishes equality between men and women as an explicit goal of the EU.[64] In the declaration to Article 119, the commission states: "When adopting measures referred to in Article 119(4) of the Treaty establishing the European Community, Member States should, in the first instance, aim at improving the situation of women in working life."[65] The Amsterdam Treaty goes beyond any other existing European legislation regarding equality between men and women in the workplace.

The Amsterdam Treaty expands the scope of the EEC Treaty's Article 119 by adding two paragraphs. First, the Amsterdam Treaty incorporates the principle of equal pay for work of equal value and requires the council, under qualified majority voting, to adopt measures to ensure nondiscrimination in employment.[66] Second, the treaty allows member states not only to adopt and maintain positive action programs with respect to access to employment, but also to adopt positive measures or programs that provide for specific advantages "in order to make it easier for the underrepresented sex to pursue a vocational activity or to prevent or compensate for disadvantages in professional careers."[67] In the current version of Article 119, the term "under-represented sex" replaces "women."

The amended and new provisions of the Amsterdam Treaty affirm the EU's commitment to promote equality between men and women and requires the council to adopt measures to ensure that gender discrimination in employment does not occur. Unfortunately, the treaty does not go far enough. Member states are permitted to implement positive action programs, but are not required. Furthermore, the Amsterdam Treaty does not specify which measures member states should take to correct gender discrimination.

CONCLUSION

In the EU, what began as an economic incentive, equal pay for equal work, has slowly evolved into a social commitment to gender equality in employment. The Treaty of Amsterdam further raises EU awareness of gender discrimination in employment and in other areas. But as with EU action in general, implementation rests primarily with member states. Experience with the EPD and the ETD indicates that the states will continue to require prodding from the courts and the commission to fully implement the new equality provisions in the Treaty of Amsterdam.

NOTES

1. Treaty of Rome, Mar 25, 1957, 298 UNTS 3. The EEC Treaty is also known as the Treaty Establishing the European Economic Community and the Treaty Establishing the European Atomic Community.

2. Convention for the Protection of Human Rights and Fundamental Freedoms, Nov 4, 1950, 213 UNTS 22. See Peter Leuprecht, *Innovations in the European System of Human Rights Protection: Is Enlargement Compatible with Reinforcement?* 8 Transnat'l L. & Contemp. Prob. 313 (1998).

3. Treaty of Rome, supra note 1, at art. 119.

4. The United States Constitution contained no equality provision until the adoption of the Fourteenth Amendment in 1868. The effectiveness of this provision, even as it applied to its core purpose, race, was virtually nonexistent until the latter half of this century. Gender discrimination was excluded from its scope until 1971, and even today, the Constitution's applicability to gender discrimination is limited.

5. See June Neilson, *Equal Opportunities for Women in the European Union: Success or Failure?* (Aberdeen: University of Aberdeen, 1998), 65.

6. See George A. Bermann et al., *Cases and Materials on European Community Law* 1158 (1993).

7. See id.

8. Council Directive 75/117, 1975 OJ (L 45/19) (Feb 10, 1975).

9. Id. at art. 1.

10. Id.

11. See Neilson, supra note 5, at 66.

12. See Council Directive 75/117, supra note 8, at art. 1.

13. Id. at art. 6.

14. See id. at art. 2.

15. Id. at art. 7.

16. See Case 12/81, *Garland v British Rail Engineering Ltd.*, 1982 ECR 359 (voluntary travel concessions for retirees); case 170/84 *Bilka-Kaufhaus Gmbh v von Hartz*, 1986 ECR 1607; case C-33/89, *Kowalska* (temporary postemployment payments); case 171/88, *Rinner-Kuhn* (maintenance of salary in case of sickness); case 69/80, *Worringham* (severance allowances); case 262/88, *Barber* (redundancy payments).

17. 29 USCA § 201 et seq. (1982).

18. 452 US 161 (1981).

19. Id. at 166.

20. See *Spaulding v University of Washington*, 740 F2d 686 (9th Cir 1984); *American Nurses' Association v Illinois*, 783 F2d 716 (7th Cir 1986).

21. See *Enderby v Frenchay Health Authority*, case C-127/92 [1994] 1 Common Mkt. L. Rev. 8.

22. EUROSTAT, *Statistics in Focus,* 15 Population & Social Conditions (1997) (visited May 20, 1999) <http://europa.eu.int/en/comm/eurostat/compres/en/9597/6309597a.htm>.

23. 143 Cong. Rec. S80403, (daily ed. Jan. 29, 1997) (statement of Senator Tom Harkin).

24. S232, 105th Cong., 1st sess. (1997).

25. Id.

26. See 145 Cong. Rec. E545, (daily ed. Mar 24, 1999) (statement of Delegate Eleanor Holmes Norton).

27. Council Directive 76/207, 1976 OJ (L 39/40) (Feb 9, 1976).

28. Id. at art. 1(1).

29. Id. at art. 2(1).

30. Case 184/83, 1984 CMR 15,497.

31. See id. at 15,516.

32. See id. at 15,515.

33. See id. at 15,514.

34. See Council Directive 76/207, supra note 27, at art. 2(3).

35. Id. at art. 2(2).

36. See Elena Noel, *Prevention of Gender Discrimination within the European Union,* 9 N.Y. Int'l L. Rev. 77, 86 (1996).

37. See case 222/84, *Johnston v Chief Constable of the Royal Ulster Constabulary,* 1986 ECR 1651.

38. See Noel, supra note 36, at 8687.

39. Case 222/84, supra note 37.

40. The "determining factor" limitation in the ETD can be paralleled to the narrowly interpreted Title VII bona fide occupational qualification which permits an employer to hire on the basis of religion, sex, or national origin where those qualities become a bona fide occupational qualification necessary to the normal operation of the business. See 42 U.S.C.A. § 2000(e)(2); see also 29 CFR § 1604.2.

41. Council Directive 76/207, supra note 27, at art. 2(4).

42. See case C-450/93, [1996] All ER(EC) 66; [1996] 1 CMLR 175.

43. Id.

44. Id. at 21213.

45. Id.

46. Id.

47. Communication on the Kalanke Ruling, 1996 COM (96) 88 final 29.

48. See id. at 31.

49. Id.

50. Case C-409/95 [1997] All ER(EC) 865; [1998] CEC 7720.

51. Id. at 168.

52. See id. at 169.

53. See id.

54. Id. at 170.

55. See *Equal Opportunities: Disagreement about How to Interpret the Marschall Judgment,* European Reports, Jan 28, 1998.

56. See id.

57. Id.

58. 438 US 265 (1978).

59. 91 F3d 1547 (3d Cir 1996), cert. granted 117 S.Ct. 2506 (1997), cert. dismissed 118 S.Ct. 595 (1997).

60. Id. at 1551.

61. Executive Order no. 11246, 30 FR 12319, 1965 WL 7913 (Pres.). President Lyndon B. Johnson issued Executive Order no. 11246 on September 24, 1965. The order directed the federal government "to provide equal opportunity in Federal employment for all qualified persons, to prohibit discrimination in employment because of

race, creed, color, or national origin, and to promote the full realization of equal employment opportunity through a positive, continuing program in each executive department and agency." Id. § 101. Order no. 11246 encouraged and mandated affirmative action programs in employment in federal agencies.

62. See Ann C. McGinley, *The Emerging Cronyism Defense and Affirmative Action: A Critical Perspective on the Distinction between Colorblind and Race-Conscious Decision Making under Title VII,* 3 ACLR 1003 (1997).

63. Treaty of Amsterdam, Oct 2, 1997, European Commission Doc.

64. The new Treaty of Amsterdam incorporates the equal pay for work of equal value provision of the Directive of 1975 and states:

1. Each Member State shall ensure that the principle of equal pay for male and female workers for equal work or work of equal value is applied.

2. For the purpose of this Article, "pay" means the ordinary basic or minimum wage or salary and any other consideration, whether in cash or in kind, which the worker receives directly or indirectly, in respect of his employment, from his employer.

Equal Pay without discrimination based on sex means:

a) that pay for the same work at piece rates shall be calculated on the basis of the same unit of measurement;

b) that pay for work at time rates shall be the same for the same job.

Id. at art. 119.

65. Declaration on Article 119(4), Treaty of Amsterdam (1997).

66. See Treaty of Amsterdam, supra note 63, at arts. 119, 189b.

67. Id. at art. 119(4).

❖ FURTHER READING

Aharonian, Taline. *Equal Value in the European Union: Fiction or Reality?* 2 Buff. J. Int'l L. 91 (1995).

Bolick, Clint. *Jurisprudence in Wonderland: Why Judge Henderson's Decision Was Wrong.* 2 Tex. Rev. L. & Pol. 59 (1997).

Devuyst, Youri. *European Union: Consolidated Version of the Treaty on European Union and Consolidated Version of the Treaty Establishing the European Community.* 37 ILM 56 (1998).

Docksey, Chris. *Sex Discrimination.* European Union Law Anthology 360 (Karen V. Kole and Anthony D'Amato, 1998).

Fox, Eleanor M. *German Sex Bias Rules "Unlawful."* Financial Times, May 27, 1997.

———. *Vision of Europe: Lessons for the World.* European Union Law Anthology 1 (Karen V. Kole and Anthony D'Amato 1998).

Hinton, Eric F. *The Limits of Affirmative Action in the European Union:* Echaard Kalanke v Freie Hansestadt Bremen. 6 Texas J. Women & L. 215 (1997).

Manin, Philippe. *The Treaty of Amsterdam.* 4 Colum. J. Eur. L. 1 (1998).

Mazey, Sonia. *The European Union and Women's Rights: From the Europeanization of the National Agendas to the Nationalization of a European Agenda.* J. Eur. Pub. Pol'y 131 (1998).

Means, Rebecca. Kalanke v Freie Hansestadt Bremen: *The Significance of the Kalanke Decision on Future Positive Action Programs in the European Union.* 30 Vand. J. Transnat'l L. 1087 (1997).

Mertus, Julie A. *International Decision:* Marschall v Land Nordrhein-Westfalen. 92 Amer. J. Int'l L. 296 (1998).

Moens, Gabriel. *Equal Opportunities Not Equal Results: "Equal Opportunity" in European Law after* Kalanke. 23 J. Legis. 43 (1997).

Molinari, Laura. *The Effect of the Kalanke Decision on the European Union: A Decision with Teeth but Little Bite.* 71 St. John's L. Rev. 591 (1997).

Moore, Sara. *Nothing Positive from the Court of Justice.* 21 Eur. L. Rev. 156 (1996).

Reyburn, Mary J. *Strict Scrutiny across the Board: The Effect of* Aderand Constructors, Inc. v Peña *on Race-Based Affirmative Action Programs.* 45 Cath. U. L. Rev. 1405 (1996).

Roberts, Lance W. *Understanding Affirmative Action.* In Discrimination, Affirmative Action, and Equal Opportunity 145 (W. E. Block and M. A. Walker eds., 1982).

Senden, Linda. *Positive Action in the EU Put to the Test: A Negative Score?* 3 Maastricht J. Eur. L. Rev. 156 (1996).

Simpson, Stephen C. *The Self-Critical Analysis Privilege in Employment Law.* 21 J. Corp. L. 577 (1996).

The Fundamental Social Rights of Workers in the European Union

BERNARD D. REAMS JR.

A t their December 9, 1989 meeting, the member states of the European Community (EC) in the European Council in Strasbourg solemnly declared a Charter of the Fundamental Social Rights of Workers. The vote was 11 to 1, with the sole dissent coming from the United Kingdom. This was the second major step in ten years toward a community bill of rights. The first step was a 1979 proposal to the Council of Ministers that the EC should accede to the European Convention on Human Rights and Fundamental Freedoms, a document primarily to protect classic civil and political rights rather than economic and social rights.

The 1989 charter contains thirty articles elaborating ten basic social and economic "rights" of workers or citizens. The first three of these basic rights are freedom of movement, rights of employment and remuneration, and guarantees for the improvement of living and working conditions. Social protection, freedom of association and collective bargaining, vocational training, and equal treatment for men and women follow. Moreover, the charter assures workers the right to information, consultation, and participation in decisions concerning the workplace, health and safety protections, and special protection for children, adolescents, the elderly, and disabled persons.

The 1979 Proposal for Accession to the European Convention on Human Rights has several points worth noting. The commission established that the European Convention on Human Rights, designed to protect traditional civil and political rights, is indeed applicable to the

European Union (EU). These classic rights include freedom of expression, the right of due process under the law, and equal protection in community actions. As with other action in the EU, this 1979 proposal met with controversy, especially with members' concerns over the roles of the Court of Justice and the European Court of Human Rights. A coordinated effort by the Council of Europe's Human Rights Directorate helped to surmount technical problems.

The Treaty of Rome serves as the keystone for the adoption of social legislation within the EU. The European Court of Justice has declared that this "treaty constitutes the constitutional charter of the community." Just as the fundamental analysis of a field of federal legislation in the United States begins with study of its constitutional basis, so too in the EU a legislative program must be examined in light of its basis in the EEC treaty. References to social goals are not clearly stated in the Treaty of Rome and social policy is not clearly articulated as a sphere of community action. It is necessary to use Article 100, the general harmonization provision, when a social measure is to be linked to the economic goals of the common market.

Title III of the Treaty of Rome covers social policy but does not provide for an express grant of legislative authority to attain social policy goals. For example, Title III's Article 117 begins, "Member States agree upon the need to promote improved working conditions and improved standard of living for workers." But the economic nexus kicks in when these goals are to be achieved by "the functioning of the common market" as well as "harmonization of law provisions in the Treaty." Article 118 assigns the commission the "task of promoting close cooperation between Member States in the social field" through studies and consultations in labor law, employment, working conditions, social security, the right of association, and collective bargaining. Article 119, relating to mandating equal pay for equal work between men and women, has had tremendous import on the social life of the Community, due in large measure to the article's expansive interpretation by the European Court of Justice. But there is no grant of any legislative authority.

So where does the legislative authority come from? It comes essentially from the generic grant of power to harmonize laws in order to achieve the common market stated in Article 100. This article was used initially in the 1960s to correlate technical, health and safety, and quality rules in the member states in order to promote the free movement of goods. By the 1970s it had been expanded to social legislation, consumer rights, and environmental protection. Social policy is established by a stretch of the treaty. Because legislation that protects or benefits employees invariably produces economic consequences for employers, the "whereas" clause frequently refers to the need to harmonize member state rules in order to achieve equal competitive conditions among enterprises in different states—to level the playing field.

Even though everyone understands that the principal purpose of Community social legislation is to promote the interests of employees or society in general, the particular measures must be given the appearance of being necessary to attain competitive equality among member state enterprises, and an economic rather than a social goal, in order to justify the legislation as an appropriate use of Article 100. Thus, Community legislation to promote social goals is adopted through the legislative power to achieve a common market, an interesting parallel to the adoption of labor relations and employee protection measures in the United States through the use of the interstate commerce clause.

On a jurisdictional level, the Community Charter challenges the Community's adoption in fact, if not in theory, of the British common-law creation of constitutional principles. It elevates judicial decisions to the level of primary law, affirming judicial discretion and relying on the doctrine of precedent to protect Community citizens' fundamental rights. It reflects a Continental civil law bias toward text, a preference for codification rather than judicial pronouncement of basic rights, and a partial remedy for what has come to be known as the European Community's democratic deficit.

As has been alluded to earlier, during the early history of the EC, social legislation was noteworthy for its absence but for one major exception—legislation to achieve the Community goal of free movement of workers. Council Regulation 1612/68 grants migrant workers "the same social and tax advantages as national workers." The Court of Justice has interpreted this broadly to include equal status in trade unions and housing and equal access for a worker's spouse and children to education and higher education. This regulation had three major goals: to attain full and better employment within the community, to improve living and working conditions, and to increase involvement of management and labor in economic and social decisions of the Community.

SOCIAL ACTION PROGRAMS OF THE EC

The following legislative actions reflect the Community's initial Social Action Programs, which sought to protect employees' economic interests:

1975 Directive on Collective Redundancies

In the industrialized world it is not uncommon for workers to be dismissed at will for business or economic reasons. Whether as the result of an oil embargo or recessions, liberal political leaders and unions have supported legislation to protect employees threatened with layoffs. Under the 1975 directive the employer must give thirty days' advance notice of proposed dismissals to public labor authorities and employee representatives, including the number of employees affected and the period of time involved. The employer is obligated to hold discussions with employees on ways to avoid redundancies—massive layoffs of employees. The comparable statute in the United States would be the Worker Adjustment and Retraining Notification Act of 1988 (WARN).

1975 Transfer of Undertakings Doctrine

Directive 77/187, which entitled the safeguarding of employees rights in the transfer of undertakings of parts of businesses, reflects the desire for favorable treatment of employees impacted by corporate acquisitions or mergers. When a business is transferred to another via a merger, employees retain employee status and their specific contractual rights. Various decisions of the European Court of Justice has generated a substantial precedent liberalizing the protection of the employee. The comparable legal doctrine in the United States would be case law on the topic of corporate succession liability.

1980 *Directive on Employee Insolvency*

Directive 80/987 sought to shield employees who became victims of corporate bankruptcy. With the insolvency of an employer, employees are ensured that they will be paid in full, with reasonable speed, the salary and benefits owed at that time.

1980–1983 *Amended Vredeling Proposal for Employee Information and Consultation Rights*

The Vredeling Proposal reflected and affirmed the tradition of management-employee representation in a work council where employee representatives receive information from management including financial statements and operations data. These concepts serve as employee forums with management to review employee grievances, working conditions, and health-and-safety issues. Economic issues are not discussed in this forum.

Equal Rights for Women and Men in the Workplace

Community law early on paid particular attention to the need for pay equity among the sexes. This was regarded as a basic human right worthy of protection. Subsequent legislative action reflected the influence of the decisions of the Court of Justice in supporting basic human rights.

Article 119 and the Second Defrenne Judgment

The EEC Treaty, in Article 117, states that each member state will ensure the principle that "men and women should receive equal pay for equal work." Article 119 was requested by France to ensure its constitutional provision of equal pay for women in French businesses. Its purpose was to prevent France from being disadvantaged by member states that did not require pay equity. The second Defrenne case heard by the Court of Justice held that Article 119 was unconditional and must be given direct affect in national courts. This decision is regarded as giving high respect to Article 119 and the principle of equal pay as a foundation of the Community. The comparable U.S. law would be the Equal Pay Act (EPA) of 1963 and Title VII of the Civil Rights Act of 1964.

Directive 75/117: Equal Pay for Men and Women

The Equal Pay Directive expanded and made precise that pay is for work for which equal value is attributed—similar to the comparable worth doctrine in the United States. This directive requires member states to use all legal means to enforce the equal-pay principle for work performed under similar working conditions. In the United States, the comparable worth doctrine is not enforced by U.S. courts.

Directive 76/207: Equal Treatment for Men and Women

The third Defrenne case before the Court of Justice affirmed equal pay but held that Article 119 was too precise to imply an obligation to provide equal working conditions. The court felt it could only protect basic human rights within a treaty-based context. This was remedied with the adoption by the council of Directive 76/207, the Equal Treatment Directive. This directive promotes equality of the sexes in the working environment in hiring, training, and working conditions. Direct discrimination on the basis of sex and in reference to marital or family states is prohibited. The comparable U.S. law again would be Title VII of the Civil Rights Act of 1964.

Directive 86/613: Equal Treatment in Agriculture in a Self-Employment Capacity

Directive 86/613 covers all self-employed persons—specifically members of the liberal professions and farmers. This directive looks to equal treatment in commercial and professional partnerships, such as law and accounting firms, regarding both pay and working conditions. The U.S. Civil Rights Act has no parallel to this directive.

The State and Private Social Security Directive

Equal treatment of men and women in the context of the social security scheme is covered by two directives, 79/7 and 86/378. Directive 79/7, Equal Treatment for Men and Women in Matters of Social Security, covers all statutory benefit plans such as sickness, old age, workers compensation, and unemployment. Directive 86/378, Equal Treatment for Men and Women in Occupational Social Security Schemes, refers to private-sector benefit plans—these are considered pay under Article 119. These plans must be provided with equal treatment in their scope, contributions, benefits, and duration. In deference to the United Kingdom, member states were permitted to fix different ages for men and women in determining their eligibility for old-age pensions.

Worker Health and Safety Legislation

With increased public awareness of the risks of exposure to physical and chemical agents, protection of workers in these high-risk environments is an essential social goal of the European Union. Health risks from exposure to asbestos, lead, mercury, PCBs, or industrial machinery required appropriate action for worker safety. Directive 80/1107, Protection of Workers from the Risks Related to Exposure to Chemical, Physical and Biological Agents at Work, set guidelines and limits on workers' exposure. Directive 82/501, on Major-Accident Hazards of Certain Industrial Activities, was prompted by the chemical plant explosion in Seveso, Italy. Subsequently, the hazard of noise in the workplace and its adverse impact on the employee was recognized by Directive 86/188, Risks Related to Noise at Work. Lastly, recognizing the increased reliance on transient workers, signs and safety warnings are required to be in local languages to best protect the migrant workers.

THE SOCIAL CHARTER OF 1989

During the 1980s the Social Action Plan of 1974 lost momentum, except for the implementation and enforcement of the section on health and safety of the workers. The loss of momentum is generally recognized as resulting from the accession to power of Prime Minister Margaret Thatcher in the United Kingdom. The Thatcher government viewed legislation protecting economic and social interests of employees as seriously hampering the competitiveness of British commerce and industry. As in the United States under President Ronald Reagan, the major focus was on deregulation, especially in the social sector.

At the same time the Community itself became involved in time-consuming issues concerning raising of revenues, budgetary issues, agricultural policy problems, and the admission of Greece, Portugal, and Spain, among other challenges. The ultimate adoption of the Single European Act allowed the focus of concern to shift back to social problems.

During the late 1980s the new Social Charter was widely reviewed and eventually accepted by the European Council, the U.K. dissenting, in Strasbourg in December 1989. The Social Charter does not have legally binding effect; the Council of Europe is not a legislative body. The Social Charter is not a Community legislative act under the EEC Treaty, Article 189, and it is not a convention under public international law. The Social Charter is a political commitment of eleven member states to move ahead with specific new social action measures. It serves as a fundamental policy under which specific measures can be based. The Court of Justice may choose to cite it in future cases for principles of fundamental rights or as a guide to interpret future legislative acts. Substantive coverage of the Social Charter is stated in twelve sections that describe the contours of workers' rights and the obligations imposed on member states in the form of specific protections or benefits to individuals.

Freedom of Movement

This section of the Social Charter affirms the rights of workers to move freely throughout the community, to receive equal treatment in access to occupations, to receive equal treatment as to working conditions and social protection, and the right to have a residence with their families.

Employment and Remuneration

The two principles covered by the section assure the freedom to engage in any occupation without discrimination on the basis of nationality and promise that all employment will be fairly remunerated with an equitable wage, including that of part-time and temporary workers.

Improvement of Living and Working Conditions

This section provides workers with a right to a weekly rest period and annual paid leave.

Social Protection

The right to adequate social protection is covered by this section. It looks to access of social security benefits and social assistance for those unable to enter or reenter the job market when they have no means of subsistence.

Freedom of Association and Collective Bargaining

Topics covered by this section include the right of both employers and workers to consult professional organizations or trade unions to defend their economic and social interests. The right to negotiate collective agreements is assured and migrant workers are to enjoy equal treatment.

Vocational Training

Every worker is assured of access to vocational training and of receiving such training throughout his working life without discrimination on grounds of nationality.

Equal Treatment of Men and Women

This section reaffirms the assurance of equal treatment for men and women. Measures are to be made enabling workers to reconcile their occupational and family obligations—for example, parental leave and child care measures.

Information, Consultation, and Participation for Workers

This text reflects the provisions covered in the Collective Redundancy and Transfer of Undertaking directives discussed earlier.

Health Protection and Safety at the Workplace

This section is a restatement of the EEC Treaty, Article 118a.

Protection of Children and Adolescents

This section calls for new initiatives setting the minimum age of employment at fifteen years, requires equitable remuneration for young people, and requires limits on the maximum time worked and a prohibition of night work.

Elderly Persons

This section seeks to guarantee an adequate pension plus medical and social assistance to retired workers. It can be anticipated that this section will encourage a harmonization of national and private pension schemes.

Disabled Persons

An obligation is placed on member states by this section to improve and expand the social and professional integration of disabled persons into the workforce and into society.

The Social Charter of 1989 requests the commission to prepare an annual report on the implementation of the charter by the Community and by the member states. This report is to be submitted to the European Council and the Parliament for their evaluation.

▨ SUBSEQUENT ACTIVITIES

The most recent social action in the EU has been significant. Directive 92/85, to Encourage Improvements in the Safety and Health at Work of Pregnant Workers and Workers Who Have Recently Given Birth or Are Breast-feeding, contains a series of measures for protection of female employees. Pregnant women are forbidden to work at night; maternity leave is an obligation at least two weeks before and after birth, and the employee may opt for fourteen weeks of maternity leave with pay set at sick-pay levels. There is a prohibition of termination of employment of female workers throughout their pregnancy and maternity leave. In the United States, the comparative statutory guidelines would be in the U.S. Family and Medical Leave Act of 1993, which applies to men and women, provides twelve weeks unpaid leave, and includes pregnancy, births, adoptions, ill health, and injury.

The Treaty on European Union (TEU; the Maastricht Treaty) was signed on February 7, 1992. In pertinent parts the preamble of this treaty notes the parties are: "determined to promote economic and social progress for their peoples"; "resolved to establish a citizenship common to the nationalities of their countries"; and "reaffirming their objective to facilitate the free movement of persons." Title 1 (Article B) notes that the Union shall itself set forth the following objectives: "To promote economic and social progress which is balanced and sustainable, in particular, through the creation of an area without internal frontiers, through the strengthening of economic and social cohesion." The TEU is accompanied by seventeen protocols of which no. 14 is entitled Social Policy. It notes that a qualified majority of not less than fifty-two votes are required in favor of social changes. It specifically excludes Great Britain and Northern Ireland from any impact of these proposals or protocols.

Protocol no. 14 consists of seven articles and two declarations essentially expanding on existing social policies already articulated. For example, Article 2 requires the member states to support: improvement of working environments to protect worker's health and safety, improvement of working conditions, sharing of information and consultation with workers, equal work opportunities for men and women and their equal treatment at work, and integration of persons excluded from the labor market.

The council must act unanimously on proposals from the commission after consulting with the European Parliament and the Economic and Social Committee in the following areas:

social security and social protection of workers;

protection of workers where their employment contract is terminated;

representation and collective defense of the interests of workers and employees;

conditions of employment of third-country nationals legally residing in Community territory;

financial contributions for promotion of employment and job-creation without prejudice to the provisions relating to the Social Fund.

Lastly, Protocol no. 15, entitled Economic and Social Cohesion, calls on the Community to "reaffirm their conviction that the European Investment Bank should continue to devote the majority of its resources to the promotion of economic and social cohesion."

THE TREATY OF AMSTERDAM

The Treaty of Amsterdam, amending the Treaty on European Union, was signed on October 2, 1997. It contains three parts: part 1 contains substantive amendments to the three Community treaties and the Treaty on European Union; part 2 contains the results of a technical exercise carried out in parallel to the main negotiations: simplification of the three Community treaties by deleting absolute provisions and updating others; part 3 contains final provisions, including an article renumbering the provisions of both the TEU and the EC Treaty.

Articles 117 to 120 of the EEC Treaty have been replaced and reenacted almost unchanged and appear as a new Title XI with new article numbers (136–145). Article 119 has been expanded beyond simply an equal-pay provision for males and females. It now includes the application of the principle of equal opportunities and equal treatment of men and women in matters of employment and occupation. One of the major changes for the United Kingdom is its participation in the provisions formerly annexed to the old Protocol no. 14. The two directives already adopted under the Social Agreement in parental leave and the European Workers' Councils are now to be applied to the United Kingdom. The Treaty of Amsterdam had modest goals of making institutional reforms and improving the efficiency of the Union. The overhaul was only of those provisions deemed necessary; a complete revision was avoided.

CONCLUSION

The perceived prosperity of the EU has attracted new candidates for membership. The central European nations are eager to join in, whether it be Poland, Hungary, the Baltic States, etc. Also recall the prior efforts of Turkey to seek membership. An EU with thirty member states is not inconceivable, according to the experts. Certainly the social policies articulated above will have major impact on the quality of life of the citizens of the Union—and a challenge to the Union itself.

REFERENCES

Goebel, Roger, J. *Employee Rights in the European Community: A Panorama from the 1974 Social Action Program to the Social Charter of 1989.* 17 Hastings Int'l & Comp. L. Rev. 1 (1993).

Langrish, Sally. *The Treaty of Amsterdam: Selected Highlights.* 23 E.L. Rev. 3 (1998).

Part IV

The European Union:
International Impact

An American Perspective on the Euro

LARRY NEAL

The purpose of this paper is to provide a perspective on Euroland from abroad, from the United States. When I first presented my views on this topic to a seminar in Sweden nearly two years ago, a Swedish economist approached me afterward to tell me that it makes a lot of difference in Sweden how one pronounces the name of the new currency. If pronounced in German, "oy-row," it sounds like the Swedish expression for "Oops!" or "Oh, dear!" If pronounced in French, "ooh-r-r-r-oh," it sounds like the Swedish for "OK!" or "All right!" This was an appropriate comment, as I had argued that for the success of the euro the French preference for at least mildly inflationary financing was preferable to the long-standing German preference for price stability or deflation. Since then I have become less enthusiastic about either pronunciation, as I wait for necessary reforms to take place in both labor and capital markets. The delay in reform of labor markets is understandable, but it is especially disconcerting that reforms in the capital markets are not taking place faster.

The benefits of a common currency have shown up already for the governments of the participating countries, namely in reducing the interest payments required on their very large stocks of outstanding government debt. But just as the constantly rising interest payments create an ultimately unsustainable situation of rising debt and inflation (the situation that economists call unpleasant monetary arithmetic), so the current fall in interest payments and disinflation is ultimately unsustainable without changes in the labor and capital markets of

Europe. Even pleasant monetary arithmetic has its limits! There is some evidence that European banks and businesses are beginning to respond to this challenge, as they recognize the competitive pressures that are coming upon them. Governments, by their nature, are delaying their response, but the long-run pressures on them will surely rise.

I will illustrate my argument by taking up the economic history of the European Union in its monetary aspects where John Gillingham left off, with the end of the European Payments Union in 1958. From 1960 to the present, the development of European monetary unification has been determined by the various external shocks that have struck from time to time. In this respect, I am simply continuing the theme of Stephen Schuker, who emphasized the importance of external shocks in shaping the European Economic Community (EEC) in its early years. Until the German reunification shock of 1990, the tight money policy of the Bundesbank proved consistently superior to the French and Italian inflationary habits in coping with the various shocks. This historical experience has led the French and Italian central banks to bind their policies to those of the German central bank. Both resumed a pegged exchange rate with the deutsche mark after the unexpected and unpleasant consequences of German monetary unification in 1990 led to collapse of the exchange rate mechanism of the European Monetary System (EMS) in 1992 and 1993. The pegged exchange rate for France and Italy was only viable if their central banks restricted the growth of their money supply to the same extent as the Bundesbank. The result was that both France and Italy have suffered the negative economic consequences of the German failure to finance easily the reconstruction of the East German economy. Neither country, however, has managed to help ease the German transition problem. In the future, capital markets capable of mobilizing venture capital as in the American and British economies must be created in Euroland, if the problems of financing large-scale structural changes in the Continental economies are to be overcome successfully. There are hopeful signs underway as Continental stock exchanges adapt to the challenges and opportunities of the revolution in information technology. But before describing the problems of the future, let's look at the successes of the past.

▨ THE BRETTON WOODS ERA (1958–1971)

With the resumption of currency convertibility by the leading nations of Europe in 1958, the multilateral settlement of trade imbalances envisioned in the original Bretton Woods Agreement of 1944 could be realized.[1] Indeed, the following ten years saw the full flowering of the possibilities for trade expansion. France and the Netherlands joined in the export-led growth parade initiated by Germany and Italy, while those two leaders continued to grow rapidly. On the other side of the world, Japan freed the yen, and it too began its export-led ascent to economic supremacy. Underlying this expansion in world trade and world output was a system of fixed exchange rates, with all European currencies pegged to the U.S. dollar. Figure 1 shows that this golden decade was initiated by a minor devaluation of the German mark and the Dutch guilder in 1961 and ended in 1969 with a devaluation of the French franc and a revaluation of the German mark. The initial decade of the European Economic Community, in short, with its enormous expansion of trade among the member countries, was one of fixed exchange rates and effectively a common currency within the customs union.

As a result of their common adherence to the rules of the International Monetary Fund (IMF), which meant maintaining fixed exchange rates with respect to the U.S. dollar, the member states of the European Community (EC) did not have to pay explicit attention to the questions of exchange rates with one another, or move toward a common currency as mandated by the Treaty of Rome. By 1968, however, the expansion of trade between France and Germany had developed into increasing trade deficits for France, which led to the first disruption of the regime of fixed exchange rates within the EEC. The problem arose from the difference in monetary policies followed by France and Germany: mild inflation in France and strictly stable prices in Germany. With both exchange rates fixed relative to the dollar, a lower rate of inflation in Germany meant that its real exchange rate was constantly depreciating relative to the dollar while the higher rate of inflation in France meant that its real exchange rate was constantly appreciating relative to the dollar, and even more so relative to the deutsche mark. The continued real depreciation of the deutsche mark helped maintain the momentum of Germany's export-led growth in the 1960s. After further inflation was required in France to quell the labor unrest that erupted in May 1968, a major realignment was agreed upon between France and Germany. France devalued relative to the dollar by 10 percent, but only after Germany agreed to revalue against the dollar by an equal 10 percent (see fig. 1).

Before further realignments were necessary within the European Economic Community, however, the Bretton Woods era of fixed, but adjustable, exchange rates was terminated by the United States. This occurred in August 1971 when President Richard Nixon ordered the Federal Reserve System of the United States to cease paying out gold to central banks of foreign countries when they wanted to cash in part of their holdings of U.S. dollars. Closing the gold window, as this action was termed, enabled the United States to float the dollar against all other currencies, letting it rise or fall depending on the state of the balance of payments. With respect to the currencies of the original six members of the EC, the dollar fell at differing rates, most against Germany, then against the Netherlands and Belgium, and least against Italy (fig. 1). This meant that the exchange rates within the EC changed as well, creating uncertainty among traders and consternation among the bureaucrats charged with administering the price supports of the Common Agricultural Policy.

▨ THE SNAKE

In 1969, in response to the acrimony generated over the realignment of the French and Germany currencies, which was carried out bilaterally, the EC had already launched an ambitious effort to achieve economic and monetary union. Based on the Werner Report of 1970, a plan was

Figure 1. The First Six Exchange Rates on the Dollar

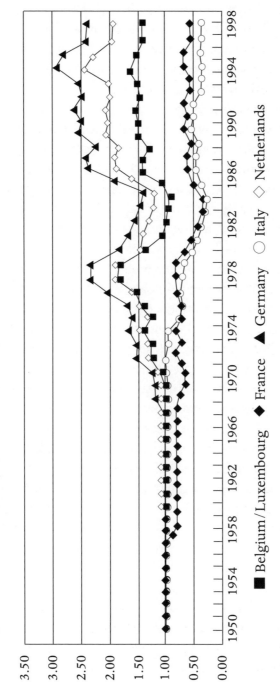

Index, 1950 = 1

■ Belgium/Luxembourg   ◆ France   ▲ Germany   ○ Italy   ◇ Netherlands

introduced to achieve a common currency by 1980 in three stages. Stage one, to begin in 1971 and last for three years, would achieve a "concertation" of national macroeconomic policies with a goal of narrowing exchange rate fluctuations among member currencies within a smaller range than authorized by the IMF (then still +/– 1 percent). Stage two would create a European Monetary Cooperation Fund controlled by the governors of the individual central banks, which would use its resources to intervene in the foreign exchange markets to minimize exchange rate variations among member currencies. Stage three would see the evolution of this fund into a European central bank managing a common Community currency by 1980.[2] Any resemblance between the Werner Plan of 1970 and the Delors Plan of 1990 is more than coincidental!

The collapse of the Bretton Woods system in August 1971 forced stage one of the Werner Plan into a series of makeshift arrangements as the individual countries struggled to cope with the final collapse of a managed international monetary system in March 1972, the first oil shock in October 1973, and the second oil shock in 1979. Concertation was largely put aside in favor of domestic political considerations, and achievement of consensus over exchange rate policies was not aided by the accession of three new members in 1973—Great Britain, Ireland, and Denmark. What emerged instead was a system of jointly floating currencies anchored to the deutsche mark, which came to be known as the snake in the tunnel, or simply the snake.

The first stage in the breakup of the Bretton Woods system was the Smithsonian Agreement in December 1971, where a new set of "central rates" among the Group of Ten[3] major industrial countries (G10) was agreed on, with temporarily wider bands of 2.25 percent on either side allowed. The initial reaction of the EEC Council of Finance Ministers to the Smithsonian Agreement was to state that the EEC currencies would maintain this +/– 2.25 percent band with respect to one another, but not with respect to U.S. or Canadian dollars. A bit later, in March 1972, they determined to maintain margins with respect to each other that were only +/– 1.125 percent from the agreed central rates (the snake), while keeping within the +/– 2.25 percent margins with respect to the other G10 currencies (the tunnel). Britain joined only briefly (May to June 1972) as a token gesture of its commitment to membership in the EC, which began in 1973, but then floated from June 1972 on. Italy left the arrangement in February 1973, just before the entire Smithsonian Agreement broke down and generalized floating began in March 1973. This ended the tunnel, but the snake continued to float, although with a varying membership. By January 1974, France had dropped out of the arrangement, rejoining briefly from July 1975 to March 1976. While Norway and Sweden participated from time to time, the joint float ended up being conducted by Germany, the Netherlands, Belgium, Luxembourg, and Denmark.[4] Obviously, it was the German Bundesbank that was orchestrating this arrangement, and not the European Monetary Cooperation Fund envisioned in the now moribund Werner Report. The disarray of exchange rate policies among the new, peripheral members of the EU is illustrated nicely in figure 2.

While each major country in the EC pursued its own national policy to respond to the first oil shock, the German economy and those linked most closely to it in the snake had the most success. This can be attributed in large part to the effect of Germany's tight money policy in absorbing a large part of the oil shock through an appreciation of the deutsche mark relative to the dollar. The oil shock consisted of the Organization of Petroleum Exporting Countries (OPEC) countries quadrupling the price of crude oil in *dollars*. When the deutsche mark and the currencies pegged to it appreciated by 30 to 40 percent relative to the dollar, they wiped out that much of the price increase for imported oil. Meanwhile, France and Italy, by continuing to depreciate their currencies relative to the dollar, magnified the oil shock for their economies. Recognizing their relative failure, the central banks of France and Italy renewed their efforts to imitate the German policy when they were confronted with the second oil shock that started in late 1978, lasting through 1979 into 1980. This led quickly to the formation of the European Monetary System, a greatly modified version of the second stage envisioned in the Werner Report.

Figure 2. Second Six, 1950–1998

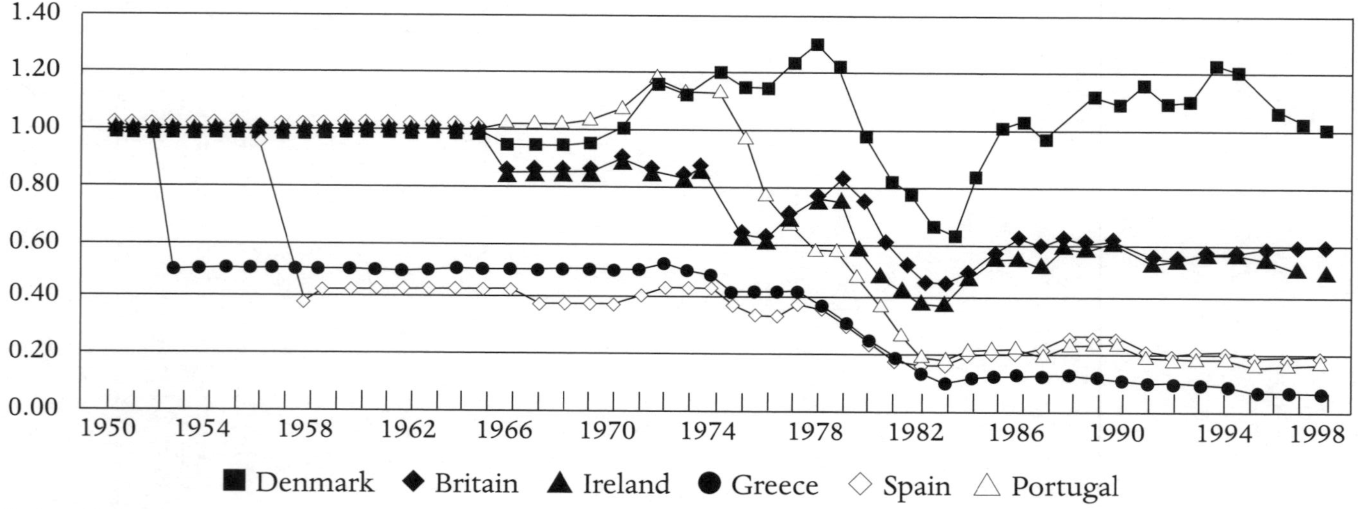

■ Denmark ◆ Britain ▲ Ireland ● Greece ◇ Spain △ Portugal

Index, 1950 = 1

⊠ THE EUROPEAN MONETARY SYSTEM (1979–1992)

The inclusion of France and Italy in the joint float with Germany against the dollar and yen required some modifications in the arrangements of the EC. While the formal initiative was launched at the July 1978 meeting of the heads of government of the member countries (the European Council), operation of the EMS did not begin formally until March 13, 1979.[5] Great Britain opted out for a variety of reasons, pragmatic and political. Its previous effort at floating with the rest of the EC had aborted after only one month in 1972; as yet its trade with the rest of the Community had not expanded to the extent hoped for when it had joined; and most important, its commitment to development of its offshore oil resources in the North Sea was coming to fruition, foretelling the emergence of Britain as a net oil exporter rather than oil importer, unlike the rest of the EC. The importance of this was that the price of oil was then (and still is) set in U.S. dollars by the OPEC cartel. Germany's tight money policies during the first oil shock of 1973–74 had meant the deutsche mark appreciated relative to the dollar, so the price of oil, while still rising in terms of deutsche marks, did not rise as much as it did in dollars. This was a definite advantage for a net importer like Germany and the rest of the EC, but a definite disadvantage for a net exporter such as Britain.

In the event, the British decision proved right—almost immediately with the launching of the European Monetary System came the second oil shock of 1979–80 set off by the revolution in Iran. This redoubled the price of oil, which had already quadrupled in response to the power of the OPEC cartel in 1973–74. The British decision forced Ireland and Denmark, two small open economies whose major trading partner had traditionally been Great Britain before they entered the Common Market with Great Britain in 1973, to decide where their future lay. Both opted to stick with Germany in essence, and take their chances on trade with Britain as the pound floated with respect to the deutsche mark. In the short run, this proved especially painful for Ireland, as it found itself priced out of much of its traditional British market and not yet competitive in the rest of the EC. No doubt the economic costs were judged worth bearing for the political independence from Britain that the decision implied.

More important than the short-run costs for these two small countries, however, was the effect of the second oil shock on the stability of the newly created system. The first oil shock had destroyed permanently the Bretton Woods system of fixed exchange rates, set with adjustable pegs to the U.S. dollar, despite the best efforts to realign rates in the Smithsonian Agreement of December 1971. Would the second oil shock destroy the more modest effort of the Europeans to have a limited area of exchange rate stability within the confines of their customs union? Surprisingly, the EMS survived, expanded in membership, strengthened in effectiveness, and eventually induced even Britain to join in late 1990.

There were two keys to the survival of the EMS in face of the second oil shock, reduced growth, greatly increased unemployment, and political turnover in most participating countries. One key was its flexibility, as European analysts argue; the other was the felicity of encountering two favorable shocks in the 1980s. The flexibility is manifest in the frequent realignments, usually to allow France or Italy to depreciate a bit more relative to the German deutsche mark and the Dutch guilder (see table 1). The felicity derived from facing first the Volcker shock of a sharply appreciating U.S. dollar in the early 1980s, and then the third oil shock in the late 1980s, when the price of oil collapsed. The felicitous shocks were far more important than the flexibility of the EMS members in realigning their rates periodically. All the European currencies, whether they were in the EMS or not, depreciated against the U.S. dollar from 1980 to 1985. This may be called the Volcker shock, as it came not from any European initiative but from the dramatic change in U.S. monetary policy initiated in 1980 by Paul Volcker, then governor of the Federal Reserve System. Volcker targeted limits on the annual growth of the U.S. money supply and let interest rates go as high as the market desired in the face of sharply reduced liquidity in the United States. The dramatic rise in the exchange rate of the dollar worsened the effects of the second oil shock for all of Europe, save Britain and Norway, who were now oil exporters. But it also had the effect of improving the export competitiveness of Europe relative to the United States. Among the oil importers, Germany was doing no worse than the rest and there was no chance for any country other than Norway or the Netherlands to imitate Britain by exploiting North Sea oil or natural gas. Even so, realignments were frequent in the first few years of the EMS system under the duress of the Volcker shock. They occurred in September and November 1979, again in March and October 1981, in February and June 1982, in March 1983, and finally in July 1985.

Table 1. Dates and Size of EMS Realignments (percent change in central rate with the ECU)

	24 Sep. 79	30 Nov. 79	22 Mar. 81	5 Oct. 81	22 Feb. 82	14 Jun. 82	21 Mar. 83
FF	0.	0.	0.	-3	0.	-5.75	-2.5
DM	2.	0.	0.	5.5	0.	4.25	5.5
IRL	0.	0.	0.	0.	0.	0.	-3.5
ITL	0.	0.	-6.	-3	0.	0.	-3.5
HFL	0.	0.	0.	5.5	0.	4.25	3.5
DKR	-2.9	-4.8	0.	0.	-3	0.	2.5
BFR	0.	0.	0.	0.	-8.5	0.	1.5

	20 Jul. 85	7 Apr. 86	4 Aug. 86	12 Jan. 87	22 Jan. 90	14 Sep. 92	17 Sep. 92
FF	2.	-3.	0.	0.	0.	3.5	0.
DM	2.	3.	0.	3.	0.	3.5	0.
IRL	2.	0.	-8.	0.	0.	3.5	0.
ITL	-6.	0.	0.	0.	-3.	-3.5	*
HFL	2.	3.	0.	3.	0.	3.5	0.
DKR	2.	1.	0.	3.	0.	3.5	0.
BFR	2.	1.	0.	2.	0.	3.5	0.
PTA						3.5	-5.0
UKL						3.5	*
ESC						3.5	0.

	23 Nov. 92	1 Feb. 93	1 May 93	6 Mar. 95
FF	0.	0.	0.	0.
DM	0.	0.	0.	0.
IRL	0.	-10.	0.	0.
ITL	*	*	*	*
HFL	0.	0.	0.	0.
DKR	0.	0.	0.	0.
BFR	0.	0.	0.	0.
PTA	-6.	0.	-8.	-7.
UKL	*	*	(+2.58)	(2.02)
ESC	-6.0	0.	-6.5	-3.5

Source: Ecustat, Supplement 10, "The Evolution of the EMS," December 1995, p. 50.

After 1985 the remaining realignments, until the breakaway of Britain and Italy in September 1992, occurred in the context of new entries coming into the Exchange Rate Mechanism (ERM) or existing members narrowing their bands from 6 percent (Italy and Ireland initially, and then Spain, Britain, and Portugal as they entered the ERM) to 2.25 percent. Europeans congratulated themselves on having made the necessary adjustments in central par rates during the shakedown part of the cruise. Having weathered the storm of the second oil shock, they launched the Single Market initiative.

The revival of investment and growth rates in Europe in the late 1980s is no doubt attributable in part to the opportunities opened up by the Single Europe Act of 1987, but already anticipated by the end of 1985. Equally striking, however, from an American perspective was the effect of what might be called the third oil shock, the collapse of crude oil prices at the end of 1985. This inaugurated a period of relatively cheap energy that was only briefly interrupted during the Gulf War of 1990–91. Moreover, the U.S. dollar fell relative to the other Organization for Economic Cooperation and Development (OECD) currencies after the Louvre Accord in 1985, making oil prices even cheaper for the European economies. With this fortuitous combination of falling oil prices and a falling dollar, small wonder that the participating currencies in the EMS had no further need for realignment.

From the middle of 1985 until September 1992, the EMS was hailed as having achieved its goal of stabilizing exchange rates among member states of the European Community, enabling them to move confidently forward to the next step—establishing a common currency. The success in this period owed everything, it appeared, to the economic benefits obtained by member states when they permitted their central banks to accept the monetary leadership of the Bundesbank. The Bundesbank, in turn, was committed by the German constitution to maintain independence from the central government and to keep inflation under control, meaning under 3 percent annually. In effect, the deutsche mark had replaced the U.S. dollar as the key currency for the rest of the European central banks.

The stability of the exchange rates encouraged the member states to press forward with plans for establishing a European Financial Common Market, allowing free movement of capital among the member states. This required, first and foremost, elimination of capital controls by individual members, at least as far as the capital exported to other member states. It also required elimination of restrictions on ownership by foreigners of financial assets in the EC, at least if the foreigners were also from the EC. The initial effects of this limited deregulation of European financial services was very beneficial to those countries that had had the most tightly controlled financial sectors—France, Italy, and Spain. German and British banks and insurance companies, especially, found previously untapped markets for their efficient operations in mutual funds in Italy, branch banks in Spain, and financial markets in France. Tying their exchange rates firmly to the deutsche mark further encouraged import of fresh capital to these economies. Consequently, all of the EC prospered during the late 1980s. It was against this background of increasing prosperity, renewed foreign investment within the EC generally and especially in the southern tier, financial deregulation, and stable exchange rates that the Delors Plan for achieving, finally, the long-cherished goal of a single currency for the EC was formulated.

Stage one, which was already in progress, was to be completed by the end of 1992, when all twelve member states would have committed to maintaining fixed exchange rates with respect to the other eleven currencies. All seemed well until difficulties began to be experienced with ratification of the Maastricht Treaty by the member states. From early 1987 to June 1992, the EMS and its Exchange Rate Mechanism (ERM) enjoyed an unprecedented period of stability in the central parities and in the fluctuations around them. Spain and the United Kingdom joined the ERM; Italy and Ireland moved from wide 6 percent bands for the allowable fluctuations in their currencies to the narrow 2.25 percent bands. Moreover, when uncertainties over the possible outcomes of the Maastricht Summit held in December 1991 began to put pressure on some currencies, coordinated actions were taken by several central

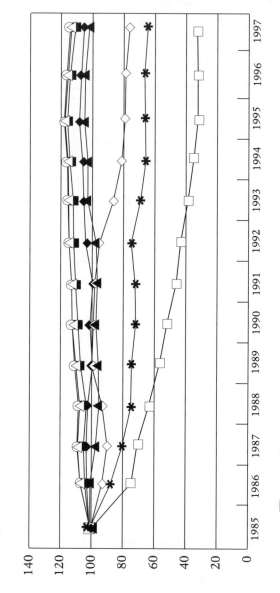

Figure 3. The EMS in Action, 1985–1997

■ BFR   ◆ DKR   △ DM   □ DR   ◇ PTA   ▲ FF   ✳ ESC   ○ ATS

1985=100

banks to maintain stability in the exchange rates. In November, the French and Italians raised their key interest rates and the British were allowed to move closer to the bottom of the 6 percent band. After the Maastricht Summit, the Germans raised their discount rate, countering inflationary pressures caused by the mounting costs of reunification, but all the ERM countries except Great Britain followed suit, again to maintain the stability of the grid of fixed exchange rates with one another.[6] By April 1992, even the Portuguese escudo had joined the ERM and only Greece remained outside the parity grid (fig. 3).

The first alarm occurred in June 1992, when the referendum presented to the Danish electorate by the government failed to elicit the necessary approval by a majority of voters. Not only did this cast in doubt the viability of the political union foreseen by the Maastricht Treaty, it undermined confidence in the future of the EMS as a stepping stone to monetary union. The political difficulties of both Italy and Britain made participants in the foreign exchange markets doubt those two governments could continue to follow the German Bundesbank in maintaining high interest rates. Moreover, the weakening U.S. dollar was putting balance-of-trade pressure on all the European economies. Nevertheless, Germany continued to raise its interest rates, and economic difficulties increased for other member states, especially Italy, Britain, and Spain. Looming in the near future was the upcoming referendum on the Maastricht Treaty in France, scheduled for September 20, 1992. The rejection of the treaty by voters in Denmark was a disturbance, not a disaster. Voters in Ireland had overwhelmingly approved it; perhaps the Danish government had mishandled the presentation of the treaty to its public.[7] But if the French referendum failed, it would be a disaster. Polls showed that this was quite possible, in fact.

In early September, Finland, which had been pegging its currency, the markka, to the deutsche mark in anticipation of applying for full membership and participating in the advantages of the single market, was forced to abandon the project and float the markka, which fell sharply. The Swedish krona came under heavy attack by speculators, leading to incredible interest rates of 75 percent and then for a spell, 500 percent. On Monday, September 14, the Italian lira was permitted to devalue by 7 percent against the rest of the currencies.[8] Speculative pressures then focused on the British pound. On Wednesday, September 16, the pound sterling was withdrawn (temporarily!) from the ERM, the Italian lira was allowed to float, and the Spanish peseta was devalued by 5 percent against all the remaining EMS currencies. This effectively ended the ERM for those countries and the prospect of uniting all the member state currencies into a common currency, as foreseen by the Maastricht Treaty. The foreign exchange markets had decided the fate of EMU before the French voters had their say.

Nevertheless, the French franc remained steadfastly linked to the deutsche mark despite enormous selling pressures against it. And the narrow approval of the Maastricht Treaty by French voters on September 20 undoubtedly helped sustain the French government in its determination to maintain the exchange rate with the deutsche mark. The speculative pressures continued to play against the various currencies that had decided to continue pegging their exchange rate to that of the deutsche mark. At the end of November 1992, both Spain and Portugal devalued their currencies 6 percent against the European currency unit (ECU). On February 1, 1993, the Irish punt finally conceded defeat and devalued 10 percent against the ECU. By May 1993, both Portugal and Spain were forced to devalue yet again.

Meanwhile, the French economy continued to suffer slow growth and rising unemployment while British exports began to rebound and the economy revive, apparently in response to the continued lower value of the pound sterling relative to its trading partners in the Single Market. At the end of July 1993, the crisis culminated when the French government decided it could no longer raise interest rates in defense of the franc and the Bundesbank decided it could no longer extend loans of deutsche marks to the Banque de France. These trends were starting to increase the supply of German currency circulating in Germany and undermining the Bundesbank's efforts to control inflationary pressures within unified Germany.

The resolution was to allow the French franc to devalue, but not by realigning relative to the ECU, as had been done by Spain, Portugal, and Ireland, nor by withdrawing from the Exchange Rate Mechanism, as had been done by Italy and the United Kingdom. Instead, a novel solution was reached—"temporary" expansion of the allowable limits of fluctuation in the values of the participating currencies to +/– 15 percent. This allowed the French franc to devalue, in fact, by as much as had the pound and lira during the September 1992 crisis. In fact, once the speculators starting taking their profits by buying back the now much cheaper French franc, it rose again to within the original +/– 2.25 percent range around its central par rate with respect to the deutsche mark.

The August 1993 solution was viewed as a temporary fix, with the goal of moving toward a common currency still held firm by the French, Dutch, Belgians, and Danes, whose central par rates had remained intact throughout the turmoil. The commitment of the Spanish, Portuguese, and Irish was maintained as well through irregular realignments. At the European Council meeting in December 1993, the composition of the ECU was fixed at its 1989 basket, when the peseta and escudo had been added to it. Hereafter, the ECU is a "hard" unit of account, meaning that in the future any change in a member state's exchange rate can be only a devaluation relative to the ECU, now called the euro.

The successive crises of the European Monetary System from September 1992 to August 1993 forced all the member states of the European Union to resolve the ambiguities of the Exchange Rate Mechanism in one way or another. Economists from the United States and Britain were nearly unanimous in proclaiming the EMS dissolved. (And good riddance, because of the confusion it caused in foreign exchange markets, whose sporadic crises caused disruptions to foreign trade.) It would henceforth be better for all countries concerned to allow their exchange rates to fluctuate freely on the foreign exchange markets. This would use the competitive forces of global product and capital markets to constrain policy makers in each country to follow sound economic policies that kept their economies competitive with those of their trading partners. If competitive in the product and capital markets, a country's exchange rate would stabilize in the foreign exchange market. Coordination, in short, would occur spontaneously by individual decision makers responding to the price signals emitted from the common marketplace.

Policy makers in both Germany and France, however, determined that the solution to the periodic instability of an adjustable-peg system would be better solved by affirming that existing exchange rates would be locked at some point on the way to a common currency. With only one currency among them, the problems of coordination will be solved once and for all by centralized authority. The "only" remaining question is how that central authority will make and enforce its decisions. The agreement reached at the Brussels meeting of the European Council on October 29, 1993, between Mitterrand and Kohl was to proceed on course with the Delors Plan and begin stage two as planned in January 1994. The Treaty on European Union, better known as the Maastricht Treaty, came into effect in November 1993. The decision to proceed with the next stage of monetary union required by the treaty was taken even as the Exchange Rate Mechanism, which had been characterized by Delors as the "glide path" to a common currency, had crashed.

Instead of a glide path for a common system of currency management that would take off into a common currency centrally managed, the more realistic analogy now was of a convoy of separate ships headed for a common destination but temporarily scattered by stormy seas. Meanwhile, serious construction of the destination site should be undertaken. So the countries remaining in the EMS agreed to maintain their previous central par rates but to allow market rates to diverge up to 15 percent in either direction from them. No longer would central banks have to stand in one place when attacked by foreign exchange speculators betting on either a revaluation or a devaluation. They could easily slip to the other side and let another set of speculators on the opposite side of the market come to their defense. Meanwhile, the creation of the framework for a single currency could go forward.

Figure 3 traces the annual exchange rate indexes of the EU15 countries over the period from 1985 to 1997, whether they were in or out of the EU and whether they were in or out of the EMS. Greece has never joined the ERM, and once Italy and the United Kingdom dropped out neither had rejoined until Italy reentered on November 25, 1996. Spain and Portugal have joined the EMS but have devalued repeatedly, preferring always to be part of the monetary integration of Europe rather than deal with volatile exchange rates. Their partners in the EMS have preferred to let them devalue rather than make interventions in the foreign exchange markets on their behalf, much less to coordinate their own monetary policies with those of the Iberian countries. Their rates within the EMS track rather closely those of Sweden and the United Kingdom, both of which have stayed out of the EMS since 1992. Finland by the end of 1995 was recovering from the shocks to its economy of the early 1990s and formally joined the Exchange Rate Mechanism of the EMS in November 1996, as did Italy on November 25, 1996. Ireland is in the unusual situation of trying to link with the deutsche mark but remains subject to much the same market forces that move the exchange rate of the British pound sterling up or down. As the pound was weak relative to the ECU in 1993 through 1995, so was the Irish punt. Although it was only devalued once in February 1993, the pound was near or at the bottom of the EMS currencies relative to its new central par rate throughout 1994 and 1995. In 1996, however, the pound sterling rose from the middle of the year and with it the Irish punt. The French franc managed to stay on course for maintaining its link with the deutsche mark since the mishaps of 1992–93, although by the end of 1996 the franc was the weakest of the ERM currencies. The Danish situation was dominated by the course of the deutsche mark, but like Ireland's punt, the Danish krone was pulled down by the importance of its remaining links with Great Britain and with the other Scandinavian economies until those currencies began to rise in 1996. Next on the graph is the Belgium-Luxembourg franc, which seems caught between tracing the course of the French franc or the German mark. In the 1990s, the choice has been clear—to follow the mark, much to the satisfaction of the Flemish part of Belgium. What appears as a very thick and ornately marked line at the top of figure 3 is actually the combination of the German mark, the Austrian schilling, and the Dutch guilder. The latter two currencies have consistently been pegged over this period with the deutsche mark.

Figure 3 is a useful diagnostic device because it shows the recent vicissitudes of the EMU adventure very clearly and also because it reveals starkly the fault lines that exist in the monetary structure of the EU. There is clearly a deutsche mark bloc in northern Europe, with the French and the Danes trying to maintain their currencies as part of that bloc and Finland trying to rejoin it. There is a second group of ins and outs who have let their currencies depreciate through 1995, either as deliberate policy (Britain, Italy, and Sweden) or as the unintended consequence of monetary policy dominated by other goals (Ireland, Spain, and Portugal). Greece is entirely another story, as seen in figures 2 and 3. How can a stable monetary structure be built on such a foundation?

THE FUTURE

The major advantage of the common currency is the reduction in transactions costs for individuals and firms doing business across the national boundaries within Europe. But to provide these cost savings to individuals and businesses, banks must make costly investments and find alternative ways of recouping lost revenues from commissions on foreign exchange transactions. A survey of European banks by *Euromoney* magazine estimated that the costs of converting to euros between 1999 and 2002 would be ECU 8 to 10 billion or an additional 1 to 2 percent of their operating costs each year for three or four years. For at least three years, banks' information technology must maintain a dual-payment system, denominated in two currencies, its national currency and the euro. From the second half of 2002 on, for an uncertain period, they must cope with euro and national currency banknotes and coins circulating together. Further, the loss of commissions on foreign exchange will be a permanent reduction in their revenue base of 5 to 10 percent.[9] The correspondent banking business across European borders will now be substantially reduced, as any one bank's business can now be consolidated into the largest, most efficient correspondent bank. The article concludes, "In terms of simple return on investment, no sensible banker would actually suggest such a project."[10] This means that the large banks in Germany and the state-owned banks in France will be arguing that they should be compensated with an alternative source of revenue.[11]

Exchange rate risks are typically hedged effectively for exporters and importers by offsetting contracts with their counterparties, by buying forward contracts in the desired currency, or by selling the current receivable in its currency to a third party. All of these require additional market contacts and do have some fixed expenses. The larger the scale of the transactions, typically, the smaller the percentage of the fees will be, so for the bulk of foreign trade these commission costs are not a serious impediment. Moreover, the larger and more competitive the market is for forward-exchange contracts, the lower the fees will be. It is precisely in the trade-off between going to a market-based solution or going to a financial specialist, such as a Continental-style universal bank, that the British and German businesses differ in their assessment. For the French and Germans, the markets are much less competitive than for the British, and so they are more concerned to get special deals from their customary banking houses, who do all their financial business for them, including funding long-term investment projects.

Governments with weak tax bases, such as Greece, Portugal, and Spain, not to mention the EU government-in-waiting, necessarily have weak markets for their debt issues as well. How can an investor be confident that a government with uncertain tax receipts and unpredictable demands on its expenditures will pay interest faithfully and redeem the principal when called on? These governments must rely on increases in the money supply they control to cover their expenditures. A counter to the EMU proposal, then, would be to broaden the potential market for the debt issues of governments with weaker tax structures. Indeed, participation in the EMS was a boon for Italian and Irish debt issues, as they continued to pay higher interest rates on their bonds than either the Germans or the French, but had a commitment from the other countries to maintain their exchange rates from depreciating very much. Alternatives, of course, would be to issue debt in the foreign currency of choice for the potential investors. It is not accidental that the first major Euro-bond (debt denominated in dollars by a foreign borrower) issue in the 1960s was to finance construction of the Italian autostrada. But this alternative denies the government in question the possible benefits of seigniorage. Excessive issue of its currency would increase the burden of servicing the debt denominated in foreign currency. Moreover, the government then has to compete with other issuers of bonds to keep its creditworthiness competitive. No European government has enjoyed doing this.

The existence of different levels and kinds of government debt already issued by the member states, however, raises further problems. Each government will still be required to service its own debt from its own tax base, even though every government's debt is denominated in the same currency—the euro. There is no intrinsic problem with this: every state in the United States issues its own debt denominated in the common currency of the U.S. dollar. But nearly every state has a balanced budget requirement, so each new issue of debt has to be backed by a specified source of revenue dedicated to servicing it. This is necessary because no state now has the right to redeem its debt with money that it has created. The problem, however, arose at the outset when the currency union of the United States was formed by adoption of the Constitution in 1789. Alexander Hamilton, the first U.S. secretary of the treasury, decided to assume the debts that the separate states had issued during the preceding years, including the expensive years of the War of Independence. Combining all their bond issues into one large issue that was backed by the customs revenues and land sales of the new federal government enabled Hamilton to create a broader market for U.S. debt than was possible otherwise. Nothing is foreseen at present for a similar refunding operation in Europe, but the same pressures of differential debt burdens and abilities to service them that prompted Hamilton to undertake his assumption of state debts will surely emerge in the early stages of the European Monetary Union. (See fig. 4)

Figure 4. Long-Term Interest Rates "Euroland," 1980–1998

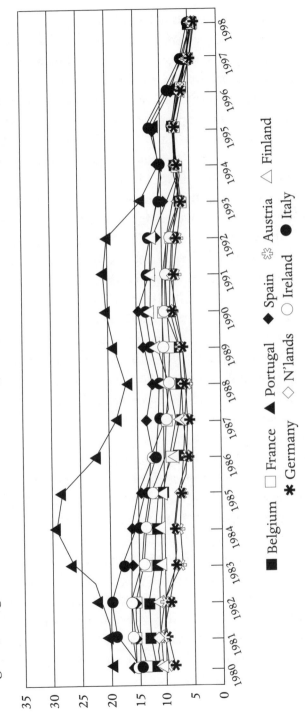

■ Belgium □ France ▲ Portugal ◆ Spain ✳ Austria ● Italy
✳ Germany ◇ N'lands ○ Ireland △ Finland

1985=100

The commission's counterargument to this scenario is that the sheer volume of euros will create a demand for them in other countries to hold as a reserve currency. Indeed, if demand for a country's currency by others depends on the size of its trade with the rest of the world, it would appear at first sight that the euro will be in greater demand than the U.S. dollar, given the greater importance of the European countries as a group in world trade. If true, then the euro will become the world's favorite currency to hold for reserves by central banks and international businesses. However, it is not true that demand for a reserve currency is determined this way. First, the EU trades mostly with itself, which is why it dominates world trade when intra-EU trade is counted as foreign trade. If we take just the trade of the EU with the non-EU world, it turns out that in the 1990s the United States alone has more trade with the rest of the world than does the EU. Another way to see the point is to realize that the deutsche mark reserves currently held by central banks and businesses in the rest of the EU will no longer be necessary for them, because their own currency, the euro, will be the same as the German currency needed for payments there. Euros will not be foreign reserves for any European bank or firm that is within the EMU, by definition. Only the rest of the world will still need a European currency for financing trade, and it will need dollars more than euros.

This point has been readily recognized. What is less obvious is that the value of the dollar as a reserve currency for central banks and especially for banks and firms around the world engaged at all in foreign transactions rests not so much on the volume of trade flows denominated in dollars as in the volume of capital flows denominated in dollars. It is the liquidity of the U.S. capital market, seen first in the size and ease of transfer among secondary holders of its national debt, and then made truly unmatchable by its broad and deep markets for private equity and bonds, that makes the U.S. dollar, or rather U.S. dollar–denominated financial instruments, so attractive to the rest of the world, including Europe. A study by the Bank for International Settlements concludes that the superior liquidity of U.S. dollar financial instruments explains "why virtually all mean-variance analyses of optimal reserve portfolios find the actual proportion of U.S. dollar holdings to be well above that suggested by efficiency considerations alone."[12] The same study concludes that increased volatility in exchange rates experienced by currency peggers, such as members of the ERM, tended to boost the U.S. dollar share of reserves. If reserves are held to offset volatile changes in a country's, or firm's, balance of payments, then it surely will see the advantage of holding those reserves in the most liquid financial asset available. Again, we come to the conclusion that it is not the common currency that is so important for the success of the Single Market but the additional market for credit.

With such an uncertain future for the euro and a present economic situation characterized by continued high unemployment and slow growth, the question for an economist is what economic motivation could be driving European governments toward adoption of the common currency? I believe a good part of the answer can be seen in Figure 3, which shows the dramatic fall in the rates of interest paid by European governments on the stock of their outstanding debt and their convergence to historic lows. With the average debt-to-GDP ratio now in Euroland of 80 percent, and average interest rates falling to 3.5 percent, the reduction in interest payments alone has enabled governments to reduce their deficits by nearly 1 percentage point of GDP on average.[13] The deficit reduction from the effect of falling interest rates is obviously highest for those countries with the highest ratios of debt to GDP and with the highest interest rates at the beginning (Italy, Portugal, and Spain), but it has been significant for all. I suggest that the reduced interest payments have enabled governments in Euroland to sustain payment of continued unemployment benefits, thereby reducing the political pressure to reform wage policies or remove structural rigidities in their labor markets.

This is unfortunate, because the long-run pressures on all European governments are mounting in terms of future pension liabilities. High unemployment as now concentrated among older and younger workers is continuing to exacerbate the problem of future funding of retirement benefits for an aging population. High unemployment among older workers encourages early retirement, speeding up pressures on pension funds. And high unemployment among younger workers reduces their future employability and productivity, reducing the growth of the tax base. In short, the continued high unemployment in Euroland that has characterized the adoption of the common currency under the tutelage of the Bundesbank is generating greater fiscal pressures for their governments in the future, even as the transition has reduced fiscal pressures in the present.

Ultimately, each country will have to turn to greater use of capital markets, both to encourage the funding of new enterprises that can create new employment and to provide investment opportunities for pension funds. Hopeful signs of this necessary transformation can already be seen in Germany. The financial sector there is trying to surmount the daunting costs of reunification by developing venture capital mechanisms and equity markets for small and medium-size enterprises. The "relationship banking" that has been the hallmark of German universal banks since the nineteenth century has proven incapable of mobilizing adequate finance for the reconstruction of the East German economy. If there is no "relationship" between West German banks and East German entrepreneurs, there can be no lending! At the same time, German banks are beginning to reform their practices to approach more the arm's length lending and investment practices of their American and British counterparts. Perhaps the German financial sector, if it is reformed rapidly enough, can provide more useful leadership for the rest of Euroland in the coming years than the Bundesbank is providing at present. In short, the future of the euro depends on the growth of capital markets in Euroland.

NOTES

1. This section is drawn from Larry Neal and Daniel Barbezat, *The Economics of the European Union and the Economies of Europe* (New York: Oxford University Press, 1998), chap. 7.

2. Charles Kindleberger, *A Financial History of Western Europe,* 2d ed. (New York: Oxford University Press, 1993), 443–44.

3. The Group of Ten was formed in the early 1960s as a caucus of the leading members of the IMF to discuss and initiate changes in IMF legislation. It consisted of the G7—United States, Germany, Japan, Britain, France, Italy, Canada—plus the

Netherlands, Belgium, and Sweden. Although Switzerland is not a member of the IMF, a representative of that country is often included in the meetings.

4. The history of the snake is given in *European Economy*, no. 12 (July 1982).

5. Horst Ungerer, *The European Monetary System: The Experience, 1979–1982* (Washington, D.C.: International Monetary Fund, 1983), 1.

6. "The ERM in 1992," study no. 5 in *European Economy*, no. 54, (December 1993), 145.

7. In contrast to the Irish government's technique of distributing brief pamphlets that highlighted the advantages Ireland would enjoy in a single market, the Danish government, at great expense, made widely available complete copies of the full treaty. Even Jacques Delors admitted later that the wording required in EC documents to gain approval of the entire European Council made many parts of them unintelligible.

8. This was done by devaluing the lira 3.5 percent against the ECU and revaluing all the other currencies 3.5 percent against the ECU.

9. *Euromoney*, September 1996, 94–95.

10. Ibid., 99.

11. One such source would be preferred access to TARGET, the interbank payments clearing system among banks on the European continent. Already in 1996, the French and German banks had proposed this, with the implicit support of both governments. Needless to say, the British banks objected mightily and in response have hastened implementation of their more advanced computer technology to facilitate payment clearings with allied banks elsewhere in Europe.

12. Scott Roger, "The Management of Foreign Exchange Reserves," Basel: Bank for International Settlements, Economic Papers no. 38 (July 1993), 68.

13. Ungerer, *European Monetary System*, 126, 132.

◈ BIBLIOGRAPHY

de Grauwe, Paul. "The Economics of Monetary Integration." *Euromoney*, September 1996. *European Economy*, no. 54 (December 1993).

International Monetary Fund, *World Economic Outlook, October 1998*. Washington, D.C.: IMF, 1998.

Kindleberger, Charles. *A Financial History of Western Europe*. 2d ed. New York: Oxford University Press, 1993.

Neal, Larry, and Daniel Barbezat. *The Economics of the European Union and the Economies of Europe*. New York: Oxford University Press, 1998.

Roger, Scott, "The Management of Foreign Exchange Reserves," Basel: Bank for International Settlements, Economic Papers no. 38, July 1993.

Ungerer, Horst, *The European Monetary System: The Experience, 1979–82*, Washington, D.C.: International Monetary Fund, 1983.

The Euro and the Dollar— Partners or Rivals?

RODNEY THOM

R ecent events in Asia and elsewhere suggest that the international monetary system may be in need of reform, or at least radical repair. Politicians, economists, and policy makers have, of course, been quick to offer opinions on what is wrong and what needs to be done to put it right. Although this paper is not directly concerned with the causes of and cures for financial crises I will nonetheless suggest two probable features of any new international financial architecture: the free movement of capital and, to the extent that national currencies survive, the predominance of flexible rather than fixed exchange rates. As the growth of free trade, the integration of international financial markets, or, more generally, the process of globalization, appear to conflict with restrictions on international capital movements, individual countries face a choice between what Paul Krugman has called confidence and adjustment. Confidence means stabilizing the external value of the currency and adjustment means using monetary and fiscal policies to stabilize the domestic economy. However, given the free movement of capital across exchange frontiers, these aims are incompatible because a rigid peg to a major currency such as the dollar necessarily requires a sacrifice of monetary independence lest deviations from the policies of the anchor country lead to speculative attacks and destabilizing devaluations. For example, contrast the experiences of countries such as Ireland and Italy with that of Holland in the European Monetary System (EMS) from its inception in 1979 to the currency crisis of late 1992. While the Dutch monetary policy effectively cloned the Bundesbank, Irish and Italian policies diverged from those in Germany. Hence the Irish punt and the lira lost 40 percent of their value against the deutsche mark (DM), while the guilder-DM rate remained stable.

In practice the choice facing individual countries is simple. They either maintain independent policies and let the exchange rate absorb the external effects (flexible exchange rates) or abandon adjustment and opt for a permanent exchange rate arrangement such as a currency board or monetary union. Europe has chosen the second. Of the fifteen member states of the European Union (EU), eleven have now eliminated their national currencies and adopted the euro as their common currency, and the popular consensus is that the remaining four (Sweden, Denmark, Greece, and the United Kingdom) may join within five years. Further, many of the emerging economies in central and Eastern Europe, which experienced monetary disintegration following the collapse of the Soviet empire, are now aspirant members of both the EU and the euro zone.

On the other side of the Atlantic the picture is less clear. There is, to my knowledge anyway, no serious proposal that the North American Free Trade Agreement (NAFTA) should emulate Europe and establish a common currency to parallel the ongoing process of trade liberalization and market integration. On the other hand, Argentina has now locked the peso to the dollar and its central bank has recently proposed that the former should be eliminated and replaced by the latter.[1] Although it is far from certain that this will lead to a domino effect with countries such as Brazil and Mexico following Argentina's example, it is nonetheless valid to argue that some form of dollarization is a viable proposition. The alternative, national currencies and flexible exchange rates, merely gives countries like Brazil the freedom to choose their own inflation rates and pay a high-risk premium on their debt.

It should be stressed that I am neither advocating nor predicting an American monetary union based on the dollar. However, it seems reasonable to argue that we are now living in a world which is increasingly dominated by three major currencies—the dollar, the euro, and, to a lesser extent, the yen.[2] The key difference between this scenario and the one which prevailed prior to January 1, 1999 is the introduction of the euro. The euro has important consequences for at least three groups—the citizens of Euroland, the candidate countries of central and Eastern Europe, and the United States.[3] It is clear why the euro is important for the first two, but why is it important to the world's largest economy? I suggest two reasons. First, the euro eventually will rival the dollar as the world's major currency. Second, the euro gives European policy makers both global influence and responsibilities which, prior to its introduction, were the preserve of the United States.

It is on these issues that I wish to address the question of whether the dollar and the euro should be partners or rivals. On the first, the euro and the dollar must be considered as rivals for the seigniorage gains associated with an international currency. The second issue is different and has been given greater urgency by recent financial crises. If we are prepared to accept that the international financial system is in need of reform, then both the United States and Europe must be seen as key players in determining its future shape. However, the design and success of any new financial architecture may depend on the extent of cooperation between America and a larger more integrated Europe.

▨ WHAT IS AN INTERNATIONAL CURRENCY?

The dollar's role as an international currency is an undoubted source of economic, and political, advantage to the United States. Most important, the United States gains from seigniorage, or the process by which foreign residents are prepared to hold dollar liabilities at relatively low, or even zero, interest rates. Seigniorage arises in two forms. First, foreign holding of non-interest-bearing dollar currency is equivalent to an interest-free loan. Most estimates suggest that 50 to 60 percent of the total United States money stock is held externally, yielding an annual seigniorage gain equal to 0.1 percent of gross domestic product.[4] Second, the dominance of the dollar on international capital markets means that the United States can finance external deficits by borrowing in its own currency with the benefit of a liquidity discount, estimated by Richard Portes and Hélène Rey to be worth twenty-five to fifty basis points on foreign holdings of U.S. government debt, which is equivalent to $5 to 10 billion annually and is approximately equal to the gains from currency seigniorage.[5]

Given that an international currency confers benefits on the issuing country, then Euroland will gain at the United States' expense if the euro can make significant inroads into the dollar's position. Before we consider this possibility it may be useful to start by defining what we mean by an international currency. A currency has three functions. First, it is a unit of account, or the measure used to record prices and debts. Second, it is a means of payment, or the commodity used to facilitate transactions between buyers and sellers. Third, it is a store of value, or a means of holding wealth. Hence Americans use the dollar to buy and sell goods and services whose prices are expressed in dollars and they also use dollar assets—such as bank deposits, bonds, and stocks—to accumulate wealth. An international currency is one which performs these functions on a global basis. For example, prices of internationally traded commodities such as oil are normally expressed in dollars, while financial institutions in Europe and Asia hold portfolios of dollar-denominated assets such as U.S. government Treasury Bills. How does the euro rank with the dollar under these headings?

Unit of Account: The dollar is a unique currency, for there is a significant difference between its use internationally and the United States' weight in world trade. For example, the share of world exports denominated in dollars is about four times greater than the United States' share of world exports (the coefficient of internationalization). The equivalent ratio for the euro is just over one.

Means of Payment: The use of a currency as a means of payment is reflected by the composition of transactions on international currency markets. About 80 percent of foreign exchange turnover has the dollar on one side of the transaction as opposed to 60 percent for the euro currencies and 10 percent for sterling. While these figures are relatively close we should note that the monetary union will automatically reduce the euro's share relative to its constituent currencies. For example, as DM–French franc transactions are now euro-euro transactions the euro must account for a smaller percentage of daily foreign exchange turnover than the aggregate of its constituent currencies.

Store of Value: The international importance of a currency as a store of value can be gauged by the extent to which it is used to denominate internationally traded financial assets and liabilities. Recent estimates (Organization for Economic Cooperation and Development, 1977) indicate that 33 percent of international bond holdings are denominated in dollars as compared to (prior January 1999) 22 percent in deutsche marks and in French francs. For new bond issues, the figures are roughly comparable, and for total funds raised internationally, bonds plus bank loans, the dollar's share exceeds 50 percent. In addition, approximately 56 percent of official European Central Bank (ECB) reserve holdings are held in dollars as compared to 17 percent (excluding sterling) in euro currencies.[6]

Hence, on all three criteria the dollar remains the dominant currency. To what extent can the euro's arrival erode the dollar's position?

WILL THE EURO RIVAL THE DOLLAR?

The euro's potential to rival the dollar as a leading international currency will depend on three related factors—the liquidity of the euro market, the European Central Bank's (ECB) monetary policy, and the growth of the European economy relative to the United States. To a large extent the euro's attractiveness as an international currency depends on the size and depth, or liquidity, of Euroland's financial markets. Liquidity measures the ease and cost with which traders can switch from one currency to another. Generally, the greater the volume of trading in a currency the greater the liquidity and thus, the lower the cost of transacting in that currency. Also, when the use of a currency increases, the opportunities to exploit economies of scale will further reduce transactions costs and create "network externalities" if the currency is used as a vehicle for transactions between other currencies.

For example, consider a transaction which involves selling South African rand and purchasing Swedish kronor. Because the dollar market is liquid and transactions costs are low, the dealer who undertakes the trade may find it cheaper to sell rand for dollars and then purchase kronor rather than exchange the currencies directly. In this sense the dollar's widespread use as a vehicle currency results from the size of the United States' financial market and the volume of trading in dollar-denominated assets. Based on data from the OECD and the Bank for International Settlements, the United States market, as measured by the sum of domestic debt outstanding and stock market capitalization, is almost twice as large as Euroland. Nonetheless, while the dollar is currently in the leading position, this gap could be narrowed by the integration of European financial markets, British (or more precisely, London's) participation in the euro, and a shift from bank-based finance to securitized finance.

An integrated euro market must be larger and more liquid that the sum of its constituent components. By eliminating national currencies, market integration also eliminates exchange rate risk, resulting in narrow interest rate spreads and lower transactions costs. Also, the introduction of a single monetary policy and a unified interbank market will intensify competition leading to efficiency gains and lower costs for euro transactions. Further, as government debt is now denominated in euros rather than national currencies, monetary union will create a market in government securities which will be larger that of the United States. Hence, as the integrated market will be more liquid than markets in the legacy currencies (DM, FF, etc.), lower transactions costs will increase the attractiveness of euro-denominated assets. Indeed, after only one month there is evidence that the euro has been successful in attracting the interest of investors, with 50 percent of the January 1999 international bond issues denominated in euros as compared to 40 percent in dollars.

Although not generally recognized, or admitted, by the citizens and governments of Euroland, British participation can be a key factor in establishing an international role for the euro. Not only is the London stock exchange the third largest in the world, with a capitalization value greater than Euroland's, but approximately 30 percent of daily foreign exchange transactions are conducted in London, as opposed to 15 percent in the United States and 16 percent in Euroland. In short, the euro may need London as much as London needs the euro.

Further, the position of London and New York as dominant financial centers is in part due to the fact that Anglo-American corporate finance tends to be security based rather than bank based. That is, whereas funds are raised on the New York and London markets by the issue of marketable securities (bonds and equity), most corporate borrowing in Continental countries is obtained from bank lending, which goes some way to explaining the greater volume of transactions and liquidity in British and American markets. For example, bank loans account for more that 50 percent of all financial instruments in Europe as compared to just over 20 percent in the United States. As an integrated market with enhanced liquidity and lower transaction costs will encourage a move towards security-based finance, it can result in both an increase in the volume and, by stimulating trading in secondary markets, the depth of trading in euro assets.

At a more general level, the international use of the euro will depend on the success of the ECB in maintaining low and stable inflation and the growth of Euroland's economy relative to the United States. Neither of these are guaranteed. Article 2 of the statute states that the ECB's primary responsibility is to "maintain price stability," while Article 107 of the Maastricht Treaty prohibits national governments and EU bodies from influencing ECB policy. In simple terms the logic of these arrangements is that an independent central bank free from political influence will be more successful in securing price stability. Can we be confident that the ECB will achieve its primary goal of low and stable inflation?[7] The answer is probably yes, but there are several reasons for concern.

First, the European political map has changed in the last two years. The new currency was conceived in a Europe dominated by right-of-center governments but it has been born into a Europe which has moved toward the left, and the new breed of politicians may be less respectful of central bank independence than their predecessors. For example, if we take the not unreasonable view that disputes over the first ECB president masked a deeper argument over political influence on ECB policy or, even worse, reflected internal political pressures within one large member state, then it is not too difficult to believe that the new political composition of Europe's governments may pose some threat to ECB independence.

Second, we can be reasonably confident that Euroland is not an optimum currency area. Economic structures differ and business cycles between the "core" (Germany, France, Austria, Netherlands, and the Benelux economies) and the "periphery" (Ireland, Finland, etc.) are not highly correlated. For example, Germany and France are currently experiencing low growth and high unemployment whereas Ireland has the highest growth rate in the OECD and falling unemployment. Hence a one-size-fits-all monetary policy is not necessarily appropriate. Whereas Germany and France might favor low interest rates and a competitive value for the euro, Irish conditions require higher interest rates and a strong currency. Asymmetries can also arise in the transmission of monetary policy to the real economy. That is, the effects of interest rate changes on economic activity may differ within Euroland. A recent survey by Rudiger Dornbusch, Carlo Favero, and Francesco Giavazzi suggests that the effect of a change in interest rates on inflation is approximately twice as large in Belgium and the Netherlands as in Italy and France.[8] The problem is that asymmetries of this type may lead to more volatile inflation if conflicts within the ECB governing council result in a policy which caters to coalitions of national interest rather the interest of the European economy.[9]

Management of exchange rates, and the dollar-euro rate in particular, may create an additional source of conflict and threat to price stability. Despite their international importance, external trade counts for relatively small proportions of GDP in both the United States and Euroland. Hence, as in the United States, the orientation of monetary policy in Euroland will be geared to domestic objectives with policy toward the dollar-euro exchange rate characterized by an attitude of benign neglect. That is, in normal circumstances both central banks will set interest rates to achieve domestic targets with the exchange rate left to absorb the external effects. For example, if the ECB decides that lower interest rates are consistent with its inflation objective then, other things equal, it must accept a depreciation of the euro against the dollar. This, however, raises two important questions—who has responsibility for exchange rate policy in Euroland and what do we mean by normal circumstances?

The Maastricht Treaty assigns responsibility for exchange rate policy to the European Council, which consists of the fifteen heads of government. Although the council is required to consult with the ECB, there is no requirement that they should agree and "should the views of the Council and the ECB diverge, those of the former would prevail."[10] This is unlikely to matter in normal circumstances but what about abnormal circumstances? What, for example, might happen in the event of a downturn in the American economy and a significant dollar depreciation against the euro? As extra-EU imports are a relatively small proportion of Euroland's GDP, it is unlikely that the deflationary effect of an appreciating euro would be sufficient to accommodate an interest rate cut by the ECB. However, the council may see supporting the dollar as politically expedient, leading to a possible conflict with the ECB and an undermining of the latter's credibility. Further, movements in the external value of the euro are unlikely to produce uniform effects across Euroland. For the larger economies these effects are likely to be relatively minor, but they will be much more significant in smaller countries such as Belgium, Ireland, and Finland, where exports outside Euroland account for nontrivial proportions of GDP. Hence, persistent movements in the euro's external value, and the dollar-euro rate in particular, may affect trade flows between Euroland and its trading partners and, as these effects are unlikely to be symmetric, they have the potential for creating tensions both within the council and between the council and the ECB.

While these concerns are real they can be exaggerated. As integration proceeds via the common currency and the Single Market, Europe's economies may become more similar and asymmetries less prevalent.[11] Also, we should not ignore the fact that a significant amount of political capital has been invested in the euro's success and it is unlikely that governments or the ECB will, in the short run at least, permit national interests to override the bank's mandate for price stability. However, there is an additional, and perhaps more fundamental, cause for concern. For the euro to rival the dollar as an international currency it is necessary that economic growth in Euroland at least match that in the United States. We should note that this is not the first time that the dominant currency has been challenged. The dollar replaced sterling as an international currency because sustained growth created an American economy much larger than any of its rivals. However, there is no reason to believe that economic growth in Europe can exceed that in the United States. Indeed, the poor growth performance of the 1990s suggests the opposite. Paul de Grauwe puts the point as follows: "[Europe's] financial markets may be relatively large in 1999, but they will become progressively smaller in relative terms afterwards. Put differently, it is difficult to see how Europe can provide for a leading international currency when its relative size in the world continues to shrink."[12]

Given these caveats it seems reasonable to proceed on the assumption that the euro will be an important international currency. Regardless of whether the euro can replace the dollar, the economic size of Euroland suggests that it should, like the United States, be regarded as, in President Clinton's terminology, an indispensable economy.[13] That is, the euro has given Euroland both global influence and responsibility.

GLOBAL INFLUENCE AND RESPONSIBILITY

The United States accounts for approximately 20 percent of world GDP and 15 percent of world exports. It also has the largest financial markets and its currency plays a pivotal role in financing international trade. As a consequence, decisions taken by American policy makers, and by the Federal Reserve Board (Fed) in particular, have global implications. Hence, when the Fed cuts dollar interest rates we can expect similar adjustments to interest rates in other currencies. Europe has now emulated the United States. Euroland's share of world GDP and exports is approximately equal to that of the United States and the integration of Europe's financial markets has created a currency which, if not dominant, must be regarded as a world player. In short, policy decisions made in Europe will also have global implications. However, global influence also brings global responsibility. The question is, how will Europe manage that responsibility? In particular, will the ECB follow policies which are firmly locked to domestic objectives or will it, when required, synchronize with the Fed and attempt to maintain order in the world's financial system?

The potential dilemma this raises can be outlined as follows. On a strict interpretation of its mandate, the ECB must set interest rates to achieve price stability in Euroland. Now, consider a situation in which the Fed cuts dollar interest rates in response to an external crisis. Other things equal, we would expect capital flows from the dollar to the euro, which would increase liquidity in the European banking system and exert downward pressure on euro interest rates. If the ECB permits euro interest rates to move with dollar rates, then it is assisting the Fed in attempting to restore order and confidence. However, if the ECB considers that lower interests will threaten price stability, it may adhere to a high-rate policy by sterilizing inflows leading to a possible misalignment of the dollar-euro exchange rate and further problems for the international monetary system.

These issues can be made more precise by considering a repeat of the recent Asian crisis. As in October 1998, we could expect the Fed to cut interest rates and, through the International Monetary Fund (IMF), ensure an adequate supply of liquidity to the international financial system. Actions such as these can, of course, be interpreted as being domestically motivated. Recession in key Asian economies, accompanied by significant depreciations of their currencies, reduces the demand for American exports and intensifies import competition on the domestic market. Nonetheless, recession in the United States is bad news for everyone and appropriate action by the Fed can only help to stabilize both the American and world economies. Would the ECB cooperate with the Fed by cutting euro interest rates, or would it pursue an independent policy anchored to the domestic goal of price stability? Consider an alternative scenario in which the crisis starts not in Asia, but in the United States. To some Europeans, and I suspect some Americans, this is far from improbable. A consumer boom underpinned by credit, a low personal savings rate, an overvalued stock market, a current-account deficit, and increasing net foreign liabilities all suggest that the current growth performance of the American economy may be unsustainable. If the stock market bubble were to burst, with the dollar depreciating and the economy pushed toward recession, would the ECB follow the Fed in assisting recovery by cutting interest rates or would it retreat to fortress Europe by rigidly adhering to its primary mandate of price stability? More generally, in the face of a global shock will the ECB and the Fed act as partners in finding a solution, or will they follow different agendas and pursue different objectives?

Clearly, some form of synchronization between the two central banks is important to global stability. Large interest rate differentials and a misalignment of the dollar-euro exchange rate cannot be good for world trade or the international financial system. Also, a serious appreciation of the euro could lead to a slowdown in the European economy and cause difficulties for the economies of central and Eastern Europe, who have close trading links with the EU and are increasingly tying their currencies to the euro. The reverse is also true in that an appreciation of the dollar would have detrimental effects on the American economy and the economies of countries linked to the dollar. Hence, in the face of a crisis, partnership or policy synchronization is the preferable alternative. By synchronization I do not mean explicit cooperation or agreement on interest rates. Rather, it implies that the Fed and the ECB should follow similar policies in the face of a global shock.

At first sight the prospects for synchronized responses are not good. Ironically, monetary union may actually weaken European interest in the dollar exchange rate. Prior to the euro, the relationship between the dollar and the European currencies was heavily influenced by what became known as dollar–deutsche mark polarization. That is, when the dollar weakened against the DM, some European countries had a preference to depreciate their currencies against the latter in order to avoid appreciation against the dollar. In the old narrow-band European Monetary System (EMS) this could, and did, lead to speculative attacks against the weaker currencies, resulting in exchange rate realignments and instability within the EMS. However, as the euro eliminates national currencies it also eliminates dollar–deutsche mark polarization. As there is no longer a prospect of a weak dollar leading to an overvalued lira or punt, then there can be no devaluation of these currencies against the DM and no speculative pressures on European currencies. In this sense, the movements in the dollar are now less important to Europe.

Further, remarks by the ECB president also suggest that the short-term prospects for policy synchronization are not encouraging: "Generally speaking, the commitment of the ECB to successfully fulfilling the mandate of the Maastricht Treaty, that is, to maintain price stability in the euro area, will also shape the ECB's international role. This is, without doubt, the best contribution the ECB can make to a stable international monetary system."[14] Statements such as this smack of fortress Europe and are in stark contrast to the Fed's response to the Asian crisis, when it not only accepted its global responsibility but was also seen to act decisively. Both the European Union and the United States have experienced price stability for the best part of a decade yet the international monetary system still experiences bouts of severe turmoil. However, the ECB president's views must be put in perspective. From the outset the ECB's overriding concern must be to establish credibility with financial markets and, given its mandate, this can be most readily achieved by adhering to the price stability target. Indeed, to do otherwise could seriously damage the credibility of the entire euro project. Further, whereas the Fed has over many years acquired a deep understanding of how the American economy works, the ECB is still at the bottom of its learning curve. Hence we should not be surprised if its public stance is totally orientated toward the domestic objective of price stability.

There are, however, several reasons to be optimistic about the future stance of the ECB. Strict adherence to rigid rules is not the only, or the best, way to achieve credibility. The Fed is the clearest example of this. Rather than following a single policy goal the Fed has, over the last decade anyway, taken a more pragmatic approach by striking a balance between price stability and growth. For example, when unemployment increased in the late 1980s the Fed prevented a prolonged recession by cutting interest rates. However when inflation threatened in 1993 and 1995 the Fed responded by increasing interest rates.[15] As a result the Fed has acquired credibility by responding to the needs of the real economy in an appropriate manner.[16]

Once the ECB establishes its anti-inflationary credentials, it may be possible to reassess its role in the world economy. It should be stressed that I am in no way suggesting that the price stability mandate should be downgraded. Nor am I suggesting that the global implications of monetary policy should be given significant weight in what may be called normal circumstances. Rather, the ECB can learn from the Fed's example in that it is possible to secure a credible anti-inflationary reputation and, when appropriate, respond to the needs of the domestic and international economies. Flexibility of this sort requires that the ECB is prepared to relax monetary policy when appropriate, but remains committed to tightening policy whenever inflation threatens. However, this type of reputation is built on repeated and reliable behavior over a period of years and cannot be achieved instantaneously.

The evolution of monetary policy will also be influenced by the Stability and Growth Pact, which attempts to restrain deficit spending by national governments.[17] There are several rationalizations for the pact, but the one I favor is that its main purpose is to enhance ECB credibility. Unlike central banks in nation-states, the ECB faces eleven governments and eleven independent fiscal authorities—a situation which makes the coordination of monetary and fiscal policies difficult if not impossible. Hence, by imposing coordination and discipline the pact reduces uncertainty and permits the ECB to choose its monetary policy in the knowledge that fiscal policy is constrained. Further, an effective constraint on fiscal policy also permits a more flexible and pragmatic monetary policy. However, as with reputation building, this will take time to evolve. In particular, the European Commission and the council must demonstrate that the pact is credible by enforcing sanctions on errant governments.

CONCLUSIONS

This paper has considered two issues—the extent to which the euro can replace the dollar as the world's major currency and the global influence and responsibility of the ECB. On the first issue, the dollar is still in the pole position and likely to remain there for some time. On the other hand, if Euroland develops as a low-inflation, low-interest-rate and high-growth economy, then the euro's role as an international currency will be greatly enhanced. This, however, is far from certain. On the second issue, the initial signs are that the ECB will assign a low weight to global objectives. However, we are speculating about a currency and a central bank which are less that two months old, and it would be surprising if the ECB were not preoccupied with the need to establish its credibility for price stability. Once this is achieved, monetary policy in Euroland may evolve along more flexible lines. There are no guarantees that this will happen but it is certainly desirable. Europe and America share common interest in many areas including foreign policy, defense, and the smooth functioning of the international monetary system. Neither "country," and by implication the rest of the world, can benefit if their central banks follow different policies when faced with the same global problems.

NOTES

1. Note that the peso-dollar link goes beyond a fixed exchange rate in that Argentina uses a currency board which issues the domestic currency only in exchange for the reserve currency.

2. This appears to be the view of the European Central Bank president Willem Duisenberg, who used January's World Economic Form in Davos, Switzerland, to announce the arrival of a "tri-polar" international currency system.

3. Euroland refers to the eleven countries comprising the euro zone. That is, the existing EU15 less Denmark, Sweden, Greece, and the United Kingdom.

4. Hence General de Gaulle's assertion that the international use of the dollar "enables the United States to be indebted to foreign countries free of charge." Quoted in D. Kunz, "The Fall of the Dollar Order: The World the United States is Losing," *Foreign Affairs* 75 (July / August 1995).

5. Richard Portes and Hélène Rey, "The Emergence of the Euro as an International Currency," *Economic Policy* 26 (1998).

6. The dollar's role as a reserve currency has declined from 79 percent in 1975 to 56 percent today. However this figure has been relatively stable since the mid-1980s.

7. Price stability is not defined by the Maastricht Treaty, but statements by the ECB suggest a target inflation figure which is positive but less than 2 percent.

8. Rudiger Dornbusch, Carlo Favero, and Francesco Giavazzi, *The Immediate Challenges to the ECB*, NBER Working Paper 6369 (Cambridge, Mass.: National Bureau of Economic Research, 1998).

9. C. R. Bean, "Monetary Policy under EMU," *Oxford Review of Economic Policy* 14, 3 (1998).

10. European Commission, *External Aspects of Economic and Monetary Union*, Commission Staff working paper SEC(97) 803, 1997.

11. For an opposite view, see Paul Krugman, *Geography and Trade* (Cambridge, Mass.: MIT Press, 1991).

12. Paul de Grauwe, "Comment on Portes and Rey," *Economic Policy* 26 (1998).

13. The president was referring to the United States and used the word *nation* rather than *economy*. Fortunately or unfortunately, depending on your perspective, Europe is still best regarded as an economy rather than as a nation.

14. Willem Duisenberg, speech to the Council of Foreign Relations, Chicago, February 1, 1999.

15. The Fed fund rate was cut from 9.8 percent in mid-1989 to 3 percent in 1993 and then increased to 6 percent by 1995.

16. The first of these examples is of particular interest. The recession of the late 1980s in the United States was followed by rising unemployment in Western Europe. However, unlike the Fed, the Bundesbank, which effectively set monetary policy for the EMS, refused to countenance an interest rate cut. The reason was, of course, the pursuit of price stability in the wake of German unification. However, the result was a serious appreciation of European currencies against the dollar, persistently high unemployment, policy conflicts within the EMS, and the collapse of the exchange rate system in 1992–1993. In short, a good example of how a lack of synchronization between large central banks can lead to turmoil on international money markets.

17. The pact puts an upper limit of 3 percent on government deficits with, under certain circumstances, sanctions when the reference value is exceeded. Over the course of the business cycle the pact probably requires a balanced budget.

Part V

The European Union, National Security, and NATO

An Informal Roundtable

National Security and Defense Implications of the European Union

A Continental European Perspective

GLENDA G. ROSENTHAL

Much attention is currently devoted to the economic and monetary policies of the European Union (EU), a natural reaction to the launching of the final stage of the monetary union in January 1999, with eleven of the fifteen EU member countries committed to a single monetary policy, managed by a single European Central Bank, with a single currency, the euro, being used for all commercial transactions.

But that is seemingly a far cry from the subject matter of this roundtable: defense and security. I assert, however, that European security, defense, and indeed foreign policy, is coming increasingly to the fore in European Union policy concerns and in the concerns of the individual member states of the EU. It has been said that the EU is an economic powerhouse but that it lacks political clout; that it has a foreign trade policy that ranks with the United States in international importance, but that when it comes to foreign and security policy, there is no single person in any single place in the EU for American policy makers to call, as then Secretary of State Henry Kissinger reminded us in the early seventies. In 1992 the member countries of the EU signed the Maastricht Treaty on European Union, which provided for a common foreign and security policy in its second pillar and, eventually, a common defense. All well and good but, as events clearly showed during the fighting in the former Yugoslavia, the European Union appeared no closer to a common foreign policy and security goal in the nineties than it had in the seventies. It was recognized on both sides of the Atlantic that the

European Union failed in its peace-making mission in Bosnia and that is why it was necessary for the United States and NATO to step in and resolve the conflict. Once, again, we heard the accusation that "those Europeans cannot get their act together and deal with security problems in their own backyard." And once again, we heard the defensive European response that its common foreign and security policy was not yet up and running and that the necessary institutional and policy-making mechanisms were not yet in place. The old refrain it seemed.

Recently, things have been starting to change. To illustrate this change, I call attention to three important moves. The first of these was an initiative taken by British Prime Minister Tony Blair on November 13, 1998, in a speech delivered to the North Atlantic Assembly in Edinburgh and in an op-ed piece entitled "Europe's Defense Capability," published in the *New York Times* on the same day. What was Prime Minister Blair's message?

In reference to NATO, "Europe has always been the weaker of the twin pillars of the Alliance," he said, "both in its ability to decide rapidly and its capability to put these decisions into action. . . . Europe's foreign policy voice in the world is unacceptably muted and ineffective, given our economic weight and strategic interests. . . . We must change this . . . by ensuring that the EU can speak with a single authoritative voice on key international issues of the day, and can intervene effectively where necessary." But, most important of all, he went on, "Europe needs to develop the ability to act alone in circumstances where, for whatever reasons, the U.S. is not able or does not wish to participate. Why should U.S. taxpayers and U.S. troops have to resolve problems on our doorstep?" One could almost hear the sighs of relief resonating from Capitol Hill and the White House.

Prime Minister Blair made it quite clear that he was not talking about a European army. As he pointed out, no country can accept the use of its armed forces without its full consent. The decision to deploy troops can only be taken by national politicians, acting collectively and accountably. But, in order to have an effective European defense capability, it was important that a European defense be planned together at a European rather than a national level. It was also important, he asserted, to have an effective Europe-wide defense industry, joint procurement programs, planning together and planning for the long-term. It was clear that Mr. Blair had no illusions about the difficulty of this process. "We need an open debate between America and Europe," he said, "free from preconceptions and bureaucratic wrangling about institutions. Our discussions should focus on results, not theology. . . . We owe it to America to pull our full weight."

The second important initiative, although in a personal rather than in an official statement, came in a piece published on February 3 by the *Financial Times*. Emma Bonino, an active and influential member of the European Commission, went much further than Tony Blair in her piece "A Single European Army": "Now that Europe has EMU [Economic and Monetary Union], it should try for DMU—Defense and Military Union. The smooth launch of the euro shows how it can be done." Measure for measure, Bonino drew a series of parallels between the gradual establishment of monetary union and the establishment of a future diplomatic and military union. The EMU process, she asserted, needed to be rerun in the realm of EU Common and Security Policy. There would be a replay of the Delors Committee on EMU. The committee would include the fifteen military chiefs of staff and senior diplomats from member states and independent experts. "If the committee chose to follow the Delors model," she explained, "it could recommend a similar multi-staged plan, stretching over several years. As with EMU, the process would be overseen at all stages, and ultimately be decided upon by member governments." Bonino herself has few illusions about her suggestions. "The whole idea," she wrote, "will surely be met with a deluge of skepticism. But so was EMU until a few months ago. . . . There will be considerable wrangling over the length of the multi-staged period to phase in a full DMU." After all, from the Delors Committee to the actual circulation of euro notes and coins, it will take Europe fourteen years to achieve a full EMU. In between, there were referenda and opt-outs, all sorts of doubts and second thoughts. But in spite of everything, the euro is now flying. "Why should this not be the case for the DMU?" Bonino asked. "No one will honestly be able to claim to have been rushed into such a union. Supposing we took 2015 as the deadline for a full DMU; it will be seventy years from the end of the second world war."

The third initiative that I would like to touch on briefly is the most recent of all—the lead being taken by the British, French, and EU in the Rambouillet negotiations in order to achieve some kind of peace settlement in Kosovo. No one at the time suggested that the negotiations could lead to a settlement, and if they do reach a settlement of some kind, it would probably be partial and relatively short term. But, note that the talks were being held in Rambouillet, not in Dayton. The negotiations were spearheaded by Robin Cook and Hubert Vredine, not Richard Holbrooke. I suggest that Europeans are beginning to act on the sentiments expressed in the statements I referred to earlier and not rely so much on American leadership and American troops. Admittedly, the Europeans insisted on some American participation in the forces on the ground in Kosovo as a precondition for their own participation in the peace force, but the American contingent was slated to be quite small in proportion to the contingents promised by various European states, not least among them the British and the French. I personally see some progress being achieved in this area; small progress, but progress nonetheless. I sympathize strongly with the sentiments expressed by Emma Bonino. Moves toward common EU policies for security and defense are slow and full of hiccups, but there is discernible movement in the right direction and that is what is important.

National Security and Defense Implications of the European Union

Looking Ahead

ELLEN L. FROST

There is an important link between economics and security, even though these two topics are normally discussed in isolation from each other. In today's world, however, the two are often closely interrelated. The challenges facing the transatlantic partnership offer many examples.

At the "highest" and most conceptual level, the formation and deepening of the European Union is itself a significant contribution to peace and stability. War in Western Europe is now inconceivable. One need only think of the last few centuries to appreciate that fact. But the emergence of the European Union as an economic superpower also challenges the United States to combine its long-standing demand for burden sharing with a new and genuine willingness to share leadership.

At the "lowest" and most nitty-gritty level, so to speak, many linkages between economics and security appear in highly specific form through technology. For some time now the driving force for most defense-related technology has been the commercial marketplace. Increasingly, the business community has acquired an important voice in removing barriers to trade and investment. The Transatlantic Business Dialogue (TABD) is the most recent and most impressive of this new role to date. Thanks to the TABD, the United States and the European Union successfully negotiated a package of "Mutual Recognition Agreements" covering testing and conformity assessment for half a dozen product areas.

The "in-between" linkages, I would argue, give rise to the most frequently voiced European complaints about the United States. These are as follows. First, Washington acts unilaterally far too often. Second, Washington extends extraterritorial jurisdiction in an effort to "punish" foreign nationals and companies beyond its legitimate reach. Finally, the United States preaches free trade but practices as much protectionism as most other developed countries.

These in-between issues are manifold. Defense industrial issues, such as defense spending, force structure, and the "two-way street" (transatlantic defense procurement), are one example. The use of economic leverage to pursue political-military goals, such as export controls and economic sanctions against rogue states and trade and investment flows, including recovery from the global financial crisis and a new round of multilateral trade negotiations, are others. Lastly, one also finds coordinated U.S.-EU policies toward important countries, such as China and Japan.

Within the U.S. government, there is a large bureaucratic and conceptual gap between economic and national security policy makers. Symptoms of this problem include the split between the National Economic Council and the National Security Council and the policy divide between the economic and political-military bureaus of the State Department. The structure of congressional committees reflects this same pattern. Compounding the problem is a lawyer culture characterized by the absence of long-term, strategic thinking and by a tendency to segregate and judicialize a number of issues that might be better handled holistically.

Looking ahead, there exists a clear commonality of interests facing the transatlantic partnership. Some of these interests are domestic. For example, government officials on both sides of the Atlantic are encountering some degree of "globaphobia" in the public at large. They need to educate their citizens about the global economy and to cope with the problems of those left behind. The mobilization of numerous nongovernment organizations through the Internet means that failure to secure political support for global economic engagement is no longer a safe option.

Similarly, the so-called information age has given rise to enormous financial instability in world markets, wreaking havoc with trade and investment and pointing to the need for improved governance of the global economic system. The transatlantic powers have agreed to launch a new round of multilateral trade negotiations; the World Trade Organization's ministerial meeting will take place in the United States at the end of 1999. Transatlantic leadership is a necessary but not sufficient condition for the resumption of global growth, with all its consequences for political stability and security.

In short, the transatlantic agenda is not primarily bilateral but global. And global challenges are a mixture of economics and security, not to mention history and culture. Despite the overtly economic identity of the European Union, Brussels is slowly becoming a foreign policy actor. All in all, this is good news for Washington, but the adjustment will not be painless on either side. What must always be kept in mind is that the two partners can achieve a great deal if they act together—and very little if they are divided.

The United States, NATO, and the Lessons of History

FRANK NINKOVICH

Someone once said that the trouble with the world is that the stupid people are cocksure and the intelligent persons are full of doubt. So I'm proud to reveal that in the debate over NATO expansion, I find myself unable to choose between the two versions of national interest currently being advanced. It's not that the two sides have done equally good or bad jobs of making their respective cases. I remain unconvinced by either set of arguments because there is no way that they *can* be convincing. There is no way that the argument can be settled in advance. Indeed, long hereafter, we are unlikely to know which side was correct. I'd like to discuss why that should be so.

Former Secretary of State Warren Christopher once insisted that "Europe's institutional arrangements should be determined by the objective demands of the present, not by the tragedies of Europe's past." The argument is fine, except for one thing: there are no objective demands of the present. Indeed, one of the problems with this debate is that it cannot be understood in terms of interests; there is nothing hard to fall back on. The best way to understand the NATO debate is to get a sense of its historical meaning, which can be objectively ascertained, rather than to talk fruitlessly about interests that don't exist.

I want to suggest that NATO expansion is going ahead primarily for some historical reasons that are themselves problematic. The debate is less about the specific merits or demerits of NATO expansion than about hanging on to the view of history that underlies it. It has less to do with specific lessons of the past, about history backing up policy, than with the sense of history from which Americans frame their foreign policies. In saying this, I realize that there are many historians who believe that there are some definite experiential lessons of history that can be applied meaningfully to this situation. The kinds of arguments found in last year's Internet discussion of NATO expansion on H-DIPLO, a forum for diplomatic historians, suggest that a surprising number of historians actually appear to believe that history can open a window with a clear view to the future. For my part, I agree wholeheartedly with Lawrence Peter's observation: "History only teaches us the mistakes we are going to make."

Before talking about the role of history as I see it, I need first to say a few words about why the debate should be as inherently inconclusive as it is. It's not the first time that a debate of this kind has occurred. We've seen its like before, most notably in the dispute between isolationists and interventionists prior to World War II. What struck me about these debates was the lack of persuasive force and the circularity of the arguments deployed by each side. How could so many people differ on a subject on which, one would think, agreement could be readily reached? Was the United States threatened or not? National security and the kind of threat facing the country are, after all, if one is to believe the realists, objectively determinable phenomena.

In the case of these debates, I would suggest that there was no correct answer to be arrived at by referring to strategic realities because these realities did not exist. The great debate of the 1930s was a quite remarkable demonstration of the difficulty of defining national security in a modern environment in which danger was not objectively manifest. Instead, the controversy was actually an argument about history, or interpretations of history, and not about strategy based on hard economic or political interests visible to everyone, like an army massing at one's border. It was a situation in which reality was itself very much in flux and its definition up for grabs. The debate over the future of NATO is one of those situations.

Now, why should things like this happen? I think it has to do with one of the defining features of modernity. Probably the best explanation I've seen comes from Arnold Gehlen, a practitioner of something called philosophical anthropology—a composite discipline that is to scholarship what the marriage between Mary Matalin and James Carville is to politics.

Contrasting the rationalist uncertainty of modern times with the prescientific certainty of earlier periods, Gehlen speaks of modernity as "blurred" or "objectively indeterminate." As he puts it: "One remains tied to a reality which is itself objectively blurred, objectively indeterminate, and which shares . . . the property of allowing for conflicting judgments. Slowly such realities are turning into a distinctive feature of our times." For Gehlen, the explanation for this state of affairs appears to lie in the rapidity of change. Modern society produces deinstitutionalization, which leads to subjectivization, according to Gehlen. Archaic institutions, by contrast, are highly objective, taken-for-granted social facts. Institutions therefore are important forces for continuity. They provide a stable background to life. But modern institutions, given their ever-changing, polymorphous character, are different in their relative lack of objectivity. Put differently, modernity shrinks the objective background of social structure and accentuates the subjective "foreground" of human existence. The search for stability and anchorage is thereby turned inward, into our minds.

There are all kinds of reasons for this tendency to objective indeterminacy that Gehlen doesn't talk about: the confusion resulting from the welter and complexity of modern issues, the simultaneous scarcity and superabundance of information, and the possibility of vastly differing outcomes in just about every massive project that human beings undertake. Modernity is an enterprise with low risks but also with great dangers when things do go wrong. It is what Anthony Giddens called "riding the juggernaut," so it is possible to imagine both worst-case and best-case scenarios in any set of social developments. It may seem paradoxical, but the more we know, the less certainty we can have about the big things, either at the time—or even, I would hold, retrospectively.

If there is anything to this idea of objective indeterminacy, one has to ask, How is policy made? Does this mean that one's policy position is a function of taste or subjective ideological preference? At least one can agree not to argue about taste, but these kinds of issues *have* to be argued; more important, they have to be decided. What provides the basis for reasoned argumentation and decision in this case? The answer, I think, lies in history.

One's position depends in part on whether one sees NATO as a Cold War institution or as an institution created to address longer-range problems of the twentieth century. A fair portion of the criticism of the NATO decision comes from those who see it—incorrectly—as a Cold War institution created to deal with a Soviet threat to Europe. If one views NATO's creation simply from a Cold War standpoint, then it makes perfect sense to argue, now that the threat is gone, that NATO ought to be given an honorary discharge, pensioned off.

Yes, NATO was indeed a Cold War organization, but it also spoke to some longer-range needs: the European problem, the German problem, the Soviet problem, and the American problem. Allow me to deal briefly with each of these four.

A significant change has taken place in American thinking about Europe. In the 1950s, the belief was that the U.S. presence on the continent ought to be temporary. A president such as Dwight D. Eisenhower, when pressing for the creation of the European Defense Community, shuddered at the thought of an ongoing American responsibility for Europe. Now the belief is that it ought to be permanent. The reason for the change, I think, comes from the understanding that NATO, like the Marshall Plan, was not simply a Cold War institution. We tend to treat the Cold War as this deus ex machina that explains the emergence of all our major foreign policy institutions. But I would suggest, had there been no Cold War, that it might still have been necessary to create something like NATO. Indeed, the Cold War itself is not understandable simply from the perspective of the Cold War.

According to my reading of the past, the Cold War addressed a set of problems that first became apparent to Woodrow Wilson in World War I, reemerged much more powerfully prior to World War II, and became axiomatic in the minds of Cold War policy makers. The problems generally revolved around the failure of the European balance of power, which Wilson, as I understand him, assumed was not simply a temporary failure, but a historical failure: that is, the European balance of power had become obsolete and could no longer function effectively as it had in the past. Which is not to say that it could not be restored—it could—but if it were, the consequences were likely to be disastrous.

Events in the interwar and postwar years proved Wilson to be correct. Despite efforts by Britain, France, and the USSR in the 1930s, no stable equilibrium was put in place. And the Second World War, while eliminating the threat from Nazi Germany, from the standpoint of realpolitik made the problem of the European balance even worse by leaving a vacuum in the heart of Europe.

NATO also was created to deal with the problem of Germany, or, to be more precise, the problem of the Franco-German relationship, which is also a problem that precedes the Cold War and succeeds it. That NATO took on a collective security aspect was not simply a way of throwing dust in the eyes of UN lovers. It was a genuine, if limited, successor to the League of Nations in its attempt to rein in the German problem. By assuring an American presence, it was able shortly after its creation to provide security guarantees to France while German re-armament proceeded. From this standpoint, an American-led NATO was a necessity. Thus, while in realist terms the United States moved in after 1945 to fill a power vacuum, it must be understood that Americans were not operating simply from that kind of perspective. The problem antedated the Soviet threat and it has turned out also to postdate it.

Of course, keeping Germany under wraps was only part of a solution to postwar Europe's problems that has come to be called double containment or dual containment, in which the objective was to resolve both the German problem and the Soviet problem, which also precedes the Cold War. If one is to believe historians such as John Lamberton Harper, what he calls a sensibility of "proto-containment" can be found long before the emergence of the Bolshevik state. Well, proto-containment and Cold War containment have now given way to meta-containment.

Russia is still there, not as threatening as the USSR was in its heyday, to be sure, but with the potential to cause big trouble.

The last pre–Cold War historical element—and I think the most important—has to do with America's role in Europe and, by extension, America's role in the world. Despite having participated in two wars in Europe, it was still not clear in the immediate aftermath of World War II whether and how the United States would commit itself to managing these problems on the Continent. NATO provided the institutional basis for an ongoing, hegemonic American presence.

Now, it is possible to argue that these four problems that predated the Cold War have not been resolved. Bosnia and Kosovo seem to suggest that Europe is still a powder keg. And while a reunited Germany is a solid citizen of the European Community, probably its most solid citizen, the reunification drama of a decade ago disclosed the existence of substantial doubts among policy makers in the rest of the Continent about the rise of another powerful German state. By these lights, the German problem, though transformed, has not gone away. German integration into Europe simply raises it in a new form. As for Russia, the argument is obvious. Weak and unsettled for the moment, an irrational and aggressive Russian nationalism might succeed in the wake of a failure of Western-style liberal democracy to take root.

The historical argument for dealing with the American problem was stated succinctly by Strobe Talbott in the August 10, 1995, issue of the *New York Review of Books* in an essay titled, "Why NATO Should Grow." "Three times in this century," he wrote, "Americans have come to Europe's defense, and one of the lessons of those experiences is that the United States must remain permanently engaged in helping to preserve the security of Europe. The NATO Alliance remains the principal mechanism for American involvement. But if NATO is to continue to be useful, it will have to adapt to the post–cold war era."

Thus it would appear that the basis for policy remains what NATO's first secretary-general, Lord Hastings Ismay said it was: "to keep the Russians out, the Americans in, and the Germans down." If we accept all this, it would seem that the current proposals for NATO expansion cannot be characterized as an example of diplomats and generals refighting the Cold War, because policy is being made on the basis of time-tested assumptions that have been around for the better part of a century.

There is no way of knowing with any certainty whether these historical assumptions about the intractability of the European, German, and Russian problems are true. It *is* possible, however, to assert without a doubt that the American problem continues to exist.

An inactive American presence in Europe would be akin to no presence at all; there would be a danger of atrophy and the consequent difficulty of taking action if trouble emerged outside the current boundaries of NATO. If something were to go seriously wrong on the Continent, political inertia might make it exceedingly difficult to act—recall George Bush's close call with Congress over the Gulf War. If the United States withdrew, there would be no easy way back; de-institutionalization would be akin to subjectivization; that is, policy would once again be up for grabs.

Put differently, leaving NATO or allowing it to rust would mean abandoning a century-long worldview. The globalization of American foreign policy tradition in the twentieth century was hard earned. It was nearly not institutionalized; and when it was, I doubt that a majority of the American people understood it or would have agreed with it if they had. During the Cold War, American policy makers believed—correctly, I think—that the American people were, at heart, still isolationists. To allow this worldview to atrophy would be to leave the country with no foreign policy orientation at all.

Thus the desire to continue American hegemony in Europe is rooted less in a lust for power than in a fear of being unable to act in the event of an emergency should the United States leave the Continent. From this perspective, the expansion of NATO is a historically conservative, prudential step because it is not clear that the kinds of problems that long antedated the Cold War have been resolved once and for all. Working through NATO is preferable because it is a going concern, already institutionalized.

However, to say that there is a deep historical rationale for NATO expansion is not to say that growing the alliance is the historically correct thing to do. Institutions, to work, require rules, underlying understandings that are the basis for their ongoing vitality and renewal. Unfortunately, in the post–Cold War context, those rules do not exist. At one time, they did. They had been provided by a sense of Cold War crisis that was internalized by policy makers and public, which itself was part of a larger sense of crisis that went back to the beginning of the twentieth century.

The problem is that the sense of crisis indispensable to effective institutionalization is no longer present. The absence of public debate suggests that there is no deeply felt sense of threat among the public. That is because the kinds of dangers that American policy makers perceived earlier in the century—the threat of a civilization-ending global conflict or a global threat to democracy—are not the kinds of perils that are being talked about in this case. Would a crisis in Eastern Europe be the kind that threatened the security of the Continent as a whole and, by extension, American security? Maybe, maybe not. Maybe it would be like Bosnia and Kosovo: an annoyance, an embarrassment, a great pity, perhaps a tragedy—but hardly a grave threat. In any event, it is unlikely that Eastern Europe can be made the kind of symbolic token that Berlin became during the Cold War.

Without this sense of threat, the Wilsonian historical sensibility that made the Cold War a crisis for the United States in the first place has vanished. And Wilsonianism without a vivid sense of threat is like Christianity without a deep terror of hellfire and damnation. In other words, policy makers are attempting to expand NATO on the basis of a historical outlook that is out of touch with the historical sensibility of the times. It risks becoming an abstract intellectual exercise without any cultural depth or roots in public opinion.

Thus institutionalization is important because it is almost all that remains. The Clinton administration is attempting to preserve through institutional means a set of policies and a global position that had been rooted in a sense of historical crisis at a time when that sense of crisis has disappeared and been replaced with a very different kind of sensibility. The Cold War was difficult enough to understand, but it could be understood by many people nevertheless in a meaningful way. This institutional expansion, by contrast, is an attempt to sustain an American role in the world on the basis of a historical perspective that today seems so strange that it is almost a curiosity to students.

But the critics of NATO expansion are not above criticism in this debate. There is no more hard reason to take seriously their dire prophecies than there is to accept the optimistic projections of the Clinton administration. If the critics are really serious, they will have to take on the worldview and the view of history that lies behind the decisions. More than that, they will have to come up with an alternative view of the world's problems and of America's world role. If they don't, by default NATO expansion will go forward, whatever the uncertainties about the depth and credibility of this American commitment.

We are left with two different wagers: the bet that the old view of history is still correct; as opposed to the insistence by critics of NATO expansion that the old view no longer applies. The United States went into Europe with the intention of staying until Europe was self-sufficient; but now it is afraid to leave Europe, which is the only way that Europeans can show that they can handle their own affairs. As a result, the United States is faced with the following choice. It can either make a historical act of faith, grounded in European developments of the past half century, that the new Europe, unlike the old, will now be able to manage its own affairs. Or it can continue to make a weak historical case, based in the attempt to apply a Wilsonian historical sensibility that no longer exists, for continuing to play the leading role in Europe, a signature role without which its identity as a foreign policy actor would be thrown into question.

Either way, that's far removed from foreign policy based on objective interests backed by the lessons of history.

National Security and Defense Implications of the European Union

Summary, Commentary, and Discussion

JERALD A. COMBS

D r. Ellen Frost argued that the European Union, even though it was almost exclusively devoted to economic concerns, was a security organization as well because it made war in Western Europe inconceivable. Dr. Frost then went on to provide an extraordinarily informed analysis of how closely economics and security were linked in the relations between the United States and the European Union over such issues as technology regulation, defense procurement, and the use of economic sanctions as military-political weapons. She worried especially that the lack of communication between economic and security officials in the United States contributed to economic and strategic policies that threatened U.S.-European relations. Economic policy makers might push for protectionist policies that undercut the political goals of the security organizations while security offices might push the use of economic leverage for political goals without proper consideration of the economic consequences. She concluded by emphasizing the common economic and security interests facing the European Union and the United States, especially the growing fear of globalization among the people on both sides of the Atlantic and the need for coordination of world trade and financial policies to secure political stability and security.

Professor Glenda Rosenthal highlighted the tension between the intra-European economic orientation of the European Union and the transatlantic security orientation of NATO. The European Union did provide for a second pillar to add to the economic pillar—a common foreign, security, and eventually defense policy. Yet in Bosnia it had been the power of the United States and NATO that had rescued the European peace effort and brought at least a temporary peace to the area. Professor Rosenthal noted, however, that the Europeans were chagrined by this outcome and were beginning to move toward a greater independent European capability to maintain the peace in the European area. She noted the November 13, 1998, speech of Tony Blair in favor of a European defense initiative; the February 3, 1999, article by Emma Bonino of the European Commission calling for a single European army; and the fact that the Kosovo negotiations being held at the time of the conference were in Rambouillet rather than Dayton. Of course, she could not have known that in Kosovo, as in Bosnia, the primary military contribution would again come to be that of the United States. Nevertheless, the aftermath of Kosovo seems to bear out her view that the Europeans are contemplating a stronger second pillar. The Europeans rather than the Americans will be the primary peacekeepers in Kosovo and the Europeans have taken the Kosovo crisis as further evidence of the need for greater and more unified European military capabilities.

Dr. Frost and Professor Rosenthal both argued that greater European unity and self-sufficiency should be welcomed by the United States and should not interfere with the continued close partnership of the United States and Europe in both economic and security affairs. But Professor Frank Ninkovich took another view. He argued that the national interests and security threats that supposedly bind the United States to Europe in the post–Cold War era cannot be clearly and objectively defined. Thus, it became very difficult to determine whether the United States should support the expansion of NATO or intervene in the Balkans.

Ninkovich argued that the United States founded and joined NATO not just to contain the Soviet Union, but also to contain Germany, maintain stability throughout Western Europe, and keep the United States involved on the continent. "Realists" would argue that all these problems still obtain in a transmuted form and that the United States therefore has an objective national interest in continuing its relationship with Europe. Russia is down but could revive, Germany is increasingly powerful and therefore still troubles the rest of Europe, and the Balkan crisis proves that Europe is still a powder keg. Ninkovich argued on the other hand that neither the Russian, German, nor European problems are so clear or of such magnitude that they require America's continued active intervention in Europe. None of them pose the threat to Continental security and therefore to American security that inspired America's previous willingness to involve itself in Europe. Moreover, he argued that the American people followed their leaders into Europe very reluctantly even when the threat was obvious, so that NATO, which institutionally compels American participation, is all that is really holding the United States in Europe against the public reluctance. And he is not at all sure that it is worth it.

In summarizing these papers at the conference, I remarked that Professor Ninkovich's paper was one of the few instances in which the entire ethos of the conference, the assumption that the United States should stay closely intertwined and identified with Europe economically and militarily, was challenged or answered. I said that I differed from Professor Ninkovich and thought World War II and the Cold War had brought most Americans to construct a definition of American national interest that included the belief that maintaining stability and prosperity in Europe and in the oil countries of the Middle East was vital to the United States. I said that I thought Americans had internalized that belief sufficiently that the United States would stay fully involved there for the foreseeable future. That set off a firestorm of debate. Professor Paul Schroeder argued that a truly realist evaluation of the Balkan situation would dictate an American avoidance of military intervention in the Balkans on the grounds that it would alienate Russia, and Russia—rather than Bosnia or Kosovo—had the means to affect the European and world balance of power. Dr. Ellen Frost argued that Asia also should be considered as one of the areas, along with Europe and the Middle East, that the United States was willing to defend at considerable risk, especially given America's specific military commitment to South Korea and Japan and its implied commitment to Taiwan. I replied that I thought the American people if not the government made such a commitment in Asia far more reluctantly than they did to Europe or the Middle East, but in retrospect I think Dr. Frost had the better of the argument. Professor Betty Unterberger noted that many of the people around her in Texas cared not a whit about Europe or the Balkans. One member of the audience wondered whether the American commitment to Europe was in part racist and would fade as the ethnic composition of the United States changed. Professor Stephen Schuker thought the commitment to Europe on the basis of World War II and the Cold War was generational and would fade as the younger generation came to power in the United States. The consensus seemed to be that the closeness of American ties to Europe might indeed wane over the next few years in the absence of the vital threat noted by Professor Ninkovich.

 Contributors

JERALD A. COMBS is Chair and Professor of History at San Francisco State University. He is the author of several works on the history of American foreign relations, including *The Jay Treaty: Political Battle-ground of the Founding Fathers; American Diplomatic History: Two Centuries of Changing Interpretations;* and *The History of American Foreign Policy.* Most recently he has published articles on the conventional balance of power in Europe during the early Cold War.

ELIZABETH F. DEFEIS, Professor of Law and former Dean at Seton Hall University School of Law, is the author of *Women's Legal Rights: International Covenants—An Alternative to ERA?* and various articles on International Law and European Union Law.

IRENE FINEL-HONIGMAN, author and editor of *European Monetary Union Banking Issues: Historical and Contemporary Perspectives,* is Adjunct Professor in the MBA program, Johns Hopkins University. Previously Visiting Professor at Columbia University School of International and Public Affairs and Chair of Foreign Languages at New School University, she served in the Clinton administration as Senior Adviser, finance policy and EMU initiatives at the U.S. Department of Commerce.

ELLEN L. FROST, a Visiting Fellow at the Institute for International Economics, is currently co-chairing a study of globalization for the Department of the Navy and the National Defense University. In her last government job, she served as Counselor to the U.S. Trade Representative. She is the author of *For Richer, For Poorer: The New US–Japan Relationship* and *Transatlantic Trade: A Strategic Agenda.*

JOHN GILLINGHAM is editor of two volumes and the author of another three, the most recent of which, *Coal, Steel and the Rebirth of Europe, 1945–1955* (Cambridge University Press, 1991), received the George Lewis Beer Prize for international history. He has published extensively on the economic history of twentieth-century Europe and is presently engaged in researching the economic dynamics of European integration. Gillingham is Professor of History at the University of Missouri/St. Louis.

JOAN HOFF is Director of the Contemporary History Institute and Professor of History at Ohio University. She is author of *American Business and Foreign Policy, 1920–1933; Ideology and Economics: United States Relations with the Soviet Union, 1918–1933; Herbert Hoover: Forgotten Progressive; Law, Gender and Injustice; Nixon Reconsidered;* and *The Cooper's Wife Is Missing: The Ritual Murder of Bridget Cleary in 1895 Ireland.*

HUGO M. KAUFMANN, Professor of Economics at Queens College of the City University of New York (CUNY), is Director of the European Union Studies Center at the Graduate School–CUNY. A specialist in international economics, with a focus on the EU, he has held visiting assistant professorships at Tel Aviv and Bar Ilan Universities in Israel. He has received numerous grants and prizes, including the Ugo Foscolo Medal at the University of Pavia, Italy. His most recent and best-known publications include "The Importance of Being Independent: Central Bank Independence and the European System of Central Banks"; "The European Economic and Monetary Union: An Experiment Whose Time Has Come—Or Has It?"; "European Economic and Monetary Union—Prospects and Pitfalls: Is EMU Premature?" and "The Political Economy of the European Monetary Union."

DEAN J. KOTLOWSKI is Assistant Professor of History at Salisbury State University in Maryland. A specialist in twentieth-century United States and world history, he has held visiting professorships at Pepperdine University and Ohio University. His articles have appeared in *Presidential Studies Quarterly*, *Business History Review*, *The Historian*, *New England Journal of History*, and *Journal of Policy History*. Harvard University Press will publish his book *Nixon's Civil Rights* in 2001.

LARRY NEAL, Professor of Economics at the University of Illinois at Urbana-Champaign, is Director of the European Union Center at the University of Illinois. He is author of *The Economics of the European Union and the Economies of Europe;* and *The Rise of Financial Capitalism*. He was editor of the journal *Explorations in Economic History*, 1982–98, and was president of the Economic History Association in 1998–99.

FRANK NINKOVICH, Professor of History at St. John's University in New York City, is the author most recently of *The Wilsonian Century* and a forthcoming book entitled *The United States and Imperialism*.

BERNARD D. REAMS JR. is Visiting Professor of Law at Seton Hall University School of Law and Professor of Law at St. Johns University. He is the author of twenty books, including *A Legislative History of the International Antitrust Enforcement Act of 1994*. For the summers of 1996, 1997, and 1998 he was a research fellow at the Max Planck Institute for Foreign and International Private Law in Hamburg, researching issues involving the law of the European Union.

HENRY H. H. REMAK, Professor of Comparative Literature, Germanic and West European Studies at Indiana University, Bloomington, Indiana, co-organized and chaired the West European Studies Program at Indiana University in the 1960s. He has, over the years, personally interviewed or talked to a number of associates of Monnet, read additional interviews done by third parties, consulted the resources of the Fondation

Jean Monnet pour l'Europe et Centre de Recherches Européenes at the University of Lausanne, and is an elected member of its Conseil. He has also been active in the American Council for Jean Monnet Studies.

GLENDA G. ROSENTHAL is Adjunct Professor of International and Public Affairs at Columbia University and Co-director of the European Union Center of New York. She is the co-editor of *The State of the European Community: The Maastricht Debates and Beyond* and *The Expanding European Union: Past, Present, Future.*

GEORGE ROSS, Morris Hillquit Professor in Labor and Social Thought at Brandeis University, is Acting Director of the Minda de Gunzburg Center for European Studies at Harvard University and Executive Director of the European Union Center at Harvard University. He is also co-editor of *French Politics and Society,* chair of the West European Politics and Society section of the American Political Science Association, and executive secretary of the Conference Group on French Politics and Society. He has published more than 150 articles. His most recent books include (with Andrew Martin) *Brave New World of European Labor* (1998) and *Jacques Delors and European Integration* (1995).

STEPHEN A. SCHUKER is William W. Corcoran Professor of History at the University of Virginia. He is the author of *The End of French Predominance in Europe* and *American "Reparations" to Germany, 1919–33;* most recently, he has edited *Deutschland und Frankreich vom Konflikt zur Aussoehnung: Die Gestaltung der westeuropaeischen Sicherheit 1914–1963.*

RODNEY THOM is Jean Monnet Professor of Economics and chair of the Department of Economics at University College Dublin. He has held visiting professorships at the University of Delaware and McMaster University in Ontario. A specialist in Irish and European economics, he has published chapters in several anthologies, and his articles have appeared in such journals as *Economic and Social Review, Irish Business Administration Review, Weltwirtschaftliches Archiv, Journal of Urban Economics, Review of Economics and Statistics,* and *Applied Economics.*

RICHARD K. VEDDER is Distinguished Professor of Economics at Ohio University, specializing in twentieth-century American economic history and public policy issues. Professor Vedder's last book, *Out of Work: Unemployment and Government in Twentieth-Century America*, co-authored with Lowell Gallaway, was published in 1997 by New York University Press. He has also written over two hundred scholarly papers for journals such as *Economic Inquiry, Journal of Economic History, Scandinavian Economic History Review, Weltwirtschaftliches Archiv*, and the *Journal of Labor Research*, and opinion articles in such newspapers as the *Wall Street Journal, Washington Post, Christian Science Monitor*, and *USA Today.*

 Index

Acheson, Dean, 94
acquis communautaire, 48
Action Committee for a United States of Europe, 60, 83–84
Adenauer, Konrad, 16, 25, 26
affirmative action, 121, 125–27
Alphand, Hervé, 20, 22
Amsterdam Treaty. *See* Treaty of Amsterdam
Argentina, 178
Aron, Raymond, 90
Article 100, 134–35
Article 117, 134, 137
Article 118, 134, 142
Article 119: and Defrenne cases, 137–38; and Equal Treatment Directive, 122; France's role in, 118, 137–38; and gender equality, 111, 117–19, 134; and Maastricht Treaty, 145; and Treaty of Amsterdam, 127–28
Asian economic crisis (1998), 38, 177, 187–89
association, freedom of, 141
asymmetric shocks, 40, 109
asymmetries, 109, 184
Atlantic Partnership, 94, 200–201
Austria, 107, 114

Baker, John C., 6, 11
Baker Peace Conference (Ohio University), 1, 6
Bakke, Regents of the University of California v, 125–26
Baltic countries, 1, 145
Bank of England, 42, 46, 49
bankruptcy, 137
Belgium, 10, 103, 155, 167

benchmark rates. *See* interest rates
Bergsten, C. Fred, 47, 51
Beyen Plan, 26
bills of rights, 133, 140–43
Blair, Tony, 196–97, 214
Bonino, Emma, 197–98, 214
Bosnia conflict, 93, 196, 208, 214
Bossuat, Gérard, 84, 85
Brazil, 178
Bretton Woods Agreement: breakdown of, 41, 79–80, 100, 154, 158; and capital mobility, 85; economic developments under, 151–52; formation of, 80–82
Briand, Aristide, 20
Briand line, 18
Bush-Baker Transatlantic Declaration, 94

Calleo, David, 27
capital markets, 149–50; and EMU, 106; and the euro, 43, 110, 174; in the U.S., 172
capital mobility, 38–39, 80, 85–86, 161, 177
center-left political parties, election of, 108, 113–14, 158, 183–84
central bank independence, 44–46, 183–84
Charter of the Fundamental Social Rights of Workers, 111, 114, 133, 140–43
children and adolescents, employment of, 142
Chirac, Jacques, 88–89
Christopher, Warren, 203
Churchill, Winston, 21
Civil Rights Act of 1964 (U.S.), 123, 125–26, 138
Clayton, Will, 27
Clinton administration, 30, 89, 210–11
Cockfield, Arthur, 29

Cogan, Charles, 91
collective bargaining, 114, 119, 141
Collective Redundancies, Directive on, 136, 142
Common Agricultural Policy (CAP), 26, 33, 152
common currency. *See* European monetary union
Common Foreign and Security Policy, 30
Common Market. *See* European Economic Community
comparable worth standards, 119–21, 138. *See also* equal pay for equal work
competitiveness, 29, 36, 76, 87–96, 109, 165–66
Completing the Single Market. *See* "1992" Plan
containment of problematic nations, 207–8
Convention for the Protection of Human Rights and Fundamental Freedoms, 117, 133–34
convertibility, currency, 23, 79, 83–84, 151
corporate succession liability, 137
Coudenhove-Kalergi, Count Richard, 19
Council of Europe, 25
Council of Ministers, 8–9
Couve de Murville, Maurice, 21, 24
Cuba, 88
currencies, international, 179–81
currency unification. *See* European monetary union
customs-free zones, 100
customs unions, 3–4, 20, 26, 151. *See also* tariffs

D'Amato bill, 88
Danish National Bank, 46
Debray, Régis, 89
Debré, Michel, 24
debt issues, government, 169–70
de Charette, Hervé, 30
deflation, 46, 102, 114
Defrenne cases, 137–38
de Gaspari, Alcide, 16
de Gaulle, Charles, 80; and Churchill, 21; on European integration, 20–21, 87, 90; and Monnet, 7, 19, 60, 87–96; return to power of, 26–27; and Roosevelt, 90, 92–93; vetoes British entry into Common Market, 27, 94
de Grauwe, Paul, 186

Delors, Jacques, 29–30, 94
Delors Plan, 154, 161, 166, 197
"democratic deficit," 9, 135
democratic markets, 10
Denmark, 157; and exchange rates, 167; and gender equality, 118; and Maastricht Treaty, 37, 163; and the "snake," 155
deregulation, 10, 113, 140, 161
Deutsche Bundesbank (DBB), 102; monetary leadership of, 160; tight money policy of, 38, 150, 155, 157
deutsche mark (DM), 102–3; as anchor currency, 28, 160, 164; East German adoption of, 4; and the euro, 47; and oil shocks, 155, 157
diplomatic and military union, 197–98
Directive on Collective Redundancies, 136, 142
Directive on Employee Insolvency, 137
Directive to Encourage Improvements in the Safety and Health at Work of Pregnant Workers and Workers Who Have Recently Given Birth or Are Breast-feeding, 143
disabled persons, 142
discrimination: and Civil Rights Act (U.S.), 123, 125–26, 138; employment, 121–25, 141; gender, 118, 122–23; wage, 117–21
dollar, U.S., 27; and Bretton Woods Agreement, 81–82, 151–52; and euro, 48, 181–86, 188; as international currency, 179–81; and NAFTA countries, 178; and oil shocks, 158, 160; as a reserve currency, 172–73; and the "snake," 154; and Volcker shock, 158
dollar-deutsche mark polarization, 189
dollar exchange standard, 81, 83, 85
Dornbusch, Rudiger, 184
Duisenberg, Willem, 45, 46, 90, 189, 191 n. 2

East Germany. *See* Germany
ECB. *See* European Central Bank
Economic and Monetary Union (EMU), 8, 28, 33–53; and central bank independence, 44–46; characteristics of, 36–37; competitiveness with U.S., 36; criticisms of, 30; and the ECB, 43–44; and the ESCB, 42–44; and Eurosystem, 43–46; and

exchange rate movements, 47–48; expectations about, 35–43; and inflation, 41–42; and international financial systems, 47–51; membership, costs and benefits of, 34, 36, 37–41, 48, 105; population of, 36; and sovereignty over economic policies, 9, 36–37; and unemployment, 41–42, 51–53, 102–3; and the U.S., 30, 50–51

economic unification. *See* integration, European

EDC. *See* European Defense Community

EEC Treaty. *See* Treaty of Rome

Eichengreen, Barry, 80

Eisenhower, Dwight D., 206

elderly persons, 142, 173–74

emerging economies, 178

Employee Information and Consultation Rights, Vredling Proposal for, 137

Employee Insolvency, Directive on, 137

employment: discrimination in, 121–25, 141; full, 42, 80; policies on, 113

EMS. *See* European Monetary System

EMU. *See* Economic and Monetary Union; European monetary union

Entente Cordiale, 23

entitlements, 107, 112

equality principle, 118–23

Equal Pay Act of 1963 (U.S.), 119–21, 138

Equal Pay Directive, 118–19, 138

equal pay for equal work, 111, 117–19, 128, 134, 137–38. *See also* comparable worth standards

Equal Treatment Directives, 121–23, 138–39

Erhard, Ludwig, 25

ERM. *See* Exchange Rate Mechanism

Ersatzkasse, Hofmann v, 122

Estonia, 1, 6

EU. *See* European Union

Euratom, 26, 60

euro, 177–92; and capital markets, 43, 110, 174; conversion costs of, 168; and the deutsche mark, 47; and dollar-deutsche mark polarization, 189; and ECB, 183, 186–91; and election of center-left parties, 108, 113–14, 183–84; and Great Britain, 182–83; impact of, 47, 87–88; as international cur-

rency, 181–86; and international financial system, 47–51; pronunciation of, 149; as a reserve currency, 172; and social policies, 99–115; and U.S. dollar, 48, 181–86, 188; valuation of, 1, 40–41. *See also* European currency unit; European monetary union

European Central Bank (ECB), 45–46, 109; and Asian economic crisis, 187–89; and EMU, 43–44; and euro, 183, 186–91; and European Council, 185; and exchange rates, 109, 185; inflation policies of, 41, 184–85; and interest rates, 109, 185, 187; and Maastricht Treaty, 183; presidency of, 90; and price stability, 43–44, 46, 183, 186, 187, 189; reserve holdings of, 181; and unemployment, 52; and U.S. Federal Reserve Board, 187–88, 190

European Coal and Steel Community (ECSC), 23–25, 26, 100; de Gaulle and, 7; Monnet and, 17, 60, 93

European Commission, 8–9

European Council, 185

European Court of Human Rights, 117

European Court of Justice (ECJ), 29, 117, 118, 120–21

European currency unit (ECU), 90, 164–65. *See also* euro

European Defense Community (EDC), 25–26, 60, 93, 206

European Economic Community (EEC), 83; competitiveness of, 76; economic growth in, 27, 28–30, 151; and external shocks, 150; Monnet and, 7, 60, 93, 100; and sovereignty over economic policies, 84

European Federal Union, 20

European Free Trade Association (EFTA), 27

European Monetary Authority, 85

European Monetary Cooperation Fund, 154, 155

European Monetary System (EMS), 38, 100; economists' views of, 165–66; and exchange rates, 150, 157–68, 189; formation of, 155, 157

European monetary union (EMU), 16; and capital markets, 106; and Clinton administration, 89; costs and benefits of, 30,

37–41, 149, 168; and debt issues, 170–71;
economic motivation for, 173; and external shocks, 150; and France, 102; and interest rates, 41; and Maastricht Treaty, 104;
Monnet and, 79–86, 92; and the "snake,"
152–55; and Treaty of Rome, 83, 151; Triffin's plan for, 85; and the Werner Report,
101, 152, 154. *See also* euro
European Parliament (EP), 8
European Payments Union (EPU), 23, 80,
82–83, 150
European Recovery Act. *See* Marshall Plan
European System of Central Banks (ESCB),
42–44
European Union (EU): affirmative action in,
121, 127; competitiveness with U.S., 29,
87–96; development of, 15–31; and equality, 117–32; inflation in, 41–42, 46; judicial
process in, 135; and Kosovo crisis, 198; legislative process in, 134–35; membership in,
145; positive action in, 121, 123–25, 128;
security and defense issues of, 93, 195–211,
213–16; and social policies, 111, 133–45
European Works Councils, 112, 145
Eurosystem, 43–46
eurozone, 99, 109
Exchange Rate Mechanism (ERM), 29, 38, 41,
150, 160–67
exchange rates: in Bretton Woods Agreement,
81–82, 100, 151–52; dollar-euro, 184–85, 188;
and ECB, 109, 185; and EMS, 150, 157–68,
189; and Maastricht Treaty, 185; management of, 184; monetary autonomy, 80;
and monetary union, 177–78; movements,
47–48; risks, 38, 169, 182; and shocks, 40;
and the "snake," 100, 152–55; Triffin on, 85.
See also names of countries
Executive Order 11246 (U.S.), 126
export growth, 151–52
external shocks, 85, 150

Fair Pay Act (U.S.), 121
Family and Medical Leave Act of 1993 (U.S.),
143
family assistance programs, 104
Favero, Carolo, 184

FDI flows, 10
Federal Reserve System (U.S.), 85, 186–88, 190
financial services, deregulation of, 161
Finland, 163, 167
Flanner, Janet, 92
Fleming, J. Marcus, 80
foreign direct investment flows (FDI), 10
foreign policy, 9, 195–96, 201, 209, 211
Forsyth, Douglas, 86
France: and Article 119, 118, 137–38; and central bank independence, 45; deregulation
of financial services in, 161; election of
center-left parties in, 108; and exchange
rates, 35, 150, 152, 164–65, 167; export
growth of, 151; health care system financing in, 107; industry after WWII, 21–22;
and inflation in, 41, 46, 150, 151–52; and
interest rates, 38; and Kosovo crisis, 198;
and Maastricht Treaty, 163–64; and the
Marshall Plan, 22; and monetary union,
102; and oil shocks, 155; and pegged-rate
system, 150; relationship with U.S., 88–96;
and the "snake," 155, 157; social pacts in,
114; sovereignty relinquished by, 88;
women's and men's earnings in, 120
Franco-German relationship, 87, 89; as economic engine, 27, 29; and Entente Cordiale, 23; and NATO, 26, 207; and rearmament, 25–26; and reconciliation, 25, 30,
90
Franco-German Treaty (1963), 27
free-trade areas, 3, 5, 23, 28. *See also* trading
blocs, regional
Frost, Ellen, 213, 215–16

G7, 35
G10, 154
GATT (General Agreement on Tariffs and
Trade), 88
Gehlen, Arnold, 205
gender equality, 117–32, 142; and affirmative
action, 125–27; and Article 119, 111, 117–19,
134; and discrimination, 118, 122–23; and
equality principle, 118–23; and positive
action, 123–25; and Treaty of Amsterdam,
127–28

Germany: and capital markets, 110, 174; deregulation of financial services in, 161; election of center-left parties in, 108; and Entente Cordiale, 23; and exchange rates, 152; export growth of, 151–52; and gender equality, 118; industry after WWII, 22–25; inflation in, 41, 46, 151–52, 160; and interest rates, 38, 163; labor unions in, 114; and NATO, 26, 207, 214–15; and oil shocks, 155, 157; and Paris Conference (1916), 18; and price stability, 102, 151; rearmament of, 25–26; reunification of, 4, 105, 150, 163, 174, 208; and the "snake," 28, 155, 157; social policies in, 114; unemployment rates in, 42, 51–52. See also Deutsche Bundesbank; Franco-German relationship

Giavazzi, Francesco, 184

Giddens, Anthony, 205

Gillingham, John, 150

Giraud, Henri, 19, 60, 92

globalization, 186–91; of trade, 9–11, 200–201; of U.S. foreign policy, 209

global shocks, 188–89

gold exchange standard, 84, 152

governmental changes in Europe, 108, 113–14, 158, 183–84

Great Britain: and Bretton Woods Agreement, 81; continental relationships of, 22–23, 27; de Gaulle vetoes entry into Common Market, 27, 94; deregulation of financial services in, 161; election of center-left parties in, 108; and EMS, 157–58; and ERM, 165, 167; and euro as international currency, 182–83; and exchange rates, 164; and free markets, 28; and gender equality, 118; and interest rates, 49, 163; and Kosovo crisis, 198; and the Marshall Plan, 22; and oil shocks, 157–58; and pegged-rate system, 38; pension policies of, 106, 139; and the "snake," 155; and the Social Charter, 140; and Treaty of Amsterdam, 145; women's and men's earnings in, 121. See also Bank of England

Greece, 36, 163, 167, 169

Group of Seven Industrialized Countries (G7), 35

Group of Ten (G10), 154

Gunther, County of Washington v, 119–20

Hanseatic League, 3

harmonization: of employment policies, 113; national, 16; of pension schemes, 142; of taxes, 6, 110

harmonized index of consumer prices (HICP), 46

Harper, John Lamberton, 207

health and safety standards, 111, 139, 142, 143

health care systems, 104, 106–7, 111–12

Heath, Edward, 27

Helms-Burton conflict, 88

Hirsch, Etienne, 20

Hitler, Adolf, 20, 61

Hofmann v Ersatzkasse, 122

Human Rights and Fundamental Freedoms, Convention on, 117, 133–34

Hungary, 1, 145

industrial cartels, 19–20

inflation, 41–43, 46, 114, 150–52, 184–85

information age, 201

information technology, 10–11, 150

insurance-based social programs, 107

integration, European, 15–31, 83, 90; and EDC, 26; historical attempts toward, 2–6, 19; Hitler's impact on, 20; Monnet vs. de Gaulle on, 20–21, 87, 90, 92; and Pan-European Union, 19; pattern of, 26–27, 101–2; and "1992" Plan, 101; political, 5, 27, 84, 87–88; and social policies, 101–2, 112; and Treaty of Rome, 100

interest rates, 38–39, 45–46; and debt to GDP ratios, 173; and ECB, 109, 185, 187; and EMU, 41. See also names of countries

International Monetary Fund (IMF), 80, 82, 84, 151

Iran, 88, 157

Iraq, 88

Ireland: debt issues of, 169–70; economic growth in, 1; and exchange rates, 164, 167, 177–78; inflation in, 41, 46; and interest rates, 109, 161, 163; and oil shocks, 157–58; social pacts in, 114; taxation in, 6

Ireland, Northern, 122

Ismay, Hastings, 208

Italy: debt issues of, 169–70; deregulation of financial services in, 161; election of center-left parties in, 108; EMU membership of, 36; and ERM, 165, 167; and exchange rates, 150, 164, 177–78; export growth of, 151; inflation in, 150; and interest rates, 38, 161, 163; and oil shocks, 155; and pegged-rate system, 38, 150; and the "snake," 155, 157; social pacts in, 114

Japan, 151

judicial processes, 135

Judt, Tony, 10

Kahn, Dominique Strauss, 95

Kalanke v Freie Hansestadt Bremen, 123–24, 125

Kennedy, John F., 93–94

Kennedy, Paul, 3

Keynes, John Maynard, 81–82

Kinnock, Neil, 8

Kissinger, Henry, 93, 195

kleptocracies, 2

Kohl, Helmut, 29, 166

Kosovo crisis, 88, 93, 198, 208, 214

Krugman, Paul, 177

labor market policies, 103, 105, 110–12, 149, 173

labor unions, 109, 114

Lafontaine, Oskar, 46

Lamont, Thomas, 18

layoffs, warning of, 136

legislative processes, 134–35

liquidity, financial market, 181–82

living conditions, 141

London Conference (1948), 24

Loucher, Louis, 20

Louvre Accord, 160

Luxembourg, 155, 167

Maastricht Summit, 29, 161, 163

Maastricht Treaty, 166; and Article 119, 145; convergence criteria of, 36, 41, 44, 80, 104–5; Delors and, 94; and democratic deficit, 9; and ECB, 183; and exchange rates, 185; referenda on, 37, 161, 163–64; security and defense provisions in, 195; Social Chapter of, 111–12; and social policies, 104–5, 143–44

Major-Accident Hazards of Certain Industrial Activities Directive, 139

Mangin, Charles, 21

Marschall v Land Nordrhein-Westfalen, 124–25

Marshall Plan, 22, 75, 82, 206

Mayer, René, 20

men: and earnings, 120; and equal pay for equal work, 111, 117–19, 128, 134, 137–38

Mendès-France, Pierre, 26

mergers and acquisitions, 43, 136–37

Mexico, 178

migrant workers, 135–36, 139

military unification, 25–26. *See also* NATO

Milward, Alan, 16

Minc, Alain, 91

Mitterrand, François, 29, 166

modernity, 204–5

Mollet, Guy, 26

monetary autonomy, 39–40, 80, 177

monetary union. *See* European monetary union

Monnet, Jean, 6–8; American proclivities of, 61, 69; and Briand line, 18; and de Gaulle, 7, 19, 60, 87–96; and EDC, 25–26, 60, 93; and EEC, 7, 60, 93, 100; and Euratom, 26, 60; on European integration, 20, 66, 76, 87, 90, 92; and French industry after WWII, 21–22, 60; life and career of, 16–19, 57–77, 83–84; and monetary union, 79–86, 92; naming new currency after, 90; and Paris Conference (1916), 18; and Schuman Plan, 7, 17, 23–25, 26, 60, 93, 100; and Treaty of Rome, 60, 93; work ethic of, 61–66

movement, freedom of, 135–36, 140–41

multinational corporations, 10

Mundell, Robert, 5–6, 80

mutual recognition agreements, 199

NAFTA (North American Free Trade Agreement), 178

NATO (North Atlantic Treaty Organization),

76, 93, 203–11, 213–15; Blair on, 196, 214; and Franco-German relationship, 26, 207; institutional nature of, 206

Netherlands: election of center-left parties in, 108; and exchange rates, 177–78; export growth of, 151; and gender equality, 118; labor market policies in, 103, 107; and the "snake," 155; social pacts in, 114

"1992" Plan, 34, 36, 100–101, 111

Ninkovich, Frank, 214–15

Nixon, Richard M., 152

North, Douglass, 3

Norway, 37, 48, 155, 158

objective indeterminacy, 205

Ohio University, 1, 6

oil shocks, 28, 154–55, 157–60

Ollenhauer, Erich, 26

Organization for European Economic Cooperation (OEEC), 22–23, 60, 82

Organization of Petroleum Exporting Countries (OPEC), 155, 157

Paeman, Hugo, 7

Pan-European Union, 19

Paris Conference (1916), 18

Pauly, Lewis W., 80

pegged-rate systems: and Bretton Woods Agreement, 158; and France, 150; and Great Britain, 38; instability of, 166; and Italy, 38, 150; and monetary autonomy, 177; and target zones, 41

pensions, 104, 173–74; eligibility for, 139; reform of, 106, 111, 112; in Social Charter, 142

Peyrefitte, Alain, 87, 92

PIGS (countries). See Portugal, Italy, Greece, Spain

Pirenne, Henri, 3

Pleven, René, 25–26, 93

Plowden, Sir Edward, 23

Poland, 1, 145

political unification. See integration, European

Portes, Richard, 180

Portugal: debt issues of, 169; election of center-left parties in, 108; EMU membership of, 36; and ERM, 163, 167; and exchange rates, 164; inflation in, 41, 46; social pacts in, 114

positive action, 121, 123–25, 128

poverty, 103–5

price stability: and ECB, 43–44, 46, 183, 186, 187, 189; and Germany, 102, 151; and interest rates, 187

privatization, 9–10

Prodi, Romano, 8

Project 1992. See "1992" Plan

Proposal for Accession to the European Convention on Human Rights, 133–34

Protection of Workers from the Risks Related to Exposure to Chemical, Physical and Biological Agents at Work Directive, 139

quota systems, 123–24, 126

Rambouillet negotiations, 198

recessions, 38, 105

Regents of the University of California v Bakke, 125–26

remuneration for work, fair, 141

Rey, Hélenè, 180

Reynaud, Paul, 25

Risks Related to Noise at Work Directive, 139

Robert Schuman Plan. See European Coal and Steel Community

Rohatyn, Felix, 87

Roman Empire, 2–3, 19

Rome Treaty. See Treaty of Rome

Roosevelt, Franklin D., 75, 90, 92–93

Rosenthal, Glenda, 213–14

Rostow, Walt, 4

Rueff, Jacques, 27, 85

"Rueffians," 85

safety and health standards, 111, 139, 142, 143

Schengen Agreement, 30, 48

Schmidt, Helmut, 28

Schroeder, Paul, 215

Schuker, Stephen, 150, 216

Schuman, Robert, 16, 60, 90, 93

Schuman Plan. *See* European Coal and Steel Community

securities transactions, 43, 182–83

security and defense issues, 30, 195–211, 213–16; Blair on European, 196–97, 214; and EDC, 25–26, 60, 93, 206

seigniorage, 179–80

self-employed persons, 138–39

Sharping, Rudolf, 52

shocks: asymmetric, 40, 109; external, 85, 150; global, 188–89; oil, 28, 154–55, 157–60; Volcker, 158–59

single currency. *See* European monetary union

Single European Act, 15–16, 29, 111, 140, 160

Single Market. *See* "1992" Plan

Smithsonian Agreement, 154–55, 158

"snake in the tunnel," 28, 100, 152–55

Social Charter, 111, 114, 133, 140–43

social exclusion, 103–4

social pacts, 114

social policies, 99–115, 133–45; and asymmetries, 109; EU programs, 136–39; and European integration, 101–2, 112; and Maastricht Treaty, 104–5, 111–12, 143–44; Social Charter, 140–43; Treaty of Amsterdam, 144–45; and Treaty of Rome, 134

social security, 139, 141

solidarity, social, 107, 113

sovereignty, 90; and economic policies, 5–6, 84, 101; and EMU, 9, 36–37; and France, 88; and monetary autonomy, 39–40, 80

Soviet Union, 81, 207–8, 214

Spaak, Paul-Henri, 16

Spain: debt issues of, 169; deregulation of financial services in, 161; EMU membership of, 36; and ERM, 167; and exchange rates, 164; inflation in, 41; women's and men's earnings in, 120

Stability and Growth Pact, 35, 39, 41, 105, 190

steel industry, 19–20

Strasbourg process, 117

Summers, Larry, 89

Sweden: economic growth in, 1; EMU membership of, 48; and exchange rates, 163–64; and the "snake," 155; women's and men's earnings in, 120

Swiss National Bank, 42, 46

Switzerland, 37, 48–49

synchronization, 187–89

Talbott, Strobe, 208

target zones, 38, 40–41, 48

tariffs, 20, 100. *See also* customs unions

taxation, 6, 106–7, 110, 112–13

Taxman v Board of Education of Piscataway, 126

technology, information, 10–11, 150

Thatcher administration, 10, 28, 140

Tietmeier, Hans, 45

trading blocs, regional, 19. *See also* free-trade areas

Transatlantic Business Dialogue, 199–200

Transatlantic Declaration, Bush-Baker, 94

Transatlantic Partnership, 94, 200–201

Transfer of Undertakings Doctrine, 136–37, 142

transnational corporations (TNCs), 10

transparency, 108–9

Treaty of Amsterdam: and Article 119, 127–28; employment policies in, 113; and EU membership, 48; and European Commission, 9; and gender equality, 127–28; and Great Britain, 145; social policies in, 144–45

Treaty of Rome, 2, 26; and European integration, 100; and human rights, 117; importance of, 84; monetary union goal of, 83, 151; Monnet and, 60, 93; and social policies, 134. *See also* Article 119

Treaty on European Union (TEU). *See* Maastricht Treaty

Trichet, Jean-Claude, 45, 90

Triffin, Robert, 27, 80, 84–85

Turkey, 145

unemployment: and EMU, 41–42, 51–53, 102–3; of older and younger workers, 173–74; and recession of 1992–97, 38, 105; and second oil shock, 158

unification, political and economic. *See* integration, European

United Kingdom. *See* Great Britain

United States: affirmative action in, 125–27; and Asian economic crisis, 187–89; and Bretton Woods Agreement, 81–82, 152; capital markets in, 172; Civil Rights Act of

1964, 123, 125–26, 138; and comparable worth standards, 119–21, 138; competitiveness with Europe, 29, 36, 76, 87–96; and EMU, 30, 50–51; and equality, 117–32; Equal Pay Act, 119–21; and European security and defense issues, 93, 199–201, 213–16; foreign policy in, 209; and the Marshall Plan, 22, 75, 82, 206; and NATO, 203–11, 213–15; relationship with Europe, 30; relationship with France, 88–96; and state debt issues, 170; and Volcker shock, 158–59; workers' rights in, 136–39, 143. *See also* dollar, U.S.

University of California, Regents of the v Bakke, 125–26

Unterberger, Betty, 216

Védrine, Hubert, 89

vocational training, 141

Volcker shock, 158–59

Vredling Proposal for Employee Information and Consultation Rights, 137

wage discrimination, 117–21

Walter, Norbert, 4

Washington, County of v Gunther, 119–20

welfare-state programs, 104, 105, 112

Werner Report, 85, 101, 152, 154, 155

Western European Union, 9

West Germany. *See* Germany

White, Harry Dexter, 81

Whitney, Craig, 89

Wilson, Woodrow, 206–7, 210

women: and earnings, 120; and equal pay for equal work, 111, 117–19, 128, 134, 137–38; health and safety standards for, 143

work councils, 137, 142

Worker Adjustment and Retraining Notification Act of 1988 (U.S.), 136

workers' rights, 117, 133–45

working conditions, 141

World Bank, 80–81

World Economic Conference (1927), 20

World Trade Organization (WTO), 88

yen, 151, 178–79

Yergin, Daniel, 79

Yugoslavia, 195

Zollverein, 3–5, 19